THE CHALLENGE OF EXISTENTIALISM

JOHN *Daniel* <u>WILD</u> · *The Challenge*
of EXISTENTIALISM

BLOOMINGTON · INDIANA UNIVERSITY PRESS 1955

Acknowledgment is made to the following publishers for permission to quote material from the works listed: Appleton-Century-Crofts, Inc., *Readings in Ethical Theory* edited by Sellars and Hospers, 1952; Barnes & Noble, Inc., *The Concept of Mind* by Gilbert Ryle, 1949; The Hogarth Press Ltd., *Later Poems* by Rilke, Leishman, tr., 1938; Alfred A. Knopf, Inc., *The Decline of the West* by Spengler, Atkinson, tr., 1926; Oxford University Press, Inc., *The Journals of Sören Kierkegaard*, Dru's edition, 1938; Philosophical Library, *The Philosophy of Existence* by Gabriel Marcel, 1949; Princeton University Press, *Training in Christianity* by Sören Kierkegaard, 1947, and *Works of Love* by Sören Kierkegaard, 1946; Routledge & Kegan Paul Ltd., *Man in the Modern Age* by Karl Jaspers, 1951.

21984

THE ARGUMENT OF *The Challenge of Existentialism* IS BASED UPON PROFESSOR WILD'S MAHLON POWELL LECTURES, DELIVERED AT INDIANA UNIVERSITY APRIL 13, 15 AND 16, 1953.

Contents

Introduction   3
    I
The Breakdown of Modern Philosophy   9
    PHENOMENOLOGY   13
    METAPHYSICS   16
    EPISTEMOLOGY AND LOGIC   18
    ETHICS   22
    CONCLUSION   24

    II
Sören Kierkegaard   27
    THE DESCRIPTIVE METHOD (PHENOMENOLOGY)   29
    ESSENCE VS. EXISTENCE   31
    PRACTICAL AWARENESS AND THE FEELING OF DREAD   33
    ETHICS AND THE EXISTING PERSON   37
    Descriptive Ethics 38 · Good and Evil as Existential
    Categories 41 · Freedom and the Masses 42
    THE BACKGROUND OF EXISTENTIALISM   45

    III
The New Empiricism and Ontology   57
    THE NEW EMPIRICISM   59
    THE REVIVAL OF ONTOLOGY   64
    Existential Protocols 64 : ESSENCE AND EXISTENCE ·
    EXISTENTIAL VECTORS · TRUTH AS IDENTITY · THE

EXISTENTIAL THEORY OF GOOD AND EVIL · CONTRADICTION
AND CONTINGENCY · POTENCY AND CHANGE
Human Ontology 72 : HUMAN EXISTENCE · BEING-IN-THE-
WORLD · WITH-OTHERS · BOUNDARY SITUATIONS · DEATH
CONCLUSION   84

IV
Human Awareness and Action   86
HUMAN AWARENESS   86
Mood and Feeling 87 · Projective Understanding 88 ·
Sartre's Theory of Awareness 90 · Logic as
Grounded on Being 95
HUMAN ACTION   98
The Feeling of Dread 98 · Care 100 · A New Theory
of Time 103 : TIME AS A NOW-SUCCESSION · TIME AS
ECSTATIC EXISTENCE · EXPLANATION OF THE ACCEPTED VIEW
History 110 : HISTORY AS A STREAM · HUMAN EXISTENCE
AS HISTORY · THE ACCEPTED VIEW AS UNAUTHENTIC

V
Existentialist Ethics. Integrity and Decision   116
HUMAN DECISION AND FREEDOM   117
Death and Human Integrity 118 · Conscience and
Guilt 121 · Projective Decision 123
AUTHENTIC VS. UNAUTHENTIC EXISTENCE   126
Being-in-the-World 126 · Being-with-Others 130 ·
Boundary Situations 139 : SITUATIONALITY · OTHER
BOUNDARY SITUATIONS · GUILT · DEATH
Awareness 145 · Care 147 · Time 148 · History 149

VI
Existentialism as a Philosophy   151
KARL JASPERS   151
JEAN-PAUL SARTRE   160
GABRIEL MARCEL   167
MARTIN HEIDEGGER   173
SOME WEAKNESSES OF EXISTENTIALIST THOUGHT   178
Method 179 · Metaphysics 180 · Epistemology 181 ·
Ethics 183
CONCLUSION   185

VII

Realistic Phenomenology and Metaphysics   187

PHENOMENOLOGY   188

Existential Description 188 · Phenomenology as a
Theoretical (not a Practical) Discipline 190 · Description,
Inference, and Explanation in Philosophy 193

METAPHYSICAL PROTOCOLS   194

The Ontology of Man 195 · Weaknesses in the Existential-
ist Ontology 197 : THE NEGLECT OF THEORETICAL COGNITION
AND ESSENCE · ALL INSIGHT AS PROJECTIVE · THE REJECTION
OF REASON AND EXPLANATION · Being-in-the-World 201 :
THEORETICAL CLARIFICATION OF PROJECTIVE WORLD
HORIZONS · THE HUMAN VS. THE COSMIC WORLD ·
Being-with 206: THE FAILURE TO ACCOUNT FOR COMMU-
NICATION · TOWARDS A REALISTIC THEORY OF COMMUNICATION ·
Boundary Situations 214 : THREE MISTAKES REQUIRING
CORRECTION · SITUATIONALITY · CHANCE · STRUGGLE ·
SUFFERING · GUILT · DEATH

VIII

Philosophical Anthropology   220

HUMAN AWARENESS, A REALISTIC VIEW   221

Cognitive Being 221 · How Do We Know Existence? 223 ·
Practical Awareness 227 · Theory 228 ·
A Humane and Realistic Logic 231

CARE   236

New Light on Human Action 236 · The Self
as Subject and Object 240

TIME AND HISTORY   242

Human Time and World Time 243 · The Intentionality
of Human Time 245 · The Historicity of Man 247

IX

Realistic Ethics   250

EXISTENTIALIST ETHICS AND NATURAL LAW   252

Essentialism and Existentialism in Ethics 253 · Classical
Ethics 255 · Existential Norms 258 · The Possibility of
A Realistic Synthesis 262 · The Ethics of the Future 266

Notes   273
Bibliography   285
Index   291

THE CHALLENGE OF EXISTENTIALISM

Introduction

THERE are many present indications of a serious breakdown in the basic enterprise of philosophy throughout the Anglo-Saxon world. At a time when there is a desperate need for the wide dissemination of sound and appealing cultural aims, *academic* philosophy at least seems bankrupt. Not only are there no great systematic syntheses with a moving inspiration; there are no great philosophic syntheses. What is the meaning of Western culture as a whole? What are its guiding aims? Great masses of people in the East and in the Middle East are asking these questions, moved by the urgent necessity of critical decision between the East and the West.

Fragments of propaganda and phrases concerning freedom and democracy have been hastily devised. But disciplined and integrated answers are almost entirely lacking. The peoples of the West are themselves in doubt concerning the basic nature of their culture. The demand for adult education is constantly increasing. The need for general education in the humanities, and in those subjects dealing with what are now commonly referred to as "values," is widely recognized. But academic philosophy has so far contributed very little towards the meeting of this need. Hence on many campuses which have felt the recent general-education ferment, philosophy has been left behind to be replaced in the exercise of its integrative function by other disciplines like history, literature, and social science.

Such disciplines, of course, have their place in the curriculum.

3

They are vital parts of wisdom; but not the integrating part. Surely this is rather that insight into the first principles and basic structure of the world which was once called philosophy. The guiding and ordering of life belongs to wisdom—*sapientiae est ordinare.* Academic philosophy is no longer thought to be wisdom. Has it lost its wisdom? Perhaps this is so. Where, then, is wisdom to be found? Where can we look for sound and integral guidance in the living of life? The philosophy of the schools is no longer exercising this function; it seems, indeed, to have lost all interest in doing so.

Every special science takes its departure from empirical facts that are observable by all. But then in view of the restricted nature of its particular object, it may be led into regions quite remote from the field of ordinary experience. This is now true of the so-called physical sciences whose sub-microscopic objects and theories are beyond the range of unspecialized observation and understanding. Such specialized sciences can proceed in relative peace and tranquillity undisturbed by any close contact or conflict with the thought of common men. Philosophy, however, can never attain such abstract peace and order. Her data are not confined to any restricted field. They pervade the world of concrete experience as well as the special fields of science. Not only do all men have access to them, but all have varying and conflicting theories about them, often vague, or biased and uncritical. This adds greatly to the normal difficulties of responsible research. The field is always a chaos of opposing views, and the verified results of critical reflection are apt to be swept aside by current fads and fashions.

From the standpoint of the abstract scientist, this situation seems utterly irresponsible and undisciplined. He is apt to conclude that philosophy is a mere bedlam of subjective speculation in which no empirical verification is possible and to wash his hands of the whole matter. This, however, is a great mistake. There is no lack of philosophical data. The trouble is that they are everywhere. It is too *much;* not too *little.* Furthermore, it is sheer delusion for anyone to think that he can wash his hands of this matter without ceasing to be human. The fact that every man is a philosopher with some view of himself and the world which he inhabits is obviously a sign of importance, not of triviality, an indication of the dire necessity for empirical and critical reflection. In fact, it is only through such investigation that the results of scientific research can be brought to bear in any coherent way on the major problems of life and culture.

A civilization is made up of vast numbers of free individuals dependent on mutual cooperation. If they are to cooperate willingly and effectively, they must be guided by a view of the world and a system of values (i.e., a philosophy) which is empirically sound and justified as well as coherent and appealing. A warped ideology that no one can clearly understand soon loses its appeal. Willing effort slackens and men sink into lethargy. Militarism, regimentation, and tyranny must then intervene if chaos is to be avoided. Many civilizations have suffered this fate in the course of human history. Nothing more awful can happen to a human culture than the disintegration of its guiding way of life or ideology. This word has taken on new meaning for us, and with good reason. We no longer think of ideas as mere abstractions, separate from the forces of life. We are slowly learning that they are the lights which guide the living forces.

We find ourselves engaged in what is primarily an ideological war against a formidable enemy, well equipped not only with physical weapons but with ideological armament as well. These ideas are not a mere jumble. They are ordered into a systematic philosophy, a coherent whole technically known as dialectical materialism, one of the great world philosophies which has drawn from the deepest springs of modern reflection.

This view of the world is based on ontological conceptions of matter and movement which are constantly exemplified in the concrete events of nature and history. It does not end with abstract metaphysics but also includes an interpretation of physical, biological, and social science, which has a strong appeal to trained minds. In close connection with this metaphysical foundation it has developed a normative social philosophy already applied with technical care and discipline to many fields of human action. It also includes a sweeping philosophy of history, which has profoundly influenced many historians, and a striking analysis of current social conflict.

These ideas have not been left in a state of abstract isolation, but have been brought into a philosophical union where they exert a mutually stimulating effect on one another. This coherent system of ideas is now being intensively cultivated and applied to all the subordinate fields of knowledge by trained minds in the schools and universities of the East. But it is not locked up in these academic halls. Thousands of lectures are being given every day; books are pouring from the presses. In a simplified form, the results of these researches are being circulated and broadcast by all means of modern communication. As we know, these ideological activities are having a profound effect in all countries except the United States and England, and even here their effect has not been negligible.

We may believe that these conceptions are distorted and unsound. We may recognize the need of arming ourselves against them. But it is naive to think that we can effectively oppose them by non-rational means. These are not material objects that can be shot down or blown up by physical weapons. These are ideas; and the only adequate weapon against a false system of ideas is the truth, or at least a closer approximation to the truth. What are we doing in this direction? How do our activities compare?

Do great multitudes of citizens in the West share any coherent view of the world and man? Do they share any integral system of norms grounded on such a view, in terms of which their own lives and their social policies may be explained and given meaning? In so far as they hold any such view, is it capable of eliciting voluntary aspiration and sacrificial devotion? The very asking of such questions must raise serious doubts in even the most sanguine minds.

In Western Europe men have seriously raised these basic questions. Certain answers have been recently formulated which should be of interest to all those who are genuinely concerned with the destiny of our culture.

An independent discipline that has long been neglected—ontology, the science of existence—is now being revived and intensively cultivated. This movement of thought, now generally referred to as existentialism, is closely allied with a descriptive empirical method known as phenomenology. Existentialism is at the present time the most influential movement of contemporary thought in France and western Germany. It has shown itself to have a marked attraction for the Latin mind, and is now intensively cultivated in both Italy and South America. Our theology has certainly felt its effects; but as a philosophy, so far at least, it has not taken root in the Anglo-Saxon countries and has borne no fruit. It is little known and is largely ignored in our colleges and departments of philosophy. My aim will be to present the reader with a critical exposition of this phenomenological philosophy of existence. I shall try to explain something about the background of this way of thought, its basic doctrines, their advantages and defects as I see them, and finally, about the way in which these defects may be remedied.

The suggestions I shall make are not made in a spirit of enmity or disparagement, but with the hope that weaknesses— which others also have seen—may be carefully corrected without any loss of sound insight. I have learned much from the existentialists. Because of the decay into which philosophy has now fallen in many parts of the world, it is a joy to learn that philosophy in the great classical sense of this word is now reviving in Western Europe. If others like myself may be helped by this work to gain further understanding of this living thought of our Western contemporaries, and to escape from the provincialism of Anglo-American analysis, it will have accomplished its purpose.

The Breakdown of Modern Philosophy

REGARDED from the point of view of that modern philosophy which began with Descartes three hundred years ago, existentialism is something radically new. Its founder, Sören Kierkegaard, the Danish thinker, and the major representatives of existentialism today all think of themselves as rebels against certain dominant trends of this philosophy. Indeed, at the present time they find themselves engaged in a radical venture of reconstruction rendered necessary by the breakdown of modern philosophy. What do they mean? Some answer to this question is required for any adequate understanding of the living movement.

Modern philosophy has been dominated by a strong subjectivist tendency which has turned attention away from the real objects presented to us in experience, to the conceptual and logical apparatus by which these objects are presented. The result has been a fading away of the object, which has receded farther and farther from the central focus of attention. What is now known as analytical philosophy is a current manifestation of this tendency. According to this mode of philosophizing, all the actual data of experience belong to the province of some one of the restricted sciences. There are no philosophic data. All that is left for philosophy is logic and linguistic analysis, a study of the tools used by science in making its empirical investigations and in stating the results.

Such a methodological conception has cut itself off *a priori* from the problem requiring solution. What is needed is an in-

9

tegral view of the world of objects, not a view of logical operations and linguistic tools, another special set of objects. How can
these objects, together with all other objects, be fitted into a
coherent world framework, verified by the facts? This is the
question.

It cannot be answered by focusing a special field of objects,
even though these objects function in another context as the tools
by which knowledge is attained and expressed. It may be that by
language and logic I understand whatever I understand. But it
does not follow that by studying these tools objectively, apart
from their references to objects, I may gain an understanding of
the objects themselves, and how they are ordered together. To
know certain instruments of understanding is not to know understanding, which may involve many other factors. And even to
know understanding is not the same as to know its objects, which
may be very different.

Vision offers us an accurate analogy. It may be that I cannot see
except by the use of spectacles. But to take off one pair of spectacles and to study them by another pair will not enable me to
gain a panoramic view. It merely gives me another object to be
fitted into such a view. To know something about the spectacles
—their size, weight, refraction, etc.—will not enable me to understand vision as such, which also involves other factors. And even
to know what vision is in general will not enable me to see real
objects. A blind man may have such knowledge. Analytical philosophy, which surrenders objective insight to focus on the logical
and linguistic tools of knowledge, is like a man who becomes so
interested in the cracks and spots of dust upon his glasses that he
loses all interest in what he may actually see through them.

But, it may be said, this is only a special tendency, fortunately
not yet in command of philosophy. Logic, of course, has its
proper place. This is a form of logicism which results from an
extreme emphasis on a partial fragment. After all, the rest of
philosophy still lives on.

Yes, it still lives on in *fragments,* but not as a disciplined, coherent view of reality as a whole. This is the most evident indication of the breakdown of philosophy in the traditional sense.
Two lines of evidence support this conclusion.

The first is the evidence of concrete experience itself. Anyone who has not forgotten himself by some exclusive obsession with abstract speculation, and who has reflected seriously on life as it comes to us in the raw, is aware of the strange and overwhelming way in which radically different entities are merged together in the concrete. The objects of all sciences are abstract. Owing to the limitations of the human intellect, they must be studied apart if they are to be understood by us. When studied in this way, they seem separate and independent. But in the concrete, as lived, they are fused together.

How is this rich fusion to be understood? How is its manifold content held together? What is the nature of this unity; and what are its laws and principles? These are the questions men ask of philosophy. They cannot be answered by principles based on highly sifted data. They can be answered only by reflections based on a disciplined description and analysis of concrete experience itself, attending to its constitutive structure (what is *always* found), and the major modes into which this all-pervasive structure falls. Such phenomenological description has been attempted on the continent of Europe. But in Anglo-Saxon philosophy, until very recently, it has been ignored and neglected. Oversimplified interpretations of immediate experience, like that of Hume, blind to vast ranges of empirical data, have won strong support. As a result of this, unity has been purchased only at the price of partiality. No insight into the order of primordial experience has been achieved. This is the privation of philosophy.

A second line of evidence is afforded by the history of philosophy itself. The classic texts do not base their interpretations on limited structures, ruling out other kinds of data *a priori* as illusory or derived. They are based, rather, on being itself, which excludes only nothing, and is thus capable of doing justice to the vast variety of given data without arbitrary reduction. The forms of order they suggest are not all equally well grounded. But they are rich in empirical content. Philosophers schooled in these texts are critical of idealistic or naturalistic syntheses based upon such arbitrarily selected data as those of mind or matter alone. These are modes of being rather than being itself. Such syntheses, in spite of their inclusive claims, are only fragments.

In attempting to support their claims of having achieved well-grounded integrations, they are forced to attempt the assimilation of data lying beyond the range of their initial assumptions. Then a clear-cut dilemma confronts them. They must either distort or reduce these data to fit the system, thus violating the first canon of sound empirical procedure, the supremacy of brute data over all theory; or they must introduce something alien into their initial concepts. In either case, authentic empirical unity is lost.

The most evident example of this disintegration is the flight from existence, the most pervasive datum of experience, and from metaphysics, the most basic empirical discipline. The positivistic dictum that ontology is meaningless has not been able to withstand careful criticism. Hence it is no longer explicitly accepted in any literal sense by this or by any other school of thought. But that many schools do accept it implicitly is shown by their widespread tendency to dismiss it as windy speculation, unverifiable by any given data.

As a matter of fact, the difficulties of metaphysics—and they are many—arise not from a paucity but rather from a vast profusion and complexity of data. Existence is given everywhere, but always with further determinations more readily focused and analyzed. This is why it is so apt to be ignored. But being is the bond of empirical unity. Everything that falls within experience, in fact everything whatsoever, is held in the unity of existence, every object of every legitimate discipline. It is only by understanding these objects in relation to being that they may be grasped in relation to one another as they actually are. If this existential unity is ignored, then either an arbitrary unity must be imposed by a special discipline, or the different sciences will fall apart into a chaos of fragments, each pursued with no relation to the rest, as is now so evidently true of the philosophic disciplines. To one who has some familiarity with the great classics of philosophy, or even to the common man looking for further light on the basic nature of things, this lack of integration among the subordinate disciplines is a sad and discouraging spectacle. If philosophy can no longer perform this vital function, where is trustworthy integration to be found?

Is academic philosophy working effectively to correct this situation? Are the pervasive philosophic data being clearly focused? Are they being accurately analyzed and used to check explanatory theories which can account for them, and provide us with some insight into the basic structure of the world? Are the results of these studies being brought to bear on the popular philosophy which guides our private life and public policy, to refine them and to purify them of error? Is academic philosophy close to the thought of the common man? Is it stirring him to think more deeply about the common problems of life? Is it clarifying his thought and helping him to choose more wisely in these times of world upheaval and crisis? Is academic philosophy really performing its cultural function?

We shall try to answer these questions by examining briefly the question of philosophic method and the present state of three basic disciplines: metaphysics, epistemology, and ethics. In each case we shall review the major trends of reflection which have led to the present situation. Such a review may help us to understand the major reasons for the present breakdown of philosophy.

PHENOMENOLOGY

The scientist is required to see aspects of things abstractly and one by one. He is interested in only one kind of thing, and must forget everything else in focusing exclusively on his peculiar object. Special machines and instruments are often needed to aid in his observations. The philosopher is interested in gaining some understanding of the structure of things as a whole, not merely that of a part. Hence he must pay attention to the vast, confused, primordial world of concrete life which is of peculiar interest to the philosopher. It is here alone that *all* the major types of data are found. It is here that their relations to one another and also their relation to those pervasive data which are of major importance to anyone seeking an adequate view of the world as a whole may be observed. The first function of philosophy, therefore, is to study this primordial world of immediate experience, to describe its unique characteristics, to distinguish and classify the major kinds of data which appear, and to analyze the constitutive structure of this concrete experience. At the present time in the

Anglo-Saxon countries, this task of phenomenological description and analysis is seriously neglected. There are several reasons for this neglect.

No one, of course, can seriously question that these data are in some sense given. But modern philosophy has produced many conceptions and arguments which tend to discredit them as objective evidence worthy of disciplined attention. From the potent influence of Descartes has come another widespread notion that the original data are twisted and distorted by cognition, so that all we directly apprehend is mind dependent. External physical things and other minds are not given at all, but are the result of elaborate inferences and unverifiable projections of our inner states. From Hume and his followers has come the theory that only objects and impressions are directly given to us. The active self and the noetic acts by which we cognize these objects are held to be not given at all, but unjustifiable suppositions grounded on no empirical evidence. Scientific theories of perception have popularized the notion that only the measurable, quantitative data of science have any objective status, and that all the secondary qualities, such as color and sound, must be disregarded as private phenomena. More and more realms of concrete data have thus been discredited and removed from the field of what is regarded as worthy of serious study.

This leaves the relatively simple data of science, which can be directly grasped without prolonged description and analysis. These alone are really trustworthy and respectable. The vastly rich and variegated fields of concrete experience are, as a friend once put it, *sloppy data,* too confused with one another and with biased interpretation to warrant careful investigation. As a result of these tendencies, philosophers in the modern tradition gradually lost the habit of careful observation and description. This distrust of the concrete has penetrated very deeply into our scientific tradition, and has actually influenced our common sense, which is often willing, at least momentarily, to grant an epistemological priority to the elaborate inferences and constructions of some science when these conflict with immediate data.

Thus we are too readily bewildered when we are told that our own body, which we immediately feel, or an object like a table that is directly presented to us, is not really there as it is given at all, but is mostly empty space with numbers of sub-microscopic entities flying through it at incredible velocities. How can a theory full of inferences and constructions be more certain than the datum it is trying to explain? We here forget the first canon of all true empirical procedure, that brute data have an absolute priority over any theory, no matter how plausible it may be. Hence if the theory really conflicts with the datum, it is the theory which must go. But we must remember also that the data are known to be very rich, and that there is doubtless ample room in them for all that science claims to be there, for all that we immediately apprehend, and for much more as well.

Unfortunately, however, without clearly realizing it, we often do not proceed in this way. It is not easy to be genuinely empirical. The contemporary analytic philosophers *think of themselves as empiricists*. But as a matter of fact, if we examine carefully what they say about method, we find that they minimize the role of direct observation and description. Only a few relatively simple. data are directly given, and they are of minor interest. More important in science are those constructive interpretations which are only indirectly verified by observed data. According to Professor Feigl: ". . . most of our knowledge, and especially all of the more interesting and important part of it, is highly indirect. It is shot through with interpretation, construction and inference. . . ." [1]

To what discipline, then, is the task assigned to describe the structure of experience as it is given? Not to philosophy, for its task is concerned with the analysis of language and meaning. All empirical facts belong to some science. As Professor Schlick has stated: ". . . the philosopher as such is not interested in facts of experience. . . ." [2]

The world as it is concretely and immediately given to us, as presented with constraining evidence, is neglected. It is no wonder that the resulting world perspectives are partial, one-sided, and out of touch with common experience. Modern philosophy has paid too much attention to the tools of logic and analysis and the building of vast constructive systems, and far too little to the wide ranges of immediate data that lie beyond the province of the restricted sciences. This is a primary reason for the breakdown of philosophy.

METAPHYSICS

Existence is an omnipresent philosophic fact. No one can be presented with a non-existent datum. It pervades all objects everywhere, both those of common experience and those of special scientific interest. But existence manifests itself in many ways. Pegasus, the winged horse which I conjure up before my mind, is not nothing. But its existence depends on mental acts. When they cease, it ceases to be. This is different from the existence of the junk man's nag that I see plodding down the street.

Some things exist only in an incomplete or potential way. They will exist on certain conditions, *if* other events occur. This partial existence is different from the full-fledged actuality of something that is all there.

A tree is substantial in that it exists in itself. Such existence is clearly distinct from that of the green color which exists only accidentally *in* something else, the leaves.

Certain modes of existence are active and diffusive. They flow over into other things. Some are passive and receptive, requiring support from the former.

Things have active tendencies not subject to what we call choice. They do what their natures determine them to do. *Persons,* on the other hand, within certain limits can direct their tendencies. They can choose what they are to be and do. They exist in a different way.

These ontological facts are often obscure to us and hard to focus. In ancient times a certain discipline was set aside to study them. Aristotle called it *first philosophy* because these data underlie and pervade all the other facts accessible to us. Some confirmed results were achieved by the careful description and analysis of these basic facts. But owing to its position *after the physics* in the Aristotelian corpus, later editors happened to call the treatise on first philosophy the *metaphysics* (the *after the physics*). In recent times, the new physical sciences claimed a monopoly on all empirical data. Metaphysics then had to be interpreted as a discipline having no access to any empirical evidence, but wholly concerned with the formulation of theories not subject to empirical verification. The unverifiable speculations of German idealistic philosophers in the nineteenth century unfortunately seemed to confirm this view. Since that time, the whole discipline has been regarded with deep suspicion, not only by scientists but by philosophers as well. Few treatises were ever written on the subject, and courses with this title gradually disappeared from self-respecting curricula. At the present time in the universities of England and America, this discipline is dead.

But even though no one is interested in them, the facts of course remain. Things do go on existing and acting. Even the failure to focus these acts results in a mistaken, but nevertheless very real, kind of metaphysics, fraught with serious consequences. What else is there to focus? With what can existence be confused?

There is something else—the determinate structure or nature of that which exists. It is this more intelligible aspect of things which is the peculiar concern of scientific analysis. Existence is taken for granted. It is the distinctive character or whatness of things, traditionally called *essence,* that is important. When this trait of scientific methodology is tacitly assumed and generalized, it takes the form of a familiar metaphysical view now commonly known as essentialism (about which we shall have much more to say). The act of existing is not clearly distinguished from that which exists. Each thing is simply *what it is,* a determinate structure of some kind, like green, blue, betweenness, and the number two. Each is self-enclosed and distinct from the rest. These things are spread out in space, and succeed one another in time. In fact, to possess spatio-temporal properties is the same as to exist. The aim of science is to discover the laws of essential succession by which the future may be predicted.

This atomistic metaphysics of *essentialism* was given classical expression in the philosophy of David Hume and was closely approximated by other influential modern thinkers. In recent times, its claim to be expressing the world view of science has given it an enormous prestige. But its failure to focus the act of existing as distinct from what exists has made it insensitive to many impor-

tant and evident phases of experience. Thus it can give no intelligible account of the difference between noetic and real existence,
between the potential and the actual, between the substantial
and the accidental, between the active and the passive. It can shed
no light on either the nature of human freedom or on that free
mode of existing which distinguishes a person from a thing. Thus
it is prone to those reductionist theories of naturalism or idealism
which oversimplify the data of experience, and which have increasingly isolated philosophy from the sound sense of the common man.

This neglect of existence and its various modes has reached a
manifest climax in the so-called "analytic philosophy" of today,
which attempts to dispense with existence as an empty epithet.
According to Quine, to speak of "existent" and "non-existent,"
"real" and "unreal," is "but a bandying of empty honorifics and
pejoratives." [3] No effort is made to account for the empirical difference between noetic and real existence, potential and actual,
substantial and accidental. Such ontological distinctions are dismissed as an "accumulation of factually meaningless verbalisms." [4]

All entities are reduced to the single level of physical being.
There is no basic difference between a person and a thing, between human science and natural science. As Feigl says: "There
are no other methods or aims in the social and cultural sciences
than exist in the natural sciences. . . ." [5] This reductive materialism is never defended in a disciplined way against other ontological views in closer touch with the empirical facts. It is simply
assumed as a clear-cut implication of science. Other views are
never criticized. They are merely brushed aside.

The failure of professional philosophers to combat this non-
empirical and anti-metaphysical point of view is one of the major
reasons for the decline of philosophy in our time.

EPISTEMOLOGY AND LOGIC

In a famous passage at the end of his treatise, the philosopher
Hume confesses that the theoretical speculations he has worked
out in his armchair are unable to answer the existential questions
of his everyday life. "Whose favor shall I court, and whose anger

must I dread? What beings surround me? And on whom have I any influence or who have any influence on me?" Abstract theory cannot help him here. As he says, "I am confounded with all these questions, and begin to fancy myself in the most deplorable condition imaginable, environed with the deepest darkness. . . ."

Nature, however, has endowed us with other modes of practical awareness to deal with such existential problems, which cause us no trouble as we converse and play with our friends. Modern thought has paid little attention to such existential awareness. It has focused on pure theory rather than practice, essence rather than existence. The two attitudes are never held together, but are always separated and opposed. As Hume concludes: "I dine, I play a game of back-gammon, I converse and am merry with my friends, and when after three or four hours' amusement, I would return to these speculations, they appear so cold, and strained, and ridiculous, that I cannot find in my heart to enter into them any farther."

Similar doubts have been expressed by many others. Theoretical awareness, the way we think in an armchair, is detached from its object, not involved with it and concerned. Such awareness gives us a *point of view* on things; it does not feel a *situation*. Modern thought has concentrated on this and ignored other modes of consciousness that are united with our practical activities. Descartes defines the human person as a *thinking thing,* that is a being which has ideas within it, like objects inside a spatial container. This ignores the intentional activity that is involved in all theoretical apprehension. Such apprehension is not wholly passive. It is an *act* by which the mind stretches out to join its object. I must open my eyes and see the color; I must hear the sound; I must actively conceive, and judge, and argue if I am to know anything. Descartes ignored this intentional activity. For him the mind is not the source of acts reaching out to an object, but rather a passive container of ideas. This is the source of that false subjectivism which has produced so many distorting effects in the history of modern philosophy.

One of these was the complete separation of theory from practice. If theory is the passive reception of ideas, then it has nothing

in common with action, which has to be viewed as a blind erup-
tion of tendency from the inside out. The only reliable knowledge
is that which we get from the cold, impersonal observations of
science, entirely divorced from our active needs and interests. As
Hume finally realized, there is another kind of knowledge, a practical knowledge fused with our acts, which we use in working, in
struggling, and in playing with our friends. This practical knowledge has been ignored. It gives us certain vital information about
ourselves and about reality that is inaccessible to pure theory.

Such knowledge is constantly given to me by what I call *mood*
and *feeling*. Thus I am feeling well or ill, in good spirits or
gloomy and melancholy. This knowledge of my own condition
may be vague and confused. But it is direct and absolutely certain. It reveals my own activities to me as they are proceeding
subjectively from the inside. This is why it is impossible for me to
doubt my own existence as it strives and struggles in the moving
world.

Our moods and feelings not only reveal our own existence to
us, they also reveal very important aspects of the external world
as it exercises its existence around us and upon us. Thus as I float
on the surface of the lake, I feel the waves rocking, and the fluid
mass supporting me. As I press against a desk I feel it resisting me.
Similarly, I sense the antagonism or friendliness of other persons
with whom I exist and try to cooperate. It is by this practical
awareness fused with my action that I become certain of alien
existences as they weigh down on me or help me.

Hence in his cogent refutation of the subjectivism of his young
friend Berkeley, Dr. Johnson does not present an abstract scientific argument, but a practical argument. He strides up to the
boulder lying by the path and kicks it with his foot. This is how
we know the existence of things. It is impossible for us to doubt
the independent being of that which opposes us and actively restricts us from outside.

Modern philosophy has paid little attention to these practical
moods and feelings. It has been exclusively concerned with abstract scientific theorizing, and has held that this is the only
source of valid knowledge. As a result, it has become uncertain of
the existence of things, and has thought of experience as though

it were a thin, unsubstantial flux of pictures on a mental screen. This is a fearful distortion of the rich and full-blooded world of existence in which we live and move and have our being. It has separated philosophy from the active life and the sound sense of the common man. It has been growing since the time of Descartes with ever-increasing emphasis, and is manifested with striking clarity in the so-called analytic philosophy of our own time.

The analytic philosopher is oblivious to the intentional structure of all awareness which is *of* some object. According to him, it is a mere property which we have within ourselves. Thus Ryle denies that a sensation is *of* some object which we sense. It does not involve any such cognitive relation. There is no such object. As he says: "To *have* a sensation is not to be in a cognitive relation to a sensible object. There are no such objects. Nor is there any such relation." [6] Sensory experiences are private events; they are *had* by each sensing organism within itself. Ryle simply ignores the subjectivism which follows from such a view.

Other analysts, however, see clearly that on this basis mind has to be regarded as wholly private. We cannot stretch out our minds to know external things or other minds. As Lewis says: "It is one such essential feature of what the word 'mind' means that minds are private; that one's own mind is something with which one is directly acquainted—nothing more so—but that the mind of another is something which one is unable directly to inspect." [7] I cannot know that you are here before me. I cannot know the mind of my child. I can only postulate that she exists. This is a blunt statement of that subjectivism which has been active in modern epistemology since the time of Descartes.

There is no practical knowledge that is capable of guiding our desires. Moral assertions cannot be verified. They are neither true nor false. They are mere expressions of feeling, hence not even propositions. As Ayer says: "They are unverifiable for the same reason as a cry of pain or a word of command is unverifiable—because they do not express genuine propositions." [8] Such irrational eruptions can, of course, be theoretically described from the outside. This is the task of social science. There is no practical reason, however, by which they may be understood from the inside, subjectively, and guided to sound and fruitful fulfilment. So far as pure theory is concerned, one is as good as another. This is, of course, the end of ethics as a rational discipline.

In modern times, logic has been pursued as a separate discipline cut off from ontology and indeed from all other sciences. Divorced from this context, the status of logical order has become unclear. Sometimes it is confused with nature itself; sometimes with mere linguistic rules, subject to arbitrary choice, which stand between us and the things we need to know. Artificial rules and languages have been technically symbolized and proliferated. But they seem to have nothing to do with the actual procedures of common sense and scientific reflection. Imposing claims are made for their possible applications. But so far they seem relevant only to the construction of calculating machines. Thus divorced from living discourse, logic seems no longer to be a humane discipline or liberal art, but rather a technological game played for the enjoyment of a few specialists.

Tremendous energy has been devoted to the disciplines of epistemology and logic. But they have shed little light on the mysterious processes of human awareness, theoretical and practical. This is one of the chief reasons for the present breakdown of philosophy.

ETHICS

Sound theoretical knowledge in a certain field should be able to guide our action so far as it touches this field. Thus physics becomes normative in directing the procedures of engineering; anatomy and physiology become normative in directing the procedures of medicine. Philosophy seeks to gain some reliable knowledge concerning man and the world as a whole. Ethics is the attempt to apply such knowledge normatively to the living of human life. It is here especially that academic philosophy approaches most closely to the conscious needs of the common man. In past periods, when more empirical methods were followed, and the basic data of metaphysics and epistemology were not neglected, some guidance was actually offered.

Thus classical ethics was close to the concrete, and full of descriptive content. One thinks of the vivid picture of Socrates in

Plato's dialogues, the description of the moral virtues and the long account of friendship in Aristotle's *Ethics*. In contrast, modern ethical theory is abstract and weak in phenomenological content. Little is said of moral habits as they are expressed in the concrete, and I know of no important modern treatise in which friendship is carefully discussed.

Classical ethics conceived of value and disvalue not as properties or essences, but rather as modes of existence. Evil is to act and to exist in a warped and privative way; good is to act in accordance with nature—to exist authentically in the highest degree. This not only requires that certain qualities be realized, but also that they be actualized freely and spontaneously by the agent himself. This existential horizon is broad enough to include the vast range of divergent values without oversimplification and reduction. In contrast, the essentialism of modern thought has led it to identify value with some fixed property, like pleasure, which leads to reductionism; or when this breaks down, to claim that it is ineffable and indefinable, which plunges the whole realm into basic obscurity.

The breakdown of modern epistemology has also had an unfortunate effect on modern ethics. Epistemological skepticism weakens moral convictions. If nothing can be known as it really is, nothing can be morally justified.

As a result of these trends in other disciplines, modern ethical theory has become increasingly remote from the concrete problems of human life. The defense of normative principles describing what men ought to do is now commonly referred to as "normative ethics," and is felt to lie beyond the province of the technical philosopher. Instead of this, the sophisticated moralist is supposed to devote his attention to meta-ethics, as it is called: the study of the meaning and syntax of those propositions by which norms are expressed. These trends have reached a manifest climax in our present-day analytic philosophy, which not only does not offer us such guidance, but declares that such guidance is impossible, and that even to hope for such a thing is to fall prey to childish delusion.

In the first place, what the ordinary man means by freedom is non-existent. No one could have acted otherwise than he did. As

Feigl puts it: ". . . the free will problem is a pseudo-issue arising out of confusions of meaning." [9]

Furthermore, it is a naive mistake to believe that any such
thing as ethics exists as a responsible discipline. We can, of course,
describe the moral attitudes of a person or a tribe. To describe
real facts is a monopoly of science. As Ayer notes: ". . . this enquiry falls wholly within the scope of the existing social sciences. . . ." [10]

Many of us sometimes seriously deliberate about our actions,
and ask ourselves what we really ought to do. Sometimes we de-
bate such questions with others who contradict us, and wonder
who is right. But as Ayer points out, this is a delusion. To say
that *x should be done* is merely to express a *pro* attitude. "It is
clear that there is nothing said which can be true or false. . . . I
am merely expressing certain moral sentiments. And the man who
is ostensibly contradicting me is merely expressing his moral sentiments. So that there is plainly no sense in asking which of us is
in the right." [11]

Moral judgments are the result of historic accident. It is silly
to believe that any one is more or less right than another. To say
that Hitler was in any sense wrong is merely to show prejudice.
Worse than this, it is really to be naive, for any belief in stable
moral standards betrays "a not fully liberated pre-scientific type
of mind. . . ." [12]

There is, of course, nothing new about this type of ethical relativism. From the time of Protagoras it has been constantly revived and defended. What is new is the intellectual arrogance
with which this time-worn point of view is dogmatically asserted
with no rational defense, except for an appeal to the authority of
modern science, and with no careful consideration of opposed positions. This sterilization of ethics is a fourth and final reason for
the breakdown of philosophy.

CONCLUSION

As moral theory has become more abstract and verbal, the sensa-
tional advances of modern technology have radically transformed
the conditions of human life. The total population of the world

has more than doubled, and a vast network of apparatus has been set up into which human beings must be fitted to perform standardized operations upon which their very existence depends. The success of mechanical methods in controlling sub-human nature has reinforced the materialistic conception that similar methods of mass conditioning and mass propaganda are the ideal means of adjusting human individuals so that they may function smoothly and efficiently in the apparatus. These methods are now being used everywhere to standardize thought in accordance with simplified conceptions and to streamline individual action. As we all know, in certain places they have achieved weird totalitarian successes with the almost complete elimination of freedom and authentic human existence.

These procedures have been justified by collectivist philosophies derived from Hegel and Marx, and from a close analysis of modern life and history. This kind of philosophy has little sense of the freedom and dignity of the individual person. But it does recognize mass injustice. Hence its normative prescriptions have a deep appeal to oppressed peoples and classes all over the world. This is a thoroughly disciplined and articulated philosophy. What have we developed in the West to meet this challenge? Have the deepest insights of Western thought been preserved and cultivated in our academies? Have they been fitted into a coherent structure and applied to the problems of the modern world?

Your attention has been called to certain facts which make it impossible to answer these questions with a confident affirmative. Academic philosophy has become a barren wasteland with little relevance to actual life and with little appeal, except to careerists and technicians. It is not surprising that many of our own enquiring youth in times of chaos and depression have turned to the Marxist synthesis. No alternative has been offered. Our philosophy has fallen into evil days. It is no longer doing the work which men have expected of it in the past.

This is the end of the gloomy history outlined in this first chapter. I have called attention to certain trends which have been deeply ingrained in the texture of modern thought: inattention to the immediate data of concrete experience; neglect of existence and first philosophy; a physicalist approach to the problem of human awareness, leading to subjectivism; and a radical separation of theory from practice, leading to the de-rationalization of ethics. It is not surprising that these trends have ended in the breakdown of a tradition that began three hundred years ago with Descartes. This tradition has now reached its end in the negativism of that so-called positivism which is now so prevalent in the universities of the Anglo-Saxon world. But the end of one thing is the beginning of another.

We have all heard at least something of that movement of rebellion and reconstruction which goes by the name of existentialism, and which is now the most active mode of philosophy in western Europe. This movement cannot be understood without considering the background against which it is rebelling. Hence this first chapter has been devoted to the study of this background. In the following chapters we shall turn to a happier side of the picture—the movement of existentialism itself. This movement also has a history. It began in modern times with the thought of the lonely Danish thinker, Sören Kierkegaard, and his cogent criticism of the reigning Hegelian philosophy. I shall try to tell you something of the novel direction of his thought, of its historic sources, and finally of its profound influence on many contemporary minds which have derived from it new inspiration and real hope for the revival and reconstruction of philosophy in our time.

Sören Kierkegaard

WE HAVE completed a study of certain trends which have become increasingly influential in the history of modern thought and are now clearly manifested in the so-called analytical philosophy of England and America. One of these is the ontological tendency to stress objective essence as over against the act of existing. We have examined this tendency with some care, and have noted the way in which it underlies all the rest.

During the last three hundred years there have been occasional rebels against the abstract intellectualism, or, as we may perhaps more accurately refer to it, essentialism of modern philosophy. Perhaps the best known of these are Pascal, who rebelled against the idealism of Descartes; Nietzsche, who rebelled against the idealistic thought of nineteenth-century Germany; and Bergson, our modern Heraclitus, who called attention to the prevailing neglect of change, and formulated a recent version of the flux philosophy. These thinkers have all exerted an influence on the existentialist mode of thought. But there is one rebel in particular whose influence has been more definitive than that of all the rest, and who may be thought of as the seminal mind of the existentialist movement. This is the Danish thinker, Sören Kierkegaard, who died about one hundred years ago in Copenhagen at the age of forty-one.

Born of middle class parents, and from his earliest youth revealing great keenness of mind and brilliance of wit, he was sent to the university to prepare for an academic or religious career.

Revolting against the reigning Hegelian philosophy then ascend-
ant in all the universities of Europe and America, he plunged
into classical studies, especially the dialogues of Plato, and wrote
his master's dissertation on the Socratic irony. Already feeling a
deep kinship with this ancient philosopher who also rebelled as
an isolated individual against the ruling ideas of his day, Kierkegaard laid the foundations for new and revolutionary modes of
thought. Having been brought up in a strict Christian atmosphere, due particularly to the influence of his father, he quickly
saw the complete failure of Hegel's attempt to absorb Christianity into an idealistic system of concepts, and decided to prepare
himself for the ministry. Then, as his interest deepened, he was
appalled at what seemed to him the shocking contrast between
religion as it was commonly preached and discussed, and religion
as it might be actually lived and authentically understood—between talking and thinking about Christianity in the prevailing
Hegelian mode, and actually *being* a Christian.

This contrast is the key to Kierkegaard's life and intellectual
development and the origin of what we now call existentialist
thought. Rejecting the Christianity of the Danish Church, he
gave up the idea of becoming a minister, and lived alone, devoting the rest of his life to the writing of those extraordinary literary and philosophical, but always primarily religious, works in
which he called in question most of the basic assumptions taken
for granted by his contemporaries. Thus he laid the foundations
of that new (and yet as he conceived it, very ancient) way of
thought which now goes by the name of existentialism.

This philosophy is best understood as a rebellion against the
abstract objectivism or essentialism of modern thought, with an
intensive emphasis on the concrete subjective existence which it
has consistently ignored. Kierkegaard attacked the four major
phases of this essentialism as they are expressed in the idealism of
Hegel. Thus in one of its most influential manifestations, he criticized the non-descriptive, speculative method of modern philosophy, its essentialist metaphysics, its neglect of practical awareness, and its repudiation of personal ethics. He not only criticized these errors, but in each case made important and often
original suggestions for their correction.

Kierkegaard's suggestions have been developed and refined by his living disciples, the existentialist thinkers of western Europe. As we shall see, they represent a cogent challenge to modes of thought which have long prevailed. What is this challenge of existentialism, and what are its historical origins?

THE DESCRIPTIVE METHOD (PHENOMENOLOGY)

Kierkegaard is radically skeptical of all attempts to fit the rich content of concrete experience into the framework of some rigid explanatory theory. Having Hegel particularly in mind, he accuses all such theories of simplifying and warping the data. Let us abandon our *a priori* theories and explanations, and simply examine the facts. In this sense Kierkegaard is a radical empiricist.

Not only does he warn us against too readily accepting plausible explanations, but also against making easy generalizations which fail to do justice to the instances they are supposed to subsume. Modern philosophy has been interested in human nature, man *in general*. Kierkegaard is interested in the individual person, not in speculating or theorizing about him, but rather in describing him as he really is, a far more difficult task. Thus he says:

> It is far more difficult to describe one actor than to write a whole philosophy of art, and more difficult to describe one of his performances than to describe the actor. The more limited the material, the more difficult the task (the Chinese drama, the Middle Ages, Nordic Myths, Spain, etc.) because it is a direct test of the powers of description. The more one can depend upon generalizations, the easier it is, for the material is so vast that all the completely abstract observations, which anyone can learn by heart, seem to mean something. But the more concrete the observations, the more difficult it is. God knows how long philosophers will continue puffing themselves up with the fantastic notion with which they deceive themselves and others, that generalization is what is difficult.[1]

This distrust of speculation, this urge to describe the phenomenon as it is given is characteristic of existentialist thought.

It has led Kierkegaard himself and many of his recent followers to utilize concrete literary media, such as the drama and the novel, for the expression of their descriptive insights. As it was said of Socrates that he brought philosophy down from the clouds into the streets and houses of living men, so it can be said of the existentialists that they have brought philosophy down from the sanctuaries of the academic classroom into the theaters, the cafés, and the homes of living men. Real entities cannot be speculated or constructed into existence. They must be described as they are experienced. Phenomenology, in a broad sense of this word, is the attempt to achieve such empirical description in an orderly and disciplined way.

This phenomenological urge is now characteristic of the major existentialist thinkers of our time. In this respect they are true disciples of Kierkegaard. Descartes found it possible to question the existence of an external world, and finally convinced himself only by a very roundabout course of abstract reflection. The existentialists find such questions hopelessly artificial and academic. Their function, as they see it, is not to question data that are thrust upon us with inexorable constraint, but rather to describe them as they are, thus breaking with the idealistic trend of modern thought.

The existentialist philosophers accept the radical empiricism of Kierkegaard. They are not interested in artificial problems, nor in theoretical constructions. They are interested, rather, in the concrete data of immediate experience, and in describing these data so far as possible exactly as they are given. This is the phenomenological method. They have applied this method to many regions not previously explored, but especially to the pervasive data of existence, awareness, and human value which lie at the root of the disciplines of metaphysics, epistemology, and ethics. In all these fields, their descriptions have revealed certain facts which are quite at variance with major trends of modern thought and contemporary analytic philosophy.

ESSENCE VS. EXISTENCE

In classical philosophy, essence refers to that factor in finite entities which determines them and marks them off from others; existence to that act which separates them from nothing and makes
them actual. Essences are grasped with relative ease by intellectual abstraction. When separated from existence in this way,
they are viewed as a system of universal, timeless, inactive objects
bound together by necessary logical relationships. Modern philosophy has been marked by a strong tendency in this direction. Instead of revealing the world in which we live, it has constructed
conceptual systems. Hence it has had difficulty in accounting for
the evident facts of individuation, time, contingency, and causal
efficacy. This essentialism, as it has come to be called, is clearly
exemplified in the great Hegelian system, but it runs through the
whole course of post-Cartesian thought as a constant trend.
Kierkegaard's writings express a cogent and bitter rebellion
against it. In the *Journals* he says:

> What confuses the whole doctrine about being in logic is
> that people do not notice that they are always operating with
> the 'concept' existence. But the *concept* existence is an ideal-
> ity and the difficulty is, of course, whether existence can be
> reduced to a concept. So that Spinoza may be right: *essentia
> involvit existentiam*, namely conceptual existence, i.e., ideal
> existence. But from another point of view Kant is right that
> with existence no new essence is added to the concept. Kant
> is evidently thinking honestly of existence as irreducible to
> a concept, empirical existence. In ideal relationships it is
> always true that essence is existence—if one may use the con-
> cept existence at all in that case . . .
> But existence corresponds to the individual thing, the indi-
> vidual which even Aristotle teaches lies outside or at least
> cannot be reduced to a concept. For an individual animal,
> plant, or man existence (to be—or not to be) is of quite de-
> cisive importance; an individual man has not after all a con-
> ceptual existence.[2]

Kierkegaard is here attacking the whole essentialist trend of modern philosophy. He singles out as a noteworthy exception the famous passage from Kant's *Critique of Pure Reason* where it is pointed out that there is no determinate difference in the order of essence between one hundred dollars actually jingling in my pocket, and one hundred imaginary dollars.[3] But there is something else of an entirely different order (existence) which makes all the difference to my actual financial status. This vital factor has been ignored by modern philosophy. We do not live in a system; we live in a world. The entities of this world are not abstract, but concrete. They are not universal, but individual; not timeless, but temporal; not fixed, but tendential; not necessary, but contingent.

These world-factors cannot be understood as essences. They are existential categories that follow after existence. Kierkegaard is recalling our attention to this pervasive factor of existence and the active, temporal contingency that comes with it. In this sense, he is an existential thinker and the founder of existentialist philosophy. All his modern followers accept his diagnosis of modern thought as preponderantly essentialist, and agree to the priority of existence over essence.

Kierkegaard did not attempt to formulate a general theory of being, an ontology. His anti-Hegelian bias obstructed any such attempt. He is primarily an ethical thinker, as he himself recognized, confining himself to the description and analysis of human existence and the world of man. Nevertheless, in this field he was forced to recognize certain data like possibility, contingency, and active tendency which had long been obscured by the essentialist trends of modern thought. He saw the way in which the unmediated opposition of being to nothing had been toned down and distorted by Hegelian idealism. Between being and non-being there is a chasm which no theoretical dialectic can bridge. There is no escape, therefore, from the law of contradiction and that radical either-or which, as he saw clearly, is involved in ethical choice.

Kierkegaard's followers also have rejected the idealistic dialectic with its spurious both-ands and neither-nors. The person cannot be all things. He must recognize his limits and choose.

They, too, have expanded their ontological horizons. Some of them, especially Heidegger and Sartre, have tried to formulate general theories of being. But like Kierkegaard, their primary object of attention has been the being of man.

PRACTICAL AWARENESS AND THE
FEELING OF DREAD

How can I gain authentic knowledge of existence? This brings us to the field of epistemology, where Kierkegaard broke with the physicalist conceptions that have been so influential in modern times, and suggested new approaches of great importance. First of all he attacked the pan-objectivist view that the world is exclusively composed of physical objects. This leaves out the important factors of existence and subjectivity. But he also rejects the essentialist view of the subject as a mental container of knowledge impressions, cut off from the surrounding world. This subject is an existing person, interacting with other persons and things. His knowledge is a phase of his existing, and therefore also active. His own existence at least can be practically known as it really is. Kierkegaard was not primarily an epistemologist. Hence he did not develop the theoretical implications of these ideas very far. But some of his followers have done so. His attack on theoretical objectivism, and his penetrating description of that existential awareness by which I know my own activity as it proceeds, have exerted a far-reaching and revolutionary influence. Let us now consider them in further detail.

Theoretical knowledge may be very clear and precise. It tells me *what* something is, but by itself it is never sure about existence. This is because it is detached and remote from its object. For this reason, Kierkegaard attacked it bitterly as useless and inadequate. "All the profounder thinkers," he says in his *Journals,*[4] "are agreed in placing evil in isolated subjectivity—objectivity being the saving factor. Oh depths of confusion! No—the whole concept of objectivity which has been made into our salvation is merely the food of sickness. . . ." He is amused at those persons who are so used to regarding themselves as theoretical objects that they seem to become permanently detached from

their own being. In conversing with them, one sometimes feels
that he is not talking to the man himself, but rather to his uncle.

> . . . Usually [he says] the philosophers (Hegel as well as all
> the rest), like the majority of men, exist in quite different
> categories for everyday purposes from those in which they
> speculate, and console themselves with categories very dif-
> ferent from those which they solemnly discuss. That is the
> origin of the mendacity and confusion which has invaded
> scientific thinking.
>   In relation to their systems, most systematisers are like a
> man who builds an enormous castle and lives in a shack close
> by; they do not live in their own enormous systematic build-
> ings. But spiritually that is a decisive objection. Spiritually
> speaking, a man's thought must be the building in which he
> lives—otherwise, everything is topsy-turvy.[5]

In spite of many variations in detail, all existentialist thinkers
hold with Kierkegaard that while an individual's thought certainly belongs to his existence, this existence cannot be truly
grasped as a mere object of thought. When I look at myself in
this way, something eludes me. When I look at another as a cognitive object, something also eludes me. And this something is
very vital. It is existence itself, the very heart of the matter. This
must be grasped subjectively in another way by another mode of
awareness. This mode of awareness is practical. By this I am
aware of myself as an existential being, committed and engaged.
To be thus committed is to be human. To regard a human person
as an object is to abstract from all commitment. It is therefore to
de-humanize the person, to reduce him to the level of a thing.
In this existentialist attack upon theoretical objectivity, as we
shall see, there is a strange mixture of truth and fiction.
    It is a major contribution to have called our attention to that
practical awareness which guides our way of life. The ancients
called this *nous orektikos*. In modern times, as we have seen, it
has been ignored and confused with pure theory. Now, once
again, it has been clearly focused. Just as theoretical reflection is
united with more primordial levels of sensory awareness, so prac-

tical reflection on projects is united with more primordial levels of practical feeling and emotion. These certainly have no theoretical significance; they cannot help the abstract scientist. They reveal the world in relation to my active existence—a situation rather than a point of view. Kierkegaard devoted his keen observational powers to a careful study and analysis of certain feelings of this sort, with results of extraordinary interest which have been extended and deepened by his recent followers.

Kierkegaard was the first to see the unique character and peculiar significance of the strange emotion of dread, which he singled out for special attention. This dread is not the same as fear.[6] When we are afraid, we can identify the object *of which* we are afraid—unemployment, sickness, loss of money, war, etc. But this peculiar feeling latent in all men is very different. It has no determinate object. No definite danger threatens. It comes from all sides. There is no defense. We cannot hide from it. The warm and friendly environment disappears. A strange curtain falls between me and the world. The color of life grows thin. There is nothing to which I can cling. I find myself alone, surrounded by alien things. What is the significance of this emotion?

Kierkegaard suggests that it brings us before "nothing."[7] As we say when the experience seems to pass, *it was nothing.* This is no doubt true. But when we think of it, this nothing is not really soothing. It is precisely the object of dread. If, as we are inclined to believe, our normal everyday existence in the world is healthy and good, then dread, of course, is a morbid phenomenon, an unfortunate disturbance. But, as the existentialist sees it, our normal existence is not authentic. It is really a fallen-ness, which we conceal from ourselves by soothing anodynes. Dread is therefore an incipient experience of arousing and awakening. For a moment the veils are torn from our eyes, and we see ourselves as we really are—in a drab and ordinary state, not doing what we might be, only half alive and half awake.

This experience of dread shocks us in all our normal habits and relations. It awakens us from our thoughtlessness, and arouses us to what we might be. "Dread is the possibility of freedom."[8] Kierkegaard holds that this is the gateway to authentic choice and human existence. The more deeply a man dreads, the

greater he is. This feeling may become the source of existential
courage and strength, not of weakness. It becomes a weakness
only if we run away and try to forget it. This running away is
the weakness. It may then lead us into a perpetual round of anxious behavior, a constant flight from dread.

But dread itself prepares us for authentic action. It enters a
man and "searches his soul thoroughly, constraining out of him
all the finite and the petty, and leading him hence whither he
would go." [9] It is like a fire which consumes all soothing delusions
and excuses, and leaves me facing myself and the actual facts.
This dread is the beginning of freedom. It is manifested in many
allied moods. What we call boredom, melancholy, and despair are
all versions of dread which call us from the distractions of everyday life. Kierkegaard has described each of these with penetrating
insight and clarity in many of his works.

There are two kinds of boredom.[10] In the first, it is something
definite that bores me, like a certain book, a task, or a particular
person. This is less interesting. But there is a second deeper type
in which one becomes bored with himself. A great cloud gathers
everything into a confused indifference. The world sinks into
this, and I am left alone with a nameless emptiness. We try to
fight this mood by plunging into busyness. We are filled with
curiosity, and seek for what is new. We may lose ourselves in this
way. But sometimes it overtakes us, and turns us to authentic
decision. Many great achievements have started from this source.
As Kierkegaard has suggested—In the beginning was boredom.[11]

When it fails to achieve any depth, and keeps leading us into
more distractions, this mood turns into melancholy.* This is not
the same as sorrow for this or that. It is essentially indefinite. If
someone asks me what is the matter, I do not know. I cannot say.
It may fall upon me in the midst of action. Why am I doing this?
It is vain and purposeless. A curtain falls between me and the
world. I may try to evade it by plunging again into distraction,

---

* Kierkegaard refers to melancholy as his "intimate, confidential friend."
Journals, no. 359; cf. 641 and 690. For a penetrating analysis cf. especially his
account of Nero in *Either/Or*, Vol. II, pp. 156-160; also *Stages on Life's Way*,
pp. 342-343 and 389-390. For melancholy as allied to despair cf. *Either/Or*,
Vol. II, pp. 172-173.

but something remains to tell me this is hopeless. I can no longer participate in routine affairs. I seem to be excluded. My daily existence is dead and joyless. This is the work of dread that slumbers within me.

When really aroused it breaks forth into despair.[12] This is more than theoretical doubt, though it may include this as a phase. Despair is a practical attitude. Doubt is specific. Despair is indefinite, involving the whole of life. It is not directed to this or that. I despair for my existence. At this point dread ceases to be a mere mood, a slumbering action. It is self-maintained and wills itself. If a person gives himself completely to this, he is freed from his delusions. Alone with his naked freedom, he may choose himself with that desperate intensity which is required for genuine existence. Dread is the narrow and painful way that leads to human freedom.

Modern epistemology has been almost exclusively concerned with the detached theoretical knowledge of objects. Such insight into essences may be clear and distinct. But it is uncertain as to existence. Kierkegaard is skeptical about all such knowledge. In place of it, he draws our attention to another way of knowing which he connects with action. Such insight is not clear, but it is certain. We cannot doubt the vague awakening of freedom which we dread in our slumbering existence. This practical cognition of mood and feeling has been neglected in modern theories of knowledge. Kierkegaard did not attempt to analyze it or to explain it in detail. But he described it with penetrating accuracy, and saw that it sheds much needed light on the discipline of ethics.

ETHICS AND THE EXISTING PERSON

These insights enabled Kierkegaard to make a new approach to the problems of ethics which breaks radically with basic presuppositions of modern moral theory. First of all, he abandoned the *a priori* procedure of Kant which has exerted a marked influence not only on intuitionism but on other schools as well. Important moral phenomena are open to natural observation. Kierkegaard not only made this assertion, but proved it by penetrating descriptions of moral action as it is lived in the concrete. In the second place, he did not conceive good and evil as fixed properties or essences, but rather as authentic and unauthentic modes of existing which can be intelligibly analyzed by the use of ontological categories. Finally, he clearly recognized and described human freedom in certain of its critical manifestations. As a result, the free person is no longer regarded as a fixed object, and the dangers of mass collectivism and the idealistic theories which have helped it develop are revealed with luminous insight. Let us now turn to these Kierkegaardian theories and examine them briefly one by one.

DESCRIPTIVE ETHICS

From a theoretical point of view, the world is made up of a great number of objects that are simply there. I am tempted to regard myself as another object which can somehow be fitted into this objective world. But when I try to perform this peculiar operation, something always eludes me. There is a vital part of myself which is essentially unfinished and subjective and refuses to become a finished object. According to Kierkegaard, this is my dynamic and contingent existential self.[13]

This self cannot be understood as an object. Nevertheless, I am present to myself, not as an object but as a subject. This kind of awareness is practical rather than theoretical. It is not an abstract point of view detached from my active tendencies and desires, but intimately united with them. It grasps these tendencies as they are proceeding, and reveals the world to me as an alien existence indifferent to my aspirations, sometimes aiding me, sometimes weighing heavily upon me and frustrating me. Kierkegaard is interested in describing this practical awareness and its divergent manifestations in opposed ways of life.

As we live our lives in different ways, so do we become aware of ourselves and the world in different ways.[14] Life and awareness vary together in mutual dependence. Thus moral materialism, or hedonism, is more than an ethical theory when it is seriously embraced. It is a way of life united with a way of looking at life. Kierkegaard calls it the aesthetic way.[15] Such a life refrains from committing itself to any long-range purpose. It recognizes no universal moral law. It makes no decisive choices to which it commits the whole of itself and by which it continues to stand. It runs away from the dread that slumbers within. It is committed only to the pleasure of the moment, which no sooner appears on the scene than it has passed away. Such a life lacks structure and continuity. There is nothing in it to resist the flux of time. It dissipates itself in passing references.

The world is revealed to such an awareness as a vast array of passing objects or events. Aside from those temporary pleasures and pains which can be visually imagined, the existent person is out of the picture. Freedom and commitment cannot be objectified. We cannot grasp them as things. Hence they remain unrecognized. Actuality is not sharply distinguished from possibility, nor theory from practice. The *things* that happen in this panobjective frame are transitory and determined. There is room for all things, but existence and freedom are excluded. Many versions of this essentialist philosophy have been formulated in our history. In Kierkegaard's day, German idealism was predominant. Hence he connects the passive aesthetic attitude with romanticism and Hegelian intellectualism. In our own time, these have been replaced by a more scientific and materialistic kind of essentialism. The aesthetic life must now accommodate itself to a naturalistic world.

There is another mode of life (Kierkegaard calls it the ethical) [16] which commits itself to long-range purposes by decisive choice, and which recognizes its own essential humanity and its responsibility to a universal moral law. In his early book, *Either/Or*, Kierkegaard vividly contrasts it with the aesthetic way of life, and describes it with great penetration and imaginative clarity. The ethical life really chooses the whole of itself, and stands by this choice. Hence it withstands the flux of time, repeating itself by taking over its past choices and reiterating them, thus preserving an existential continuity through the passing moments. To such an awareness the world is revealed as not without order and law. This law is recognized as not being self-imposed. It binds with the force of obligation. It can justify my acts or make me guilty. It bears down on me from without. Transcendence is thus dimly glimpsed.

But another possibility is open. Transcendence understood as law is abstract and outside of personal existence. It leaves us helpless in facing the evils and injustices of concrete life, which can be conquered only by an outpouring of generosity and love, beyond the rules of justice, and the natural powers of man. To make such action possible, something transcending us must break into history, and work concretely in our personal lives. Kierkegaard, as a Christian, believes that such a break-through of the eternal into history has occurred. This makes possible another religious way of life, in which duty is infused with love and love itself becomes a duty.[17] In an earlier work, *Fear and Trembling,* based upon the Abraham story, Kierkegaard emphasizes the discontinuity between the ethical and the religious. But in *Stages on Life's Way* * and other later works he no longer speaks in this way. The religious mode of life achieves a higher freedom and a greater independence. But it is not opposed to the ethical, which is transcended, not obliterated. By religion we are given the spirit of *Caritas* which enables us to fulfill the law.[18]

This law is not opposed to freedom. According to Kierkegaard: ". . . only the law can give freedom. Alas, we often think that freedom exists, and that it is the law which restricts freedom. However, it is just the other way: without law freedom simply does not exist, and it is the law which gives freedom. . . ."[19]

But freedom requires independence, and this can be achieved only by the spirit of unconditional generosity. "If one man, when another man says to him, 'I can no longer love you,' proudly answers, 'Then I can also stop loving you,' is this independence? Alas, it is only dependence, for the fact as to whether he will continue to love or not depends on whether the other will love. But the one who answers, 'Then *I will still continue to love you,*' his love is everlastingly free in blessed independence. He does not say it proudly—dependent on his pride; no, he says it humbly, humbling himself under the 'shalt' of eternity, and just for that reason he is independent."[20]

Here the ethical is no longer opposed to the religious. The moral values of independence and freedom are fully achieved

* The ethical is not an independent level, as in *Either/Or,* but "a transitional sphere," leading to religion as its "fulfilment." (P. 430.)

only with the aid of something transcending us. Hence in his later writings, Kierkegaard often brackets the two together, and speaks of the ethico-religious as a single way of life with a lower and a higher phase.[21] Both are opposed to the aesthetic essentialistic, whose concrete manifestations in both life and thought Kierkegaard had described with extraordinary poignancy and penetration in his early works.

GOOD AND EVIL AS EXISTENTIAL CATEGORIES

Values are not fixed essences or properties dwelling in some separate realm of their own. On this point Kierkegaard agrees with classical ethics, which he studied deeply in his youth. Good and evil are ways of existing. Human value is really to *be* as a human being, to think and to act in the most intensive degree as a man. Disvalue is watered down and diluted existence.[22] The word real (as against unreal) and its synonyms are used in this connection.[23] The human good is to exist authentically. Unauthentic, ungenuine existence is evil. These value-modes affect every phase of our existence, our thoughts, our words, our deeds.

Unauthentic existence remains detached and views itself as one object lying among others or as a universal mind. It does not feel itself to be an individual with an existence of its own.[24] It evades the thought of that death which the individual must die by himself alone.[25] It is easily fooled by doctrines of inevitable progress and pragmatic meliorism. Death is regarded as something morbid to be banished from polite conversation. Dread is there, but never openly faced. Choice is suppressed. It seeks for confirmation in materialistic theories of determinism which dismiss the ethical and the religious as theoretical delusions.

Authentic existence, on the other hand, is always personal.[26] This person is concerned and passionately committed, though he does not confuse his own faith with world structure. He knows himself as a limited and contingent existence, who soon must die. He realizes that he has already chosen and must go on choosing by himself. He knows the risk and feels the dread of this responsibility. Recognizing these facts, he cannot accept materialism, but guides his thought by moral and religious categories,

FREEDOM AND THE MASSES

Finally, Kierkegaard has given us poignant descriptions of the radical either-or that is involved in human choice. The issue is not merely between one thing and another. It is not so much what is chosen as that the choice should really be made.[27] Existence is at stake. Am I to be or not to be? This choice cannot be avoided. If he really chooses, he is free. If not, even then he is free, for this is a choice, though half-suppressed and unauthentic. In this sense man is necessarily free.

This freedom sharply distinguishes persons from things. It is an evident datum which must be accepted by any disciplined empiricist who looks carefully at the facts. Furthermore, it resides in the individual, not the group. Kierkegaard saw in Hegelian collectivist theory a ghastly mistake fraught with terrible possibilities for the future. Its use of the term freedom is only a deceptive cloak for an insidious form of essentialist determinism.

When the human person is viewed as an object, he is apt to be lost as a tiny drop in the ocean of humanity, swirled along by the overwhelming tides of history. When we regard things from such a theoretical point of view, our attention tends to be focused on the visible results of human decisions. We lose sight of both the actual decisions themselves as they are actually made by the living individual, and the moral and religious modes of existence of which these visible things are only by-products. This subordination of the individual to the life of the mass is a conspicuous feature of Hegelian thought. It fits in with certain social tendencies which have become accentuated with the coming of the Industrial Revolution and mass production. Kierkegaard was keenly aware of these tendencies and hated them with a passionate intensity.

Hegel had conceived of the human group as a soul substance (*objectiver Geist*), producing ideas and acts of its own and living a life quite distinct from that of its component members.[28] Individuals are viewed as tiny cells in a great encompassing spiritual organism which uses them for its purposes and crushes them when they oppose it. According to Hegel, this supremacy of the social over the individual is not only an inescapable fact, but rational and justifiable as well. This conception has played an important role in the establishment of modern totalitarian states. It is vividly expressed in a famous passage by the German philosopher Spengler who says:

> A civilization [*Kultur*] is born at the moment when, out of the primitive psychic condition of an ever infantile humanity a mighty soul awakes and extricates itself: a form out of the formless, a limited and changing existence out of the unlimited and stable. This soul comes to flower on the soil of a country with exact boundaries to which it remains attached like a plant. Conversely a civilization dies if once this soul has realized all of its possibilities in the shape of peoples, languages, creeds, arts, states and sciences, and thereupon goes back into the proto-soul from which it first emerged.[29]

Kierkegaard was keenly aware of the tendencies which were already beginning in his time to streamline individual thought and action into fixed mass patterns.[30] He saw the extreme danger of such tendencies, which threaten to stifle authentic personal existence, and attacked them bitterly, together with those Hegelian concepts * which provide them with a philosophical foundation. These processes of standardization do not lift the individual into something higher than himself. They rather level him down. Thus he writes in the *Journals:*

> There is a view of life which says that where the masses are, there too is truth, that there is an urge in truth itself to have the masses on its side. There is another view of life which says that wherever the masses are is untruth, so that although every individual, each for himself silently possessed the truth, if they all came together (in such a way however that the many acquired any decisive importance whatsoever noisy and loud), then untruth would immediately be present. . . .
> The crowd is composed of individuals, but it must also be

* Of *objective spirit* he says, for example: ". . . and instead of conscience and the spirit of God to have a community of mankind's animal exhalations, a something which they sweat out in crowds, a something which is called public opinion, and by philosophers: the objective spirit." (*Journals*, no. 515.)

in the power of each one to be what he is: an individual; and no one, no one at all, no one whatsoever is prevented from being an individual unless he prevents himself—by becoming one of the masses. . . .[31]

Truth is accessible to the individual intellect alone. Authentic human existence results from personal choice and from personal zeal in following it through. But modern society is full of demonic forces of leveling which water down the undiluted truth to the sort of thing that anyone can understand, and tone down the pattern of life to what anyone can approve. As a result of his own experience, Kierkegaard sees the Press as one of the most potent of these demoralizing forces. In a well-known passage of the *Journals* he writes:

> The demoralization that comes from the Press can be seen from this fact. There are not ten men in every generation who, socratically speaking are afraid of having a wrong opinion; but there are thousands and millions who are more frightened of standing alone, even with an opinion which is quite right than of anything else. When something is in the papers, it is *eo ipso* certain that there is always a good number of people having the opinion or about to express it.[32]

Kierkegaard also comments on the strange toneless anonymity which seems to pervade the public Press, where the authentic ring of personality has been drowned out by an even monotone. Here we are not presented with what any definite person really thinks, sees, believes, or chooses, but rather with what *one* sees, *one* thinks, or *one* prefers.

> Indeed if the Press were to hang a sign out like every other trade, it would have to read: Here men are demoralized in the shortest possible time, on the largest possible scale, for the smallest possible price.[33]

This emphatic recognition of the individual person as the bearer of all authentic human value, together with a distrust of mass mechanisms and mass attitudes has been transmitted by Kierkegaard to the whole existentialist movement.

These are the common traits of existentialist thought bequeathed by Kierkegaard. In the context of modern philosophy,
these ideas are new. But do they have no originating sources? At
this stage in our intellectual history such a conclusion would indeed be strange. Very often what seems new in a restricted context is the revival and development of something rather old.
What is the background of these conceptions? From whence do
they come? An answer to these questions may help us to see more
clearly their significance.

THE BACKGROUND OF EXISTENTIALISM

Kierkegaard was steeped in Greek philosophy, and wrote his early
Master's dissertation on Socrates (later published under the title
The Concept of Irony).[34] Thoroughly acquainted with the *Dialogues* of Plato and with the Aristotelian writings, he refers to
them in his works. He speaks of himself as employing the *maieu-
tic* method [35] and as trying to follow the path of Socrates.[36] Thus
in a striking passage with an unmistakable reference to Plato's
Republic he says:

> There was once a young man as fortunately gifted as Alci-
> biades. He went astray in the world. In his need he looked
> about him for a Socrates but among his contemporaries he
> found none. Then he prayed the gods to change him into
> one. . . .[37]

This classic literature was a primary source of his philosophical
conceptions. It is dominated throughout by a realistic attitude
towards the noetic enterprise. Being loves to hide from men.
Truth is to reveal it, to bring it out of hiding. Philosophers are
compared to hunters.[38] They must go out and find the truth, and
make it their own. Knowing is never conceived in the idealistic
manner as a process of making or creating. It is an act of discovery, a finding out of what is already there to be known. Both
Plato and Aristotle define truth as the saying of things as they
really are, falsity as the constructive saying of things as they are
not.[39] This constantly leads them to a patient investigation of the
facts as they are experienced.

Plato's dialogues are full of descriptions of the moral responses and judgments which men actually make. Aristotle always begins his discussions with an examination of the commonly received opinions of men, which are often one-sided and distorted but seldom completely mistaken. This attitude of radical empiricism is also found in Kierkegaard. He has nothing but scorn for high-flown speculation. Hence his method is descriptive and phenomenological, open to the facts as they really are. He strives not so much for systematic scope and completeness as for insight and penetration into existence as it actually is. In this he is certainly in the best classic tradition. For Plato and Aristotle also did not so much construct vast speculative systems as achieve basic insights, revealing a certain order in the world of our experience.

The notion of practical as opposed to theoretical reason is also familiar to anyone who has studied the philosophical literature of the Greeks. Thus in the *Statesman* Plato speaks of the peculiar know-how that resides in the muscles and fingers of the skilled artisan.[40] He also distinguishes between purely theoretical knowledge whose aim is simply to possess the truth, and that practical insight whose aim is to guide human activity to its natural conclusion.[41] In Aristotle, the theoretical sciences are even more sharply and clearly distinguished from the practical disciplines.[42] To know the truth theoretically is one thing, and something very valuable. But to know how to act is quite another, with a value of its own.

Both Plato and Aristotle point out how our theoretical opinions come and go. They are easily forgotten. But our habits of deliberation and choice, and the active tendencies with which they are united—these are not easily forgotten and sloughed off. They are deeply ingrained in our subjective being, and constitute our character.[43] For Aristotle, the uncontrolled man who thinks one way and acts another is headed for disaster.[44] If we are really to live authentic lives, we must not only think what is true, but this thought must penetrate into the depths of our active being. Hence Plato refers to this existential unity as "a harmony of word and deed." [45]

Kierkegaard's profound interest in practical or existential thinking is the revival of a classical conception. His famous remark about the modern philosopher whose thought moves in a lofty golden palace, but who actually lives in a squalid mud hut down below, might have been found in one of the *Dialogues*. It is definitely in the spirit of Socrates. Practical reason is not new. But Kierkegaard's discovery of the practical significance of moods and emotions is his own. The ancients had never pressed their investigations so far.

For Kierkegaard, ethics is not a special discipline that can be restricted to a limited territory and thus connected with one or more of the so-called sciences, such as psychology or sociology. For him it is an ontological discipline that plunges us into the roots of being itself. Moral choices confront us with existence as against non-existence, and we cannot understand them without gaining some insight into the mystery of being. The issue is not merely one quality (good) as opposed to another one (bad). It is rather a question of really choosing, really living, really existing, as against a diluted seeming to choose and to live. It is real existence that is at stake.

This concept of the real or authentic as opposed to the unauthentic mode of being now pervades the whole of existentialist thought. It is the revival of an ancient conception. Plato and Aristotle both agree that goodness is realized in the performance of a proper function.[46] According to Aristotle, there is no difference between a *good* flute-player and one who *really* plays it.[47] Human goodness is not a property, not a quality, not an attribute of any kind, but rather something much deeper—a mode of really living and acting, existing authentically as a man. These concepts are revivals of classical insights. But for many of his other basic ideas, Kierkegaard drew from another source to which he was even more indebted. This was the Christian tradition.

There can be no real doubt about the fact that Kierkegaard is basically a Christian thinker. He studied for the ministry in his youth, and was deeply concerned with the Christian religion for the rest of his life. At an early date, he was deeply impressed by the purely nominal Christianity of those around him, and what he could at least imagine as an authentically Christian way of life. What a difference there was between thinking and talking as a Christian on the one hand, and actually existing as a Christian on the other. This thought, which must have possessed him from his earliest youth, is vividly expressed in a passage from his book, *Training in Christianity:*

Sacred history has handed down to us the story of still another admirer—it was *Nicodemus.* In established Christendom a sermon is preached every year on Nicodemus—by all these thousands and thousands of parsons. The subject is treated thus. The Parson says: 'Fundamentally, Nicodemus was a weak man; instead of joining Christ openly, he came to Him stealthily by night, for fear of men.' The Parson pleases himself by this discourse, and it finds favour in the eyes of the congregation—and in fact it is exceedingly courteous, for tacitly the suggestion is smuggled in that the Parson and all those present are people of a totally different sort from Nicodemus—they confess Christ quite openly, without any fear of men. . . .

Everybody who has any knowledge of men, and is not restrained from being honest by regard for money—or by fear of men—must concede unconditionally that in each generation a Nicodemus is a great rarity. When danger seriously threatens—and one is a superior person, and the danger is insult, mockery, ejection from society—verily there are to be found in every generation—among superior persons, who indeed in such a case have much to lose—there are to be found very, very few, perhaps only a single individual, with feeling enough for the truth to go out at night to communicate with it. Nicodemus was an admirer; the actual danger was too much for him; personally he desired to keep aloof. Yet, on the other hand, the truth concerned him so much that he sought to get into relationship with it. Secretly by night—for he was treading forbidden paths—he stole to the despised truth; it had already cost him an effort to make this venture of seeking the society of the despised person. For dark as the night was, and carefully as he hid himself in his cloak, it was nevertheless possible that some one might have seen and recognized him, it was possible that he might have run into some one who promptly would have denounced him; and,

finally, what assurance had he that the man whom he visited
might not make such a use of it as would be injurious to
Nicodemus' good name and fame? . . .

One sees here what an admirer is, for Nicodemus never became a follower. It is as if Nicodemus might have said to
Christ, 'In case we come to an understanding, I will accept
thy teaching in eternity—but not here in this world, no, that
I cannot do. Couldest thou not make of me an exception?
might it not suffice if I come to thee from time to time by
night? But by day—oh, yes, I acknowledge it, I feel how hu-
miliating it is for me, how shameful it is, and also how in-
sulting it really is to thee—but by day I do not recognize
thee, by day I shall say, I know not this man!' You see here
in what a web of falsehood an admirer entangles himself—
and do not forget that in established Christendom there is no
real danger which might make it perfectly evident whether
one might not be only an admirer. . . .

The danger which once was involved in confessing Christ
has passed away since we have all become Christians, and to
that extent the distinction admirer-follower has passed away.
The next danger, which is brought about by taking seriously
Christ's requirement of self-denial and the renunciation of
worldly things, they have also wanted to do away with by en-
deavouring falsely to transform the Christian life into hidden
inwardness, kept so carefully hidden that it does not become
noticeable in one's life. One should be willing to deny oneself in hidden inwardness, in hidden inwardness to renounce
the world and all that is of the world, but (for God's sake!
shall I say?) one must not let it be observed. In this way, established Christendom becomes a collection of what one
might call honorary Christians, in the same sense as one
speaks of honorary doctors who get their degree without
having to take an examination. In hidden inwardness we all
take degrees, or rather we all receive them, each from the
other, as a compliment. . . .[48]

The last remarks on the "secret inner life" are worthy of note,
since certain commentators have interpreted Kierkegaard's at-

tack on speculative objectivity and his emphasis on the ethical
and religious as a defense of "spiritual" quietism. This is certainly a mistake.[49] The concept of existence which underlies the
thought of Kierkegaard and his followers is not that of mystical
communion with transcendent being nor with a pantheistic all-
engulfing being. This would run counter to that assertion of the
importance of the individual person which is a cardinal principle of existentialist thought. For the same reason it cannot be
identified with *life,* the central concept of that *Lebensphilosophie*
which was in vogue in Europe before the advent of present-day
existentialism. Existence is not to be achieved by drifting with the
great evolutionary current or by any other form of self-abandonment. The world of inorganic as well as organic objects is viewed
as something strange and alien. The existential individual is
sharply marked off from them. He stands alone in a world that is
remote and foreign to himself.[50]

But this world is not dismissed as unreal. It surrounds us. It
weighs upon us, and imposes inexorable limits on our being.
There is no real escape. To achieve authentic existence, I am
thrown back on myself. But this does not mean a retirement to
the secret recesses of my inner being. Much that I find there is
also alien and strange. Existence coincides neither with what we
refer to as the inner nor the outer. Its well-springs lie within, it
is true, in personal aspiration and choice. But unless they are
warped and frustrated they must burst forth in open public
manifestations. To exist is to struggle and act in the world of
men. It is not merely to think, but to seek for communication;
not only to remain detached, but to become engaged; not to be a
distant admirer by night, but an open follower by day.

One must not merely do this; he must really do it by straining
his capacities to the last degree. This distinction between existence and "real existence," the unauthentic and the authentic
modes, is common to all the existentialist philosophers. As we
have seen, it comes from classical sources. But it is also a Christian
conception. Kierkegaard himself first arrived at it by reflecting
(as in the quoted passage and generally throughout his works) on
the tremendous but often unfocused and even indiscernible difference between admiring Christianity from a distance, talking

and sometimes even acting like a Christian, and really being or existing as a Christian. It was from these reflections that the word *existence* gained the meaning that now lies at the root of all existentialist philosophy, whether religious or secular in form.

Many other basic conceptions of Kierkegaard were also taken from the Christian tradition, though he freed them from their dependence on a special religious context, and applied them to secular life in general. It is in this form, of course, that they have been adopted by secular thinkers in the West. But the basic ideas are found in Christian philosophy. Thus the supremacy of the practical over the theoretical is a commonplace of Augustinian thought. We should engage in philosophical reflection not merely for the sake of the truth but for the salvation of our souls. Kierkegaard takes over this conception *in toto*, but develops it in certain ways peculiar to himself.

First of all, he generalizes it beyond its specifically religious context, and states it in secular language. Thought cannot include being, but being rather includes thought.[51] The way an individual views the world is a part of his subjective existence. The primary aim of such thought, in so far as it is really aware of itself, is to chart the way to authentic existence, to attain the good. Then he applies this notion to secular life at all levels, the lowest as well the highest. He describes in detail these different levels and the practical dialectic process which, as he thinks, must lead an individual really concerned with himself, from the aesthetic, through the ethical, to the highest religious level. He develops this conception in a very original way, and is led to many new insights, but the basic conception is familiar to anyone acquainted with the Augustinian literature and that of such later representatives as Pascal.

The opposition between the Christian way and the ways of the world, and the extreme practical difficulties encountered by anyone attempting to pursue the former way, are well-known Christian themes which go back to the earliest times and to the New Testament itself. The importance of the will, and even of emotion and feeling in living the Christian life, is, of course, a familiar notion. Anxiety, apathy, and spiritual dryness have been most carefully described in the literature of meditative prayer and contemplation. But their analogous manifestations at lower levels of the Christian life have certainly been noted by many religious writers beginning with Augustine, as in his famous statement about the restlessness of the human heart: *inqueatum est cor nostrum donec requiescat in te.*[52]

Kierkegaard took over these ideas, especially those concerning the lower levels of spiritual life, stated them in modern language with great imaginative power, and developed them further with a wealth of original insight into the psychological depths of personal existence. Thus we have seen how he analyzes this Augustinian restlessness at the level of feeling into the emotions of anxiety, boredom, melancholy, and despair, each of which he then describes with great accuracy and penetration. The rational manifestations of this despair had been studied before, but this revealing excursion into the obscure depths of the emotions was very original. Its Christian sources, however, are clear.

The insight into the individual person as the center of human existence and the bearer of the supreme values of rational insight and freedom is, of course, to be found in Greek philosophy. But this insight was greatly deepened and accentuated by the influence of Christianity and the doctrine of the Incarnation. God incarnates himself first of all as an individual and in a group only through this mediation. It was from these religious sources that Kierkegaard derived his sense of the opposition of the individual person to the anonymous mass, and the equality of all individuals before the Divine.

But he carried this Christian individualism one step farther in his skepticism concerning the possibility of "direct" existential communication.[53] According to him, the individual stands alone, and he sometimes pushes this idea to the extreme of an almost morbid practical solipsism. There are certain places where he speaks of the possibility of genuine communication and of a new form of social organization in which the free person may participate without degradation and frustration. But he never developed this conception, and bequeathed the problem of authentic social existence to his successors in such a form as to render any consistent solution most difficult. His writings stand as a remarkable contradiction to this solipsistic theme that unfortunately runs through them. Here he shows not only that human insight is able to penetrate into the depths of personal existence and to shed light on its murky depths, but also that it is able to describe these regions and communicate its insights to others. His own life was lived in lonely isolation, and his writings were ignored by his contemporaries. This perhaps explains why he remained so oblivious to their methodological significance.

Kierkegaard's subjectivism is of a new type. It is not basically an idealistic or noetic subjectivism. He does not suppose that our only access to external reality is through the knowing mind, and that this mind constructs around itself a wall of impressions or sense data within which it is imprisoned. We are first of all existent beings in dynamic interaction with our surroundings. This is never questioned. But the active self is a subject possessing its own existence and thus is distinct from every other entity. This is an existential, not a noetic, subjectivism. So far it is correct. My being is my own, and yours is yours. Furthermore, the practical awareness that is joined to my activity is a part of my being, and reveals a situational world in relation to my own acts. Each person has his own practical perspective on things. This also is correct.

What Kierkegaard fails to see is that he possesses another type of awareness which is not limited in the same way, but which enables him to apprehend and to describe existence as it really is without subjective bias. Otherwise his own works would never have been written. What method is he using in his poignant analysis of the aesthetic and the ethical modes of life in *Either/Or*, and in his account of the religious attitude in the *Stages on Life's Way*? He is not merely expressing one of these attitudes. If he were, he could not compare and contrast it with the rest. It is clear that he is writing from a neutral point of view —he is describing, theorizing. And so accurate and penetrating are these theories that we are lost in the object, and forget the way by which we have been led there. Apparently even Kierkegaard forgot this way. Otherwise we would have no explanation of the bitter attacks upon theoretical reason which run through his works.[54]

If we took this irrationalism seriously,we would have to reject his writings, which are a triumph of theoretical analysis, penetrating for the first time into strange and obscure regions of experience. The description of practical awareness and its major forms is not itself a manifestation of practical awareness. Kierkegaard is a great descriptive philosopher, a phenomenologist bringing into the light of accurate analysis forms of personal existence and consciousness that had long been hidden. This fact was not clearly recognized by him nor by most of his followers because of his bitter attack on Hegel, the theoretical philosopher and system-builder. Hegel failed to see the significance of these personal phenomena, not because he was too theoretical but because his theories were not sensitive enough.

As is so often true of rebels, Kierkegaard unfortunately exaggerated the importance of that against which he was rebelling. He confused Hegel with the human intellect. In rebelling against him, he felt that he was rebelling against human reason. This, of course, was a mistake—a mistake which he has unfortunately transmitted to his successors. They, too, engage in constant polemics against all theory and objective reason, even as they are employing it. They, too, confuse the theoretical tools they are using with the practical objects they are describing. This irrationalism is the most unfortunate yet one of the most influential factors in Kierkegaard's testament to the modern age. As a matter of fact, this disruptive irrationalism rests on a misunderstanding of the nature of his achievement, a misunderstanding unfortunately shared by the author himself.

We are now able to see that Kierkegaard's achievements are rather a triumph of rational description and analysis—the revelation of new fields of experience hitherto buried in a deep obscurity. Inspired by classical and Christian sources, he recovers many insights of this tradition, applying them in novel ways to modern problems and correcting many basic errors of modern philosophy. Instead of wasting his time on constructive interpretation and system building, he devotes himself to the accurate description of facts as they are given in the concrete.

Rebelling against the intellectualistic essentialism of post-Cartesian thought, he turns his attention to existence, which he recognizes as an indubitable, immediate datum of experience. He sees that this datum cannot be understood as the object of any univocal concept. Nevertheless, it can be described as it manifests itself in certain ways in the life of the individual person. He devotes himself ceaselessly to this task.

He also sees that human cognition is not restricted to the theoretical awareness of universal objects. Men also possess a practical awareness united to their active tendencies which reveals the world to them in another way. With great penetration, he describes this awareness and its revelations, and the major forms which it takes. He recognizes moods and feelings as its most primordial forms, and presents us with poignant descriptions of boredom, melancholy, despair, and anxiety, and their peculiar existential objects. These phenomena had been almost wholly neglected by the tradition of modern thought.

Finally, as a result of these investigations, he sees that the individual person is the center of human existence, the bearer of the supreme values of rational cognition and freedom. Hence he rebels fiercely against the Hegelian notion of *objectiver Geist,* and against those tendencies which were already beginning to impose fixed patterns of thought and action upon the individual person, and to stifle his existential spontaneity.

These are important insights. It is no wonder that after almost a century of neglect they have burst into life and have kindled the fire of a new and living mode of thought. On the continent of Europe this is now the dominant philosophy, and a challenge to all living minds. Its point of view is starkly realistic. It suppresses no uncomfortable facts. Many of its leading exponents have lived through revolutions, terrors, and occupations. They have fought alone in the Resistance against hopeless odds. They express the unvarnished thought of men caught in the mass confusion and conflict of the modern age—weak and fragile men, weighed down by physical bodies, goaded by physical needs and desires, suffering from lethargy and sickness, lacking strength, and lacking knowledge. It is from such men and from such struggles that this ideal has emerged—solitary men struggling against mighty forces, alone in ignorance and in the dark. It is amazingly timely and relevant. It has been movingly expressed in poetry, drama, and novel; clearly analyzed and justified in philosophical prose. It embodies freedom and the dignity of the individual person, two of the great ideals of Western civilization. Hence it has deeply stirred the minds and hearts of multitudes of our contemporaries. I believe it will stir us, if we make a real effort to understand it.

Let us now try to make such an effort. We shall have no time to consider each of the great living existentialists one by one. We shall have to refer only briefly to individual idiosyncrasies in order to focus the common core of their teaching.

-3-

The New Empiricism and Ontology

THE existentialist philosophers accept the radical empiricism of Kierkegaard. They are not interested in artificial problems, nor in theoretical constructions. They are interested rather in the concrete data of immediate experience, and in describing these data so far as possible exactly as they are given. This is the phenomenological method. They have applied this method to many regions not previously explored, but especially to the pervasive data of existence, awareness, and human value which lie at the root of the disciplines of metaphysics, epistemology, and ethics. In all these fields, their descriptions have revealed certain facts which are quite at variance with major trends of modern thought and contemporary analytic philosophy.

Gabriel Marcel, for example, in his interesting intellectual biography, tells us how he found many of the problems of modern philosophy to be "of merely academic interest." [1] Among these last was "the problem of the reality of the outward world as it is stated in philosophical textbooks. None of the extremist forms of idealism which deny this reality ever seemed to me convincing: for to what more certain or more intimate experience could this reality be opposed?" [2] This is a characteristic comment. Before he read Kierkegaard, he said that "Hegelianism inspired me with a profound mistrust." [3] Reality as we live it cannot be squeezed within the framework of an *a priori* system. "It seemed to me," writes Marcel, "that there was a danger of making an illicit use of the idea of integration, and that the more one relied

57

on the richest and most concrete data of experience, the less this idea appeared to be applicable to reality." [4]

There is no real reason why phenomenology should be restricted to human existence. Other modes of being can also be described and analyzed. Nevertheless, Kierkegaard held that he had reliable access only to his own existence. Hence he is primarily concerned with the task of describing moral choice as he finds it in himself, and the different ways of life to which it leads. [5] This attitude also has been taken over by his modern followers.

Jaspers and Marcel have been more interested in describing the perspectives and the acts of the individual person. Heidegger and Sartre, on the other hand, have gone a step further. They attempt to describe the existential structure of human experience as such, and thus to arrive at a general descriptive anthropology.

Human existence is maintained under certain conditions which are the same for all men everywhere. A primary aim of existentialist philosophy is to describe these constant conditions as they are found to be, and then the two ways, authentic and unauthentic, in which these conditions may be understood and faced by living men in the concrete. Thus Heidegger in the early pages of *Sein und Zeit* [6] has presented a phenomenological description of that *being in the world* which belongs to all human existence.

He has recognized the vast richness of the world of immediate experience, and the presence of many pervasive structures to which modern "empiricism" has been oblivious. These phenomena lie beyond the range of the restricted sciences. The existentialists have at last embarked on the arduous task of describing them accurately as they are given. [7]

Let us now examine this new empiricism, considering first of all the chief respects in which it differs from the old; then the pervasive ontological protocols which have been found and partly analyzed; and finally the new ontology of man which has been formulated on the basis of these phenomenological investigations.

THE NEW EMPIRICISM

The oversimplified phenomenology of pan-objectivism reduces everything to an object, and that of pan-subjectivism reduces everything to a subject or some subjective state. It is clear from the account we have just given that such oversimplifications of the original data are rejected by the new empiricism. From this point of view it is pan-objectivism which is guilty of the worst error, for it ignores or reduces the existing subject, which surely lies at the very center of human experience. The existentialist literature is filled with attacks on this view, many of which are more detailed and exhaustive than that of Kierkegaard.

Jaspers, for example, in the first volume of his *Philosophie* [8] points out that pan-objectivism is an essential phase of positivism. He subjects it to a cogent criticism which brings out the internal inconsistencies resulting from its wanton reduction of empirical evidence. All the existentialists accept Kierkegaard's bitter attack on idealism, which flouts the empirical evidence by failing to distinguish between being and mental being,[9] by thinking of the free individual as absorbed in an organic whole,[10] and by ignoring time and history as they are given.[11]

The new empiricism has made an equally radical break with the Cartesian subjectivism which has so long dominated our conception of the immediate data of experience. According to this view, the mind is conceived as a passive container of subjective impressions which are immediately known, simply by being contained. External persons and things are known only through indirect inferences from these privileged internal data. This has led Lord Russell and others to speak of a private world of psychic impressions and a public world of physical things. This dualism is a figment of the logical mind, wholly unsupported by a careful study of the actual data. It is completely abandoned by the new empiricism.

I find myself not in two worlds, but in one. This ultimate horizon is not just spatial, but spatio-temporal in character. External events, internal feelings and acts, the theoretical objects of science, so far as these are verified, are all in one moving world horizon. I can think of myself alone. But this is a sheer abstraction. Being-in-the-world belongs to my very existence. No world, no subjective existence. Heidegger, Sartre, and Jaspers would all accept this formula.[12] Internal data have no special epistemological privilege. It is absurd to suppose that the carpenter knows his own act of hammering before he knows the instrument and the object he is hammering. He himself, his acts, his instruments, and their external objects are all known together as existing within the ultimate horizon.

Nor do I have to infer the existence of other "minds" from any more certain data. Being-with-others belongs to my own existence. I cannot be aware of the latter without being aware of the former. To feel alone is a privative mode of feeling-with, which is the more primitive phenomenon. Awareness is not being in a mind container; it is being towards something—a relation. Hence there is no reason why I cannot be directly aware of an external thing or an external person. As a matter of fact, I am. I am also immediately aware of my own body, a fact denied by the subjectivist. Hence Russell's fantastic assertion that he has to infer the existence of his own body. The new empiricism must reject this radically anti-empirical view, as Gabriel Marcel has shown with great clarity in his illuminating studies of the mind-body problem in the first volume of *The Mystery of Being*.[13] The body may not be physically contained in a mind thing. But nothing really is. Hence we may follow the evidence which indicates that, as against the Cartesians, I am not a mind thing cut off from my body, but that rather I am my body, and know it directly and immediately.

All awareness is intentional or relational, from a subjective pole to an object of some sort. My immediate experience always falls into a bipolar structure. Its center lies within my physical body. Around it lie various spatio-temporal fields which are terminated and replaced by others until the ultimate world horizon. The equilibrium between subject and object is very unstable and constantly ready to pass into a consistent pan-objective positivism or a pan-subjective idealism. Jaspers has given a brilliant exposition of this instability.[14] The subject is somehow a different thing from the object. He has inherited this substantive view of mind from Kant. And yet the subject leads us to the object and is somehow identified with it. So we try to identify one with the other, subjectivizing the object, and objectifying the subject. But this brings us to insuperable difficulties.[15] According to Jaspers, no stable solution is possible. "Only the passage from subjective to objective and *vice versa* is true." *

Heidegger and Sartre have broken more radically with the presuppositions of past empiricism. They cannot rest with such a confused dialectical tension. They have more clearly grasped the peculiar intentional structure of human awareness. Thus, according to Heidegger, we should not think of the mind as a thing that is simply there.[16] It has a peculiar relational structure of its own, being always of something real that it understands in the light of being, which is somehow present to it. For Sartre, all awareness is a pure relation of identity. He even goes so far as to say that it is relation as such.[17] The *pour soi* is the thing in itself (*en soi*) which it knows. The one cannot be reduced to the other. The world of experience is bipolarized. These two poles cannot be confused without distortion of the data.

The more advanced existentialist thought has also rejected the Kantian notion of the appearance or phenomenon as another entity separated from the thing as it really is, as an effect is separated from its cause. No existentialist defends this purely causal theory of awareness. The thing does not produce its appearance in something else which also helps to cause it. It is the thing itself which appears. The mind does not *make* its objects. It apprehends them by a relational act. If my act created the appearance or helped to produce it, it would at least in part belong to me. I should say that part of the appearance is *my* appearing, as part of a joint book is *my* writing. But we make no such claim with reference to an appearance. It is not I who am appearing, but the thing. I may make it possible for something to appear, but the precise determination of that which appears is not due to me. As we say, it is the thing which appears.

Thus someone might provide the funds for my book to appear. But in this case he would not claim that the book was his. In the

* "Nur das Drangen vom Subjectiven zum Objectiven und umgekehrt ist wahr." *Philosophie*, Vol. 2, p. 342.

same way it is the thing itself which appears, not my sense organs or brain or any part of me. Hence while some aspects of Sartre's analysis are less sound, he is surely right in maintaining that it is reality itself which appears, though not the thing in its entirety. This last unfortunately is a mistake.[18] But reality does exist apart from my knowing it, and may be described as it is. Phenomenalism is a misreading of the original data. Existence is given. Hence a phenomenological ontology is possible.[19] *

The analytic mind has banished vagueness and confusion from original experience in a highhanded manner. Immediate data are supposed to be presented to us in neatly separated units, red patches and square shapes, each of which is obviously just what it is. These impressions or *qualia* are simply there. We either grasp them precisely as they are, or not at all. At this level it is impossible for us to be mistaken. † Some epistemologists hold that the term *knowledge* should not be applied to this rudimentary experience, which gives us the sure foundations but not knowledge itself. Knowing begins only with the construction of interpretations and hypotheses, which may be in error. This task must be performed by reason working alone.

Views of this sort have been defended by Russell, Lewis, and many others. They have enormously strengthened those antiempirical trends of modern philosophy which have consistently disguised themselves by the use of the term *empiricism*. To those who accept such a theory, the whole idea of phenomenology—the patient attempt to clarify the data as they are originally given—is absurd. These data are already clear. A philosopher who broods over sensory data is wasting his time. The rational clarification

---

* "In the first place let us remind ourselves that today there can be no philosophy worth considering that will not involve an analysis of a phenomenological type bearing on the fundamental situation of man." (G. Marcel, *Man Against Mass Society,* p. 90.)

† Berkeley was one of the first to defend a view of this sort. According to him, ". . . sensations in the mind are perfectly known . . ." ("Principles of Human Knowledge," *Works,* Fraser ed., sec. 87, vol. I, p. 305) and when "they are actually perceived there can be no doubt of their existence" ("The Third Dialogue between Hylas and Philonous," *ibid.,* p. 446). For a fuller consideration of this issue, cf. John Wild, "Berkeley's Theories of Perception: A Phenomenological Critique," *Revue Internationale de Philosophie,* nos. 23-24, 1953, fasc. 1-2.

of immediate data is impossible. They are simply given as they are. This influential view has turned our attention away from the facts of experience. It has prevented us from correcting those gross oversimplifications and distortions which have marked the history of British empiricism. No data, no discipline. Until philosophers once again turn to the facts, their discipline will stay dead.

The revival of philosophy in Europe is largely due to such a reawakening of phenomenological interest. The existentialist philosophers are once more turning to the data. They have shown beyond all doubt that these data, as given, are not restricted to a small number of clear and distinct atomic *qualia*. They are rich in variety, manifold in order, and jumbled together in vast confusions. As Gabriel Marcel remarks: "What is given to me beyond all possible doubt is the confused and global experience of the world inasmuch as it is existent." [20] No man has ever sensed a red patch. He grasps this by sense and reason together, each apprehending the object in its own proper way. What is given to both in the first place is a blurred confusion. "What is given us to start with is a sort of unnamed and unnamable confusion where abstractions not yet elaborated are like so many little unseparated clots of matter." [21]

Clarity does not come all at once in an instant. It requires patient brooding and analysis. "It is only by going through and beyond the process of scientific abstraction that the concrete can be regrasped and reconquered." [22] All the important existentialist philosophers would agree with this recognition of vagueness and confusion as ever-present factors in experience. Reason is an apprehensive power. As such, it is able to make guesses and inferences on the basis of what it already knows. But its primary function is to clarify the original data of experience, which are certain but very confused. This task can be achieved only by phenomenological description and analysis. The existentialist thinkers have already made many important contributions to this essential phase of the philosophical enterprise.

THE REVIVAL OF ONTOLOGY

One result of the new empiricism is the rediscovery of those pervasive protocols which require ontological analysis and explanation. This means that metaphysics can no longer be dismissed as a jumble of purely speculative theories which are subject to no empirical check. Existence, awareness, and world, for example, are as indubitable as any scientific data. They involve structural patterns and modes of order which are vague and confused, like all data at first, but not necessarily opaque to disciplined description and analysis. Furthermore, these protocols are so pervasive that a clear-cut view of any one will imply a metaphysics, that is, a theory of the universe as a whole. Hence it is not surprising to find that the new empiricism has forced many existentialist thinkers to take a stand on basic issues, and to formulate and defend metaphysical hypotheses of far-reaching scope. Let us now examine these theories, turning our attention first of all to the existentialist classification and analysis of basic protocols, and then to the new light which has been shed on human existence by these discoveries.

EXISTENTIAL PROTOCOLS

There is universal agreement that being is an all-pervasive factor to which we have direct access. According to Heidegger: "Being as the basic theme of philosophy is no kind of being and nevertheless it pervades each entity. . . . Philosophy is universal phenomenological ontology, beginning with the interpretation of human existence." [23] He believes that ontology has failed to make much progress in the past because of the inveterate tendency to confuse being itself with some kind of being. Thus the materialist identifies being with the kind of existence possessed by physical objects and tries to twist everything he experiences into this limited category. The idealist similarly confuses being with mental being. Being and its structure is quite distinct from every entity and from every possible real determination of an entity.[24] Their attention to this transcendental structure, transcending all species and genera, has kept the minds of existentialist thinkers open and free for the recognition of strange phenomena, and has saved them from many prevalent forms of *a priori* reductionism. Thus Jaspers, Marcel, and Sartre openly reject both materialism and idealism.

The subjective existence of man is sharply distinguished from man as an ordinary object of consciousness. To exist is not the same as to be perceived, as Berkeley thought. Heidegger complains that the whole tradition of Western philosophy has basically misunderstood man by thinking of him in this way as a mere thing with determinate properties, and ignoring his peculiar ways of existing.[25] In his important book, *Sein und Zeit,* he has forged a new set of existential categories or existentials, as we shall call them, by which he believes that we may hope to gain a more adequate insight into the peculiar, temporal being of man. Others, like Jaspers and Marcel, go much farther, and deny that any mode of theoretical reflection can do justice to existence. They are certainly correct in distinguishing between being and being known, and thus rejecting idealism. But by refusing to recognize any union between the two, they are often led close to a self-sterilizing skepticism which is incompatible not only with the facts but with the many insights into personal existence which they manage to describe objectively and to transmit to their readers.

Essence and Existence

The existentialists clearly recognize the classical distinction between determinate structure, or essence, and the act of existing. But in violent reaction against the essentialism of modern thought, these thinkers all place an extreme emphasis on existence, and agree in asserting its priority over essence. Thus Heidegger says that "the 'essence' of man lies in his existence." * He uses the term *Dasein* in order to express not a determinate whatness (essence) but rather a mode of being (*sein*) always proceeding from a certain position (*da*) into which he has been thrown.

This mode of existing is distinguished by its peculiar futurity from that of trees, houses, and other objects. These objects have

* "Das 'Wesen' des Daseins liegt in seiner Existenz." (*Sein und Zeit,* p. 42.)

possibilities to which they are open. But these possibilities are extrinsic to what they are now, and are largely determined by external factors. *Dasein,* on the other hand, is always ahead of himself. He *is* his possibilities, and in his being somehow understands them.[26] He chooses how he is going to be. His existence is thus prior to what he is. This remains ever flexible. Heidegger does not explain fully why the realistic notion of essence or nature is inadequate to express these existential characteristics. He simply states dogmatically that it applies only to inert things that are simply there on hand before us (*Vorhandensein*).

Sartre follows Heidegger very closely, and states explicitly that "existence precedes essence." [27] If man were an artifact, like a paper-knife, his idea (essence) would have preceded his existence and determined its nature. But man is not an artifact. He was not created for any purpose. Hence he has no fixed nature, but determines this by his own choice.[28] In spite of this denial, Sartre, like Heidegger, is forced to recognize certain stable "conditions," as he calls them, like death and the need for food, which pertain to all men everywhere.[29] It would seem most difficult to explain these without assuming some such set of determining traits as has hitherto been signified by the term *essence* or *nature.* Jaspers seems to despair of discovering any stable structure anywhere, and tends towards a modern version of the flux philosophy, though in his published writings he has not yet presented any thoroughgoing analysis of change.

Marcel has spent his life fighting what he calls "abstractions" in attempting to come closer to the concrete. Yet, as we have seen, he realizes that abstractions are necessary for the gaining of clear insight. On the whole, his position is less anti-rational than that of Jaspers. In a recent work, he has come out with a qualified defense of the notion of essence. "It is clear," he says, "that reflection on the meanings of words must be directed, just as Plato wanted it to be, towards a grasp of what traditional philosophers used to call essences. One cannot protest too strongly against a kind of existentialism, or a kind of caricature of existentialism, which claims to deprive the notion of essence of its old value and to allow it only a subordinate position." [30] This is a significant criticism by one who has a thorough command of the literature.

Determinate structure is certainly found in experience. This pervasive factor cannot be permanently evaded and ignored by any philosophy which seriously hopes to be really empirical and to achieve even a minimum degree of intelligibility.

Existential Vectors

Their close scrutiny of concrete data has forced the existentialist thinkers to break with metaphysical atomism and to forge new complex concepts to express the relational structure of being. Thus human existence is never properly conceived as being enclosed within itself, but is full of vectors and tendencies. It is a being-in-the-world, a being-with-others, a being-towards-my-death.[31] These relations are not to be thought of as bonds between two already existent terms. Such a relation is usually a mere construction of reason. It cannot really relate two terms unless it passes out of itself vectorially and acts on them, as a magnet holds the filing to its surface. But then it cannot be conceived as a bond between two atomic entities. These entities are not self-enclosed. Their being is vectorial, a being-to-another. The filing is susceptible-to; the magnet is active-on. These real relations are not added to insular entities. They are not insular in the first place. Their very being is a being-to-something. Hence they retain this vectorial character even when they are not fulfilled by any real term. The filing remains susceptible-to-attraction even when there is no magnet. As Heidegger explicitly states, I retain my being-with even when no factual other is present.[32]

Sartre explains this active linking in atomistic, and therefore negative, terms. I am not externally, but internally and existentially, directed towards another. My being is relational and therefore involves an otherness within it. I really am this towards-another-I-am-not.[33] Sartre's language is unnecessarily paradoxical, but he is getting at a basic ontological truth. Real existence is not made up of discrete units juxtaposed together, but rather of vectors, each of which exists by virtue of the other. What we call a single real entity includes many such relational factors within it. Furthermore, the whole entity is never self-enclosed but full of relational valencies to things that are quite distinct.

This theory does not lead to the idealistic conception of in-

ternal relations and a monistic absolute. Because some relations
are internal, we cannot infer that all relations are. The act of
knowing internally relates itself to the object known. To attain
such knowledge makes an important difference to the knower.
But this relation is wholly external to the entity known, which
suffers no real internal change from being known.[34] There is no
reason why an entity should not be able to retain an essential
unity while still maintaining vectorial relations to other things.
The magnet is internally related to iron filings. But this does not
mean that it is an iron filing, or indeed anything other than a
magnet. Monistic idealism is incompatible with that personal existence and freedom which is a primary object of existentialist
study. Hence these philosophers have rejected it on phenomenological grounds.

Truth as Identity

It has long been known that there are certain relational structures, like truth and goodness, which follow along with being
wherever it is found. The existentialists have succeeded in focusing both of these, and have attempted to analyze them—with results that are sometimes questionable, but always interesting.

Truth is clearly distinguished from being. This follows from
the rejection of idealism. Being is everywhere. Truth is centered
in man. Nevertheless, Heidegger attacks the relational conception
of truth as agreement of thought with independent reality on the
ground that it conceives of thought or judgment as a thing related to other things. If this is so, the criticism is sound. But
Heidegger's own view, though obscured by his failure to give any
careful analysis of thought, seems to be relational in character.
We talk about reality itself, not some representation of it.[35]
Truth is allowing being to reveal itself as it is.[36]

For Sartre, all reflection is relational.[37] The act of knowing is
its object, and is separated from it only by nothing. It is the very
nature of the *pour soi* to reveal the *en soi* and itself. Nevertheless,
the reflection is distinct from its object. Sartre explains this apparent contradiction by his peculiar doctrine of the *pour soi* as a
nothing. But his view is neither idealistic nor subjectivistic. To
be is not the same as to be known. Man has a direct cognitive

access to reality, and can reveal it as it is. Truth is the identity of reflection with its object.

The Existential Theory of Good and Evil

The existentialists have completely abandoned the essentialist idea that good and evil are fixed qualities or properties. According to Heidegger, they are existential categories or modes of existing. "Because Dasein is essentially his possibility he CAN in his being win the choice of himself; he can also lose himself, that is never really but only seemingly win this." [38] The terms *authenticity* and *unauthenticity* are used for these two existential modes.[39] *Lose (verlieren)* certainly implies privation. But Heidegger seems to deny this when he says that the unauthenticity of *Dasein* does not quite mean a "lower" grade of being.[40] He is probably trying to protect this conception against the idealistic notion of degrees of being. In any case, it certainly means the privation of existence that ought to be possessed, and is used in this sense throughout the work. *

Other existentialist writers use these terms in this way without qualification. According to Sartre, I am my liberty.[41] To sink into the world of the *en soi,* to become like a thing, is the death of the *pour soi.*[42] There are variations of the way in which human reality is conceived. But value is never separated from existence. Moral choice is never a matter of mere abstractions. The ultimate issue is whether I am really to be or not to be. As Marcel puts it, "What we call value today in fact is what was formerly called the modes or perfections of being. To me personally the kind of philosophy for which 'value' is a key term seems an abortive attempt to recover through our words what we have really lost from our thoughts. For what we have to do with really is a decisive option: the choice between being and not being." [43]

The term *value* suggests an abstract separation from existence, where all true values are. This means that it is no longer possible to regard ethics as a limited subject or field, neatly marked off and isolated from ontology. It also means that for moral insight we must no longer look at language and at abstract essences but

* Cf. "Das Dasein stürzt aus ihm selbst in die Bodenlosigkeit und Nichtigkeit der uneigentlichen alltäglichkeit." (*Sein und Zeit,* p. 178, cf. pp. 130 and 259.)

rather at reality. These insights have already had an invigorating effect upon this somnolent discipline.

Contradiction and Contingency

Choice cannot be evaded. Even the failure to choose is a diluted choice with inexorable consequences. Furthermore, every choice involves rejection. Essences may be synthesized in thought. But I cannot both exist and not exist in a certain way. In being, contradiction is impossible, nothing. From their studies of choice, the existentialist thinkers have been led to a deeper understanding of the meaning of the law of contradiction and the unbridgeable chasm between existential being and non-being. Without nothingness, this law cannot be understood. The existentialist literature does not avoid this basic but difficult topic. Heidegger in *Was ist Metaphysik?*, and Sartre in his major work, have both been concerned with nothingness, especially certain of its derivative modes. Some of these studies are fanciful and distorted. But many are suggestive as well as original. Nothingness has been rediscovered. Ontology once again is alive.

Once this fundamental notion is clarified, other related ideas are bound to come into focus. One of these is the long-neglected idea of contingency, referring to a ubiquitous factor pertaining to all human experience. Once essences are brought before the mind, they are necessary and universal. Regarded abstractly in this way, they do not seem to be contingent. But an existent essence is temporal. It comes and goes. It is individual. Its nature necessarily is what it is. But what of existence? Here the question *why* is relevant.

Why does this entity exist? Why do any such things exist at all? No reason can be found within such an entity. Its nature does not demand existence. Each entity by itself, and the world composed of such entities, is contingent. They might all not exist. With the rediscovery of existence, it is not surprising that this ontological fact should once more be clearly focused. This is a constant theme of existentialism.

According to Heidegger, our human feelings reveal the factual situation into which we have been thrown from no choice of our own. Our moods reveal this sheer facticity to us in its brute contingency without any sense of where-from or where-to.[44] According to Sartre: ". . . existence is not necessity. To exist is simply to be there. The existents come before us, we meet them, but we can never deduce them. . . . Contingency is not a seeming fact, an appearance that we can avoid; it is absolute. . . ."[45] Both the *en soi* and the *pour soi* are radically contingent in the sense that they might just as well not have been. And yet there they are for no visible reason, absurd and too much (*de trop*).[46]

The prejudice against theoretical insight, which the existentialists have inherited from Kierkegaard, has led them to interpret the principle of sufficient reason along subjective lines. Thus according to Heidegger, the notion of reason, or ground, is rooted in the nothingness revealed by anxiety, and the choice that this makes possible. It is here that we experience the possibility of things being otherwise than they are, and from this that we are led to ask for the reasons of things.[47]

It is hard to know whether Heidegger believes that this question can ever be really answered. Probably not. Hence Sartre cogently affirms that from these subjectivist premises we can infer only that all (the *pour soi* as well as the *en soi*) is not only contingent, but ungrounded.* This recognition of the fact of contingency, combined with a denial of the law of sufficient reason, results necessarily in the well-known existentialist theme that life is absurd.

Potency and Change

The existentialist thinkers recognize other ontological categories, and sometimes carefully describe them in their concrete human manifestations, but without systematic analysis. Thus in Jaspers' philosophy, change is a basic category. But he is content with description and ostensive definition, and makes no attempt to determine its structure. Potentiality plays an important role in the theories of both Jaspers and Heidegger, but neither has attempted to work out an exact ontological analysis. Sartre denies all potency in the *en soi* (non-human reality) which he holds to

---

* The *en soi* is uncreated, without reason and without cause. (*L'Être et le Néant*, p. 34.) The *pour soi* is necessarily what it is, but is still contingent in its facticity. (*Ibid.*, pp. 121-127.)

be full and complete, in perfect act.[48] Presumably it is found in human reality, though never carefully explained as such. As we shall see, all these authors hold that human existence is an ever unfinished striving for uncertain goals, never fully attained. Here, at least, the notion of active tendency is often clearly recognized and sometimes vividly described, but hardly ever, except in Heidegger, subjected to an exact analysis.

HUMAN ONTOLOGY

The original data of experience are very rich and various, including existence, both subjective and objective; essence; and forms of order that are internal as well as external, temporal as well as spatial; value and disvalue; contingency; potency; change; and active tendency, all intermixed and merged in a vast confusion. Many fields are incomplete and terminated by arbitrary horizons that may be transcended by persistent investigation. As originally given, these data are for the most part both vague and confused. To grasp them clearly requires accurate description and analysis. Certain types of data are objects of scientific investigation. But no such selection does justice to the world as a whole. They are all abstractions from this. If the investigations of science are to be finally understood, they themselves, together with the theories which explain them, must be fitted back into the concrete world of experience as it is given. What is this ultimate world horizon within which all the events of experience take place? Does it have an intelligible structure? These are philosophic questions to which no science can give an adequate, empirically grounded answer.

Each person has some beginning of an answer to these questions. He has at least a vague *Weltanschauung*, or view of the world as a whole. These views, as we all know, differ from individual to individual and from culture to culture. Kierkegaard described certain basic types, as we have seen. Some of the recent existentialists have also tried to describe experience as it is apprehended by the single individual. Jaspers, for example, has maintained that nothing more than this is possible. Other existentialists, however, like Heidegger and Sartre, have attempted to abstract from individual idiosyncrasies and to describe that recurrent structure which is always present in any human world. As a result of this descriptive effort, certain essential phases of world structure have been so clearly grasped and analyzed that they are now part of the common core of existentialist teaching. Let us now consider them one by one.

Human Existence

Husserl thought that existence is less indubitably given than essence. He believed that existence could be bracketed or ignored, while the phenomenologist focuses the determinate structure (essence) of things. This is true. We can abstract. But Husserl also held, finally, that the abstract world of essence had a peculiar being of its own, and that it could be exhaustively understood apart from factual existence. All the existentialists agree that this is a mistake. While the phenomenologist is intuiting an abstract essence, he is also factually existing. Essence cannot be adequately understood except in relation to this existence. It may be that existence is harder to grasp with clarity, but it is just as directly and immediately given. In the actual world, existence is prior to essence.

Man does not originate from a possibility. He possesses no common nature or essence. The question *What is man?* can be given no definitive answer. That he is, is certain. This naked factual existence is his origin. Everything else comes later. Existence is prior to essence. This assertion is characteristic of existentialist thought. What, then, is meant by existence? This question can be answered only indirectly by a set of negations.[49]

First of all, this existence is not equivalent to the concept of life as developed by Nietzsche and by certain varieties of pragmatism or *Lebensphilosophie*. It is not embedded in a great ongoing stream of evolution carrying it towards cosmic goals. It is naked and alone—a brute fact that simply is.

Existence cannot be known objectively. It is not the object of any faculty or group of faculties. It can be known only internally or subjectively by one who exists.

The philosophy of life maintains that the concrete is too rich to be known theoretically. But the concrete can be more or less closely approximated. Here we find a more radical irrationalism.

According to the existentialist, it is full of paradox and contradiction which preclude rational analysis.

Existence is not what a man has or possesses. It is what he is. All that he possesses, his house, his tools, his goods, may become indifferent to him—even the use of his senses and limbs, and his learning and culture. It is a last inner center which escapes all concepts. In this respect, it is like the Christian experience of the soul, alone before God, to which everything else is alien and external. The negative approach which is required is like that of negative theology.

Life has parts. It can be analyzed into desires and needs. Existence has no parts. It may be indifferent to desires and needs. What we ordinarily mean by life may become external from this point of view.

Existence has no degree. It either is or it is not. It is not to be conceived in spatial terms. My existence is certainly not external to myself. Neither does it coincide with what I think of as internal. My desires and thoughts and hopes and fears may sink into externality and indifference.

Existence is not to be found in any mystic absorption in an absolute. It throws us back on the individual "I."

In spite of this negative approach, existentialist thought must not be confused with Buddhist negativism and quietism. Existence is something positive and affirmative. It leads us on to dynamism and action in a world where there is no vanishing of time.

Existence is beyond conceptual analysis and definition. It can only be described and illumined. The background of this conception is the Christian experience of the soul confronting an alien world, alone before God. The individual person has no fixed essence or nature. His essence is to exist, to act. He is always more than what he now is, constantly projecting himself ahead of himself in a restless urge to fulfilment, never achieved. According to the existentialists, this is what it is like to exist as a man. The aim of this philosophy is to remind us of that existence which we all know immediately in a confused, inarticulate way, and to clarify this awareness by the accurate description of invariable factors found within it.

Being-in-the-World

My existence is not first given to me as the object of a detached mind which is separated from it. I find myself existing in the first place, and my mind is part of my existence. I find that I am aware of myself, but not myself alone. The existentialist philosophy must not be confused with solipsism or any form of idealism. My existence is active and tendential. It is surrounded not by static objects of knowledge, but by moving powers and agencies that aid it and obstruct it. I do not exist in a point of view from which I am detached, but rather in a situation determined not only by my own urges but by alien forces as well. Both are presented to me with equal immediacy. I am a being to whom existence is revealed. No attempt is made by the existentialists to explain this openness to being. It is simply described as a brute fact. I find that I am aware of the forces now resisting me, of the situation I am in, of further forces encompassing these, and finally of that ultimate horizon which I call the world. Together with all these alien forces, I exist-in-the-world, restlessly seeking for peace and fulfilment.

We have a strong tendency to interpret the word "in" as a form of purely spatial inclusion. We think of the world as a spatial container *in* which we ourselves and other objects simply lie at fixed coordinates. But this is a mistake. Things are *in* the world as *in* a field of care or concern. We often think of the world as a mere sum of all those objects which are already *in*-the-world. But this is an error. World-structure is prior to the objects which are in it. We are first aware of the entities surrounding us, not as mere "things" which are simply there on hand to be stared at, but rather as tools or instruments to be used in certain ways. They are *at hand* rather than *on hand,* stuff to be worked on rather than objects to be known. The chair invites us to rest, the pencil to write, the book to be studied or rejected. The place of such objects is not determined by Cartesian coordinates, where the zero point is purely arbitrary. They are in or out of a place determined rather by human purpose and plan. The place of the paper is in my drawer where it is ready for use.

Dasein (Man) does not occupy a place like a physical object there before me. He prepares places for himself, and takes his place in the neighborhoods he has prepared. He is not merely in space but actively spatializes himself in following his projects, which always determine the structure of the world in which he acts. In pursuing these projects, he approaches or recedes from us. This existential distance is not restricted to its spatial manifestations. In our primordial experience, distance is not merely a matter of miles or metres. As originally experienced, it is merged with time, and measured by the effort to be expended in reaching the goal. Thus there is psychic as well as physical distance. A friendly person physically separated from us may be much closer than someone in the immediate vicinity with whom it is hard to communicate.

These objects are first understood by us in relation to our existential action. They are in-the-world as the field of our ordered purpose. With reference to this, they are hostile or friendly, in place or out of place. But this does not mean that they are subjective in an epistemological sense. These relations are not in the mind, or even mind-dependent. I myself actually exist, and my existence is actually related in these ways to the forces around me. Furthermore, I can be aware of these relations as they actually are. There is no inevitable noetic transformation or distortion. It may be said that my action is biased and tendential. This, of course, is true. But I am this bias. There is nothing unreal about it, and this at least I can know as it is, together with those alien forces that help or frustrate it.

But this bias is only a tiny fragment of the world as a whole. Even the collective urges of mankind are only an insignificant island in the great ocean of being. Our vision may be true so far as it goes. But it does not go very far. And here lies a great danger. It is easy for us to confuse the relatively ordered world which we have carved from the wilderness with the universe at large. This often happens with those whose vision is restricted to the regular routines of daily life. Hence they come to think of the world itself as an ordered system, or cosmos, in which everything has its place. They even view themselves as pawns or instruments of some kind performing some function in a cosmic system they themselves imagine and project.

According to the existentialist, this is a fearful error. Man has been cast up in the world, we know not whither or how. He has established some order around him. But this stands in the midst of a vast and mysterious waste. He is himself full of paradox and mystery, and opaque to his own intelligence. Whatever else he may be, he is certainly not his own instrument. He is not merely a thing that is there to be gaped at, nor a passive stuff to be used for some purpose. He is not a thing at all, for a thing is just what it is. But a man is never just what he is. He is free and able to determine himself by his chosen projects. When he realizes this, the determinate entities of nature become alien and strange, for they certainly are not free, and seem to have no purpose at all. The ordered realm of human culture may also become strange, for its underlying purposes often fail to survive a careful questioning. The brute facts of his own origin and early history are foreign to him because he has been thrown into existence and assigned a particular place in the world without being consulted or informed. Where is the justification? He is alone with his freedom in a world that is alien and remote.

This freedom to make himself separates man radically from all subhuman entities of nature. They simply are *what* they are, and do what their natures determine them to do. Man *makes himself.* He is not merely something different. He is something different existing in a different way. Modern philosophy has toned this down. Naturalism has attempted to reduce what is peculiarly human to the level of subhuman nature, and thus to emphasize the continuity between man and the rest of the universe. Idealism, on the other hand, has attempted to elevate nature—to regard it as the expression of a spirit somehow congenial and friendly to man. All things fit together, making up a great world system in which we can feel at home.

According to the existentialists this is a delusion. There is a terrible chasm between us and all subhuman things. These entities, as science dispassionately reveals them to us, are quite unlike ourselves. We have been thrown into a universe where we are surrounded by vast ranges of speechless and unfeeling being. We stand alone in a world which is foreign to our existence; where, without comforting delusions, we cannot feel at home. Indeed, much of our own human life—yes, much of ourselves—when sharply focused, seems alien and strange. This feeling, based upon new insights into the uniqueness of human existence, runs through the whole existentialist literature, and sharply distinguishes it from all forms of naturalism and idealism. It is poignantly expressed in a well-known poem of the German writer Rainer Maria Rilke:

The Great Night

I'd often stand at the window started the day before,
stand and stare at you. It still seemed to warn me off,
the strange city, whose unconfiding landscape
gloomed as though I didn't exist. The nearest
things didn't mind if I misunderstood them. The street
would thrust itself up to the lamp, and I'd see it was strange.
A sympathizable room up there, revealed in the lamplight:
I'd begin to share: they'd notice, and close the shutters.
I'd stand. Then a child would cry, and I'd know the mothers
in the houses, what they were worth. I'd know in a moment
inconsolable grounds of infinite crying.
                              Or else, when an hour was striking
I'd begin to count too late and let it escape me.
As a strange little boy, when at last they invite him to
    join them
cannot catch the ball, and is quite unable
to share the game the rest are so easily playing,
but stands and gazes—whither?—I'd stand, and, all at once
realize you were being friends with me, playing with me,
    grown up
Night, and I'd gaze at you. While towers
were raging, and while, with its hidden fate,
a city stood round me, and undivinable mountains
camped against me, and Strangeness in narrowing circles,
hungrily prowled round my casual flares of perception. . . . [50]

With-Others

In its unquestioning acceptance of the world of nature and technology, existentialism has broken with the epistemological subjectivism of modern thought. It conceives of its function not as that of speculating about imaginary problems, but rather as that of describing existence as it is. We find ourselves existing-in-the-world. We also find ourselves existing-with-others. These facts are as evident as my own existence. Subjective data are not privileged. Hence there is no special problem of "other minds," as it has been called. This is not a problem but a misconception. Mind is not walled up within itself, but self-projective and communicable by word and deed. Human existence is transmissive. Each individual, whether he wills it or not, is constantly radiating signs to others, and receiving signs from them. He is bathed in an atmosphere filled with the light of translucent communication.

It is true that this atmosphere may become misty and opaque. Words may be used in such a way as to conceal rather than to reveal our thought. But this is due either to special, unconscious perversions of a natural function, or else to conscious techniques of deception. Our existence is open and communicable. We are directly aware of the sympathetic or antithetic moods and responses of others. If this were not true, we could not become aware of breakdown and obstruction; we could not distinguish between failure and success. Our existence is an existence-with-others. Being alone is a privative mode, the failure of an ever-present power.

Modern thought has ignored the complex phenomena of human communication. The existentialists have rightly called our attention to them as an essential phase of human existence, and have begun the arduous task of describing them as they actually occur, and distinguishing their major types. Thus Kierkegaard struggled with the problems facing one who desires to communicate personal experiences and existential attitudes to those pursuing alien ways of life, and developed his strange technique of pseudonyms. This is certainly not an adequate solution, but he clearly grasped the problems. Jaspers and Heidegger have called attention to the current overemphasis on linguistic symbols, and the serious corruptions and perversions to which this gives rise.[51] Jaspers has also clearly distinguished abstract scientific communication from that which is philosophical or existential, and has made many penetrating comments on the latter.[52]

Exact analysis and explanation have not as yet been achieved. But a new field, the phenomenology of human communication, has been opened up, and is now ready for disciplined investigation. This is a noteworthy challenge of existentialist thought.

Boundary Situations

The objects of thought may be static and fixed. But as Kierkegaard made very clear, man himself is active and tendential. He does not exist in a realm of inert objects, but in a field of shifting forces. He is himself a center of urges which these either aid or obstruct. Certain aspects of a situation may be clearly revealed by abstract analysis. The whole situation is always dimly revealed in the twilight of what we call mood or feeling. It is satisfying, irritating, gloomy, or hopeless. The mood itself is a part of the situation which usually presses upon us, and weighs on us with little reference to choice.

Some of these situations may be clearly analyzed and met by clever calculation. Others cannot be met in this way. They resist theoretical analysis and are insurmountable by any plan. They are ever present and inescapable. We can see no way of getting around them. We cannot see beyond them at all. Hence Jaspers has called them boundary situations.[53] The term is his, but the concept is common to all the existentialists. These situations limit us and hem us in. They are like unscalable walls which bear down upon us. We can recognize their presence, but not exactly what they are. We can neither plan for them nor escape from them. We can only struggle and in the end be shattered by them.

What are they? Of those considered by Jaspers,[54] six have been widely accepted and discussed by other writers.

The first is something we may call situationality,[55] the fact that while we may succeed in escaping from one situation, it is only to fall into another. We are always in some dynamic situation. From this we can never escape.

The second is the fact of chance and fortune.[56] Human existence is always at the mercy of chance eruptions and coincidences. No one is ever safe. Plans of the highest import may be ruined by the smashing of a teacup; existence of the highest order wiped out by a falling brick. Once in being, we are ever subject to this threat. But this is not all. Who can say to what degree our very existence is not conditioned by such random factors? Who can say? In this sense, life is absurd. Why are we here? Who can answer this question? We have been cast into the world without rhyme or reason, a random happening, a sad mischance.

The third is suffering (*Leiden*),[57] which dominates many situations and threatens others but can never be altogether ignored. It assumes many forms: corporeal pain, illness, mental disease (the loss of myself without death), old age and its weariness, torture and enslavement by alien power, hunger, and starvation. It is always a shrinking of life. Behind all suffering is death. There are great differences in the modes and degrees of suffering, but at last they all come to the same. Each must bear his own suffering. No one is spared.

The fourth is the fact of human struggle and conflict.[58] Two human individuals never completely agree. There is always some measure of forceful domination. In ordinary conversation and in scientific discourse, basic opinions and attitudes are not expressed. When that rare phenomenon, philosophical or existential communication does occur, it always takes the form of "friendly combat." At the social level, this omnipresent fact of conflict takes a cruder and more evident form. Social peace is purchased only at the price of physical force or the threat of force. Thus American life at the present time is conditioned by the atom bomb.

A fifth limiting situation is the fact of guilt.[59] Who can escape it? Whoever we are, whatever we do, we are guilty. We may try to forget this fact and suppress it. Nevertheless it is certainly there.

The sixth and final one is the fact of death.[60]

These facts are inescapable. They implacably confront us when we make any honest review of our existence in the world. They are opaque to understanding. We can do nothing about them. They show us the essential limits of our being. They restrict us and weigh upon us. They reveal the harshness and the strangeness of the world in which we live. This is a unique feature of existentialist thought. The idea that man is finite is, of course, not new. But it has often been slurred over, and even dealt with as an accident which may be mitigated in various ways. The existentialists have brought this fact once more into the clear light, and have emphasized it with a new poignancy and penetration. It is a clear-cut challenge to the idealist notion of a friendly universe, and to the innumerable forms of sentimental optimism which this modern conception has spewed forth in recent times.

Death

All men know that they must die; [61] the time is uncertain. As the ancient saying has it: *Mors certa; hora incerta*. It is inescapable and opaque to theoretical analysis. There is no evidence. That it will be, we are certain; what it is, we do not know. At the best, we may postpone it for a time, but in the last analysis we can do nothing about it. Like an impenetrable barrier, it stands before us limiting us and hemming us in. This is the ultimate boundary situation, and as such it deserves special treatment. In it, the general features of a boundary situation are marked with a peculiar evidence, which is clearly brought out by the existentialist descriptions.

These analyses have often been misunderstood because they conflict with certain idealistic and naturalistic attitudes which actually rest on a very shaky foundation, as the existentialists have shown.

Science regards everything as an object from a detached point of view. It abstracts from subjectively lived existence. Deceived by this attitude and its monopolistic claims on truth, I may conceive of death exclusively in terms of observed phenomena and generalizations based upon these. I will think of death in terms of heartbeats, loss of consciousness, respiration rate, and a host of similar phenomena. But alas, I am deceiving myself. This is no doubt all very true, but really irrelevant to my own death, which is the central question for me. This death I shall not be observing from the outside with cardiographs and stethoscopes. This death I shall be actually dying by myself. No one can die my death for me. This thing at least I must do alone.

We have all been influenced by a naturalistic view of death as the culmination of a gradual ripening process in which, after youth and maturity, the harvest is finally reaped. This vegetative analogy, however, simply does not hold. It ignores the sad fact of senility. Death often waits too long. Furthermore, young persons are often struck down in their prime, or even before. Human death is not the harvesting of a fully ripened and undamaged fruit.

Misled by the vague pantheism so often associated with naturalism, we are apt to identify ourselves with the life cycle of the species which, of course, survives. We then think of death as a process of rejuvenation by which old and outworn individuals are constantly replaced by the young and energetic. But I am not the species; and I do not survive.

The naturalist tends to underestimate the role of awareness and anticipation in human existence. Reducing this to the biological functions of life, he easily persuades us to think of our existence as a long cord stretching on and on from a first beginning. Death is then conceived as a shears approaching this cord from the outside, and snipping it off at the end. As the Epicureans argued, this end is wholly external and does not concern us at all. When we are, it is not. When it is, we are not. Life and death are separate from each other; they do not interpenetrate. But unfortunately (for this view) the human individual not only exists, he knows that he is existing. He not only knows this, he also anticipates the future. He knows that he is going to die. Death has to be faced here and now. In the conscious existence of man, life and death do interpenetrate. Man exists only in the face of death.

From these criticisms, the stark reality to which the existentialist descriptions refer emerges in naked clarity. Actual death confronts the human person with the dizzying possibility of nothingness, his not existing at all. As such, it is an impenetrable limit of his real existence. It is an actual act to be lived through by the individual alone. So far as he is a conscious person, it is something that he must face now. It is this last fact that is underscored by the existentialist thinkers. When they speak of death, they are not thinking primarily of death-bed scenes, last agonies, and the pains of expiration. About all this, of course, much can be done by others. What they are thinking of is my way of facing death here and now. There are many ways of facing it. I may forget it, suppress it, evade it, or sharply focus it. But face it some way I must. However I may respond, it is an essential limiting fact of existence. Harsh, mysterious, and inexorable, it places all else in question, and reveals the uncanny strangeness of the world.

CONCLUSION

In this chapter we have studied the new empiricism and the ontological data it has discovered, especially being, which pervades every aspect of our experience in many different modes. According to Heidegger, the aim of philosophy is not merely to describe this being or that being, but rather to shed some light on being itself. The study of human existence which he has completed in *Sein und Zeit* is only an approach to this basic problem, an ontological fragment rather than a complete ontology. Aside from Sartre, this is also true of the other existentialist thinkers. They recognize the presence of ontological data which have been revealed by phenomenological research. Here and there they have given us painstaking analyses of such data. But as yet they have refrained from any attempt to interpret being as such, and in the light of this to fit the isolated bits of ontological structure into an intelligible framework. Some, like Jaspers, insist that no such theory can be anything more than plausible myth, or a personal theory. But even those like Heidegger and Sartre who are not so skeptical, have restricted their attention primarily to man.

Man has been studied from various quantitative perspectives as physiological, as behaving, as economic, etc. But now it has become evident that man also *exists*. What light can be shed, if we regard him from the point of view of those basic categories we have just been discussing? This ontological approach has already led to many new insights and suggestions in the fields of epistemology and ethics. But these disciplines are no longer conceived as isolated fields or islands. Their objects are kinds and modes of being. With this ontological setting in mind, new truth becomes accessible.

When we regard man from an ontological point of view, we find that he is marked off from other beings not merely by certain determinate traits (essences), but by a peculiar mode of being which marks him off even more radically. This human way of being is now called existence, and has given its name to the new philosophy we are studying. This existence is active and temporal. It has many peculiar structural modes which Heidegger calls existentials, and which he and others have described. In this section, we have considered some of these: being-in-the-world, being-with-others, and the unsurpassable boundaries which limit his finite being, including the final boundary of death. These are not fixed properties of a finished thing, but tendential phases and limits of his relational being. Each one of these involves awareness. Each man at least vaguely knows that he exists-in-a-world. He not only interacts with others but communicates his awareness to them. He not only comes to an end like the other animals, he knows that he must die.

Awareness is always a phase of human existence. What role does it play as a part of our being? How does it really work in the concrete? How is it to be accurately described as an existential mode of man? The existentialist thinkers have raised these questions, and have been led by them to suggest answers of great interest which often seem very strange in the context of modern philosophy. It is to these answers that we shall now turn.

- 4 -

Human Awareness and Action

REAL KNOWLEDGE belongs to the being of man, and is itself a mode of action. All the existentialist thinkers bring awareness into a close relationship with human practice. Some, like Sartre, assert an ultimate identity between the two. To choose and to be aware are one and the same.[1] As we shall see, even those who do not go so far, interpret human knowledge in the light of action. It is practical reason in which they are primarily interested. Theoretical reason, so far as it is recognized at all, is seen as a subordinate derivation.

HUMAN AWARENESS

Jaspers' epistemological views never escape from the confines of a Kantian subjectivism, or critical realism, so we shall not refer to him in this section. Marcel has been moving steadily away from idealism towards a more realistic position.[2] His thought is phenomenologically very suggestive and always stimulating, but often hard to interpret in any exact detail. His ideas about human awareness and action seem to be very close to those of Heidegger. Sometimes, however, there are significant differences, which we shall note. On the whole, we shall follow the thought of Heidegger as expressed in *Sein und Zeit;*[3] first, because of the scope and rigor of his investigations; second, because his results in this field are representative of existentialist thought in general; and third, because they are at present so little known in England and America.

86

MOOD AND FEELING

My being in the world is first of all disclosed in the primordial awareness of mood and feeling. Heidegger here follows closely in the path laid down by Kierkegaard, but adds important new observations of his own, and fits these insights together more exactly and clearly into an existential view of man as a whole. Feeling has its own peculiar mode of disclosure, and gives us access to much that is opaque to pure theory.[4] Such theory, for example, is incapable of revealing an actual danger or a threat. It may be possible to gain a certain control over our feelings by clarification from other cognitive sources. But we can never get rid of them. My moods are ever present, constantly revealing the rough situation of which I am the center, and how it is going with me. Even the most decisive action has its feeling tones. Pure theory itself has its moods of detached concentration and excitement. My mood is not a succession of psychic events proceeding within me, for it discloses external objects which aid or threaten me. It is not restricted to a single object or a set of objects there before me, since it also discloses itself and my subjective condition. Thus it is neither objective nor subjective, but transcends these categories. It is not something *there* at which I can look. It is rather an existential mode which in its way reveals my being-in-the-world.[5]

What does it reveal? According to Heidegger, it is always centered in the factual place where I am. It discloses the naked facticity of this situation into which I have already been thrown. But this facticity is not that of an object from which I am detached, and at which I can stare. It is an existential facticity concerned with itself and either turning back to take over its factuality, or turning away from this as a burden and a chain.[6] For the most part, it is the latter type of feeling that predominates. I feel myself thrown into a situation that weighs on me, that I must solve as best I can in order to pass on. I feel myself struggling in order to escape. It is through such moods that I first gain cognitive access to my being-in-the-world. Heidegger does not try to analyze its relational structure more exactly. It belongs to my being to be thus disclosed to myself.

Marcel would not disagree with the major points of this description.[7] He also deplores the way in which sense and feeling in general have been neglected by the intellectualistic traditions of modern thought.[8] Cartesian idealism denied it any purely cognitive significance, and tried to make reason altogether independent of it. This led inevitably to skepticism. Our knowledge of existence is gained only with the cooperation of sense and feeling. In actual life, sense and reason never work separately, but always in combination. Marcel has devoted himself tirelessly to the clarification of certain attitudes where both are involved —like hope and fidelity.[9] On the whole, he goes farther than Heidegger in defending the claim of such cognition to provide us with reliable knowledge, not only of ourselves but of independent being as well.

PROJECTIVE UNDERSTANDING

So far as what is ordinarily called *rational knowledge* is concerned, Heidegger's emphasis is voluntaristic and practical. Theoretical insight is viewed as derived and very narrow in scope. Mood and feeling always take me back to the facticity of what I already am in my given situation. Understanding, *verstehen* as he calls it, focuses on my essential possibilities and projects— that part of me which is always ahead of itself in the future. According to Heidegger, this is the central core of my being.[10] My projects are not added on to me as an actual and rounded being. They are not accidents of a substance already there. What is already there is essentially incomplete. This must be taken over, if I am to exist authentically. But my projects are even more important. I am the possibilities which my understanding projects before me.

It is not that I have potentialities which my cognition then understands. Heidegger says, rather, that understanding is the possibilities it projects as an essential phase of my being.[11] In this sense, of course, understanding is a kind of creation, the projection of new being. But Heidegger also recognizes the sense in which understanding must be a disclosure of something already existent in some way.[12] For example, I can become aware of a real possibility already possessed by me. But for Heidegger, any such possibility already is an act of understanding. Hence he is led to interpret the fact that I have never been without possibilities as implying that I have never been without understanding. All insight presupposes previous insight, and thus moves in a circle.[13]

Furthermore, the whole world is ordered and understood with reference to the ultimate projects I set for myself. To judge a thing is to interpret it in the light of some project, ultimately in the light of my ultimate aspiration. All understanding is relative to *Dasein* and his projects. Pure theoretical apprehension is not denied. But it is reduced to a secondary and derived position.[14] Our primitive insight into things is practical. In using the hammer, I find it is too heavy, and seek for another hammer. But when at leisure and freed from the demands of action, I may simply look at the hammer from a detached point of view, and examine its so-called properties as a hammer-thing there before me. Theoretical science arises in this way. Heidegger does not go so far as many other existentialists in disputing the claims of such theoretical knowledge. But, like them, he expresses a deep distrust. Apparently it can give us valid knowledge of only a restricted sphere of non-living entities. It is incapable of grasping human possibility,[15] but turns it always into a fixed existent of some kind. When we apply this kind of seeing to *Dasein,* it leads us to disastrous misunderstandings.

What method, then, is Heidegger himself using in describing the existence of *Dasein?*

This question is never clearly answered. He calls it phenomenology—which would suggest a detached theoretical apprehension of this being as it actually shows itself to be. But this would seem to contradict the many disparaging remarks made about seeing and theoretical intuition throughout the work. Also, he refers to his method as interpretative phenomenology.[16] This would imply the *a priori* acceptance of some practical point of view. If so, this point of view is not exactly explained, nor how such a procedure could fail to distort the data. It is implied that sound philosophy can only interpret and clarify the insight already possessed by men.[17] This is certainly true. But it does not follow that this primordial insight is exclusively or even primarily practical.

In his discussion of knowledge, Heidegger constantly wavers

between two conceptions: that of knowing as disclosure, and that of knowing as the articulation of a practical project. On the whole, it is the latter view that predominates. Our primordial and true insight into the world is derived from our active projection of possibilities ahead of ourselves. This projection is the first act of understanding. This orders ourselves and all other entities into an intelligible world. Interpretation is the detailed development of this frame, and its application to concrete objects confronting us. To fit something into such a frame is to disclose its being. Such disclosure belongs to the being of *Dasein*. He is the disclosures he makes. Some of them are true and reveal the entity itself.

What, then, is the revealing relation? Many possibilities of *Dasein* have nothing to do with this. I can swim. I can walk. These do not *reveal* anything to me unless I am conscious. How does this awareness enable me to penetrate to the being of what I know? Heidegger gives no definite answer to these questions. Like modern epistemologists in general, he evades them. He says that this awareness belongs to the being of *Dasein*.[18] He recognizes its relational structure.[19] He has placed us in a perspective where we are certainly far more likely to find a solution. But he has given us no ontological analysis and explanation of the noetic act.

Sartre noticed this in his close reading of Heidegger's text, and was left unsatisfied. He has, therefore, tried to deal with this question by developing Heidegger's ideas in his own way. Certain of these developments are worthy of serious attention.

SARTRE'S THEORY OF AWARENESS

Sartre breaks completely with the Kantian subjectivism that believes in a hidden thing in itself behind the appearances, like flesh behind the clothing which conceals it. When we describe phenomena we are not describing nothing.[20] Being is a datum, and furthermore this being is independent of our knowing it. Sartre gives several rather questionable arguments in favor of this position. But one of them at least is sound. This is based on the intentional or relational structure that is always found in awareness.[21] I cannot be conscious without being conscious *of* something. The idealist tends to merge the object with the act.

Then it is reasonable to hold that I perceive my own states or acts. But the act is not self-creative. It is always *of* something quite distinct. It is, therefore, absurd to suppose that awareness gives being to the object out of itself. If being reduces to being perceived, then consciousness must be perceived in order to be, and we are involved in an infinite regress. The intentional structure of awareness runs counter to the whole drift of idealism. It strongly suggests that the being of the object is independent of its being known. Sartre accepts this theory.[22] The object exists in its own right. There is no thing in itself back of the appearance. So far as it accurately describes this appearance, phenomenology apprehends being as it is.

According to Sartre, the first act of awareness manifests such an object. Indirectly and obliquely it manifests itself at the same time. But it is focused on the object and ignores itself.[23] Thus in the case of an internal feeling like pleasure, so close is the union of awareness with object that it is difficult to distinguish the two. There is no pleasure thing apart from my awareness. Nor can I distinguish any awareness apart from the object. The two are one. In revealing the object, awareness reveals itself. This is what Sartre calls *the pre-reflexive cogito*. The awareness does not grasp itself by a separate act. It simply reveals its real object, and thereby reveals itself. The reflexive act is very different, but derived from the former. Here awareness turns on its own act, and focuses it as an object. This is the Cartesian *reflexive cogito*, the awareness of myself as thinking I. But Descartes made two mistakes in interpreting this experience of self-consciousness.[24]

In the first place, he failed to see that this is founded on a primitive, non-reflexive experience which makes me aware of a real object. In the second place, he failed to see the intentional duality in the I-think-*about*, and interpreted it as a unified thing, the I-substance, which led him into idealism. As against these errors, Sartre rightly points out that our original awareness is always *of* some object. Until this occurs, I cannot become aware of myself at all. When I turn my attention to this awareness by a second act of reflection, I may of course abstract from the objective pole that is always present. But I cannot forget it completely without distorting the phenomenon. Awareness is always bipolar, the revealing of an object. It is not a thing, but rather a relation. This phenomenological criticism of subjectivism is very sound.

But what is this peculiar relation of disclosing? What kind of being is it? How can it be explained? As we have noted, Heidegger never answers these questions. But Sartre is not content with mere description. He boldly tries to answer them in terms of an ontological system that is a strange and suggestive mixture of truth and error. Like other existentialists, Sartre sees the gross inadequacy of physicalist attempts to explain consciousness. Hence he expressly rejects materialism as a complete account of the world.[25] Nevertheless, his view of being (*en soi*) is very similar. It is inert and inactive. It is fully complete with no room for potency.[26] Finally, it is a huge atomic plenum, wholly enclosed within itself, a being-in rather than a being-to, and thus non-relational in structure.[27]

Now let us look at the awareness which needs to be explained. It is active and not inert. Its potencies are never filled.[28] There is always more to be known. Finally, it is radically relational in structure, never enclosed within itself, but always reaching out to unite with an object distinct from itself. These traits emerge clearly from Sartre's own descriptions of awareness. It is clear that we must find something beyond his limited conception of the *en soi*, if we are to explain this strange phenomenon. We might broaden our conception of being. But Sartre is committed to his globular view of the *en soi*. So he refuses to take this course. Only one alternative then remains. Awareness is beyond being as he conceives it. What is beyond being is nothing. Hence awareness is non-being.[29] Its activity is an act of nihilating. As potency, it is not. As the privation of being, without which it cannot be understood, it is essentially relational.[30]

Forced into this desperate procedure by his limited view of being, Sartre then presents us with a brilliant and voluminous display of dialectic in which he tries to show how nothingness, taken in many different senses to which it is susceptible, can shed light on pre-reflexive and reflexive awareness, on choice and human life in general. In spite of its artificiality, this elaborate *tour de force* represents an attempt to make the original phenomena of consciousness really intelligible, which is unique in the literature of modern epistemology.

If he had stuck consistently to the notion of nothing as unqualified absence of all being, this so-called explanation would be wholly unintelligible. *Nothing* in this sense cannot explain. But fortunately Sartre is not always consistent in this way. The vagueness of the term often enables him to shift over to other allied meanings, such as "absence," "otherness," "repulsion," etc.,[31] and potencies of different sorts which are found in experience,* though for Sartre they contain a certain nothingness in themselves.[32] When these ambiguities are borne in mind, it is possible to find real significance and sometimes partially developed insight in the Sartrian dialectic.

Awareness is certainly distinct from its object and yet identified with it. If the knowing act is viewed as a fixed thing enclosed within itself, or even as a set of physical motions, all explanations must inevitably shatter. There is no way in which one physical thing or motion may become identical with other things or motions from which it is physically distinct. Awareness is not anything physical of this sort. From a materialistic point of view, it is, indeed, a peculiar nothingness, ready to be fulfilled. In this way, as nothing, it is distinct from its real object, and remains distinct even when partially filled. But as fulfilled, it can be its object. If interpreted as a mode of potency, this nothingness makes sense.

Sartre also refers to it as a pure relation. Hence it can become related to itself, retiring to a distance from its first act, and, as we say, reflecting upon it. One consciousness then becomes aware of another. The two are thus identified. No spatial distance, no interval of time, no entity of any sort—only nothing lies between the two. They are one. And yet this oneness is not absolute. Presence-to implies a duality of some kind.[33] I am never exhaustively that which I know. This is even true of self-awareness. The first is an object, and therefore merged with being. The second reflecting awareness is a potential nothing becoming fulfilled. So the two are distinct, but separated only by nothing. It is

* Thus possibility is the lack of the *pour soi*—nothing. *L'Être et le Néant,* pp. 139-145.

impossible to catch this nothingness by itself. It is pure relation to being. We tend to hypostatize it into a real thing of some kind, and thus to confuse the *pour soi* with the *en soi*.* But this leads us only into the absurdities of subjectivism.

Awareness lies at the core of our human existence. It is a nothingness which has sprung up from the heart of being and which perpetually haunts it.[34] This nothing is an existential relation. It *is* only by virtue of what it is not. Without being, of which I am aware, there can be no awareness. And yet it is not what it is. My awareness never completely coincides with its object. Wherever man comes, he brings notness with him. His intelligence begins by asking why something is not otherwise. He advances only by negating what is there. The possibilities which, as Heidegger has shown, are the central core of his being, are nothing. When we concentrate on any phase of this being, we find nothingness at its roots. Man is the source of nothingness,[35] an adventurous worm that gnaws at the heart of being.[36] No explanation of awareness can be given in causal terms, for being cannot explain nothing.[37] It is its own principle, a nihilating emptiness, a crack in the plenum of existence.

But the story is not finished. If this nothingness were purely relational, it might be filled with being as it is, and thus really disclose it. But this is not the case. It is a productive or creative nothingness like the Hegelian negation. Its nihilation is the emergence of something new. Here Sartre follows Heidegger in fusing knowing with action, thus giving his whole theory a strongly voluntaristic and idealistic twist. We have already noted Heidegger's tendency to think of all genuine potency as centered in *Dasein*. Sartre bluntly asserts this.[38] The *en soi* has no potency.[39] Indeed, it lacks all that determinate structure and order which is so characteristic of our knowledge. This certainly facilitates the passage to a practical interpretation of awareness.

The *pour soi* also lacks active being. This gives us a new sense of nothingness, and a new dialectic of action. This being, not possessed by the *pour soi,* is its possibilities. They are not discov-

* This seems to be the point of Heidegger's objection to the traditional view of truth as a relation of agreement *between* the judgment (conceived as a thing) and another external "thing." (Cf. *Sein und Zeit*, pp. 219-226.)

ered, for they neither exist anywhere in themselves nor in any realm of abstraction.[40] They are projected ahead of itself by the *pour soi,* which *is* these possibilities. I am my possibilities, and exist only by virtue of them, as they exist only by virtue of me. Being nothing, there are infinite things that I might be. Amongst these I must choose. This choice rests solely with me, and is wholly arbitrary.[41] Serious people pretend that their choices are grounded on factual laws, on natural principles, on the will of God, etc. But these are only transparent attempts to rationalize choices already made. The choice is groundless and arbitrary. But it sets up ends and goals which are the source of what we call *the order of the world.* This world, the totality of existents, is the way I have ordered things, or understood them in order to strive for my chosen projects. Every person exists-in-a-world. Without a world there can be no person; but without a person there can be no world.[42]

Thus the *pour soi* is viewed as active, and, as in Heidegger, understanding is thoroughly pragmatized. The meaning of an event is the way it fits into a plan of action, and all understanding presupposes an ultimate end that has been chosen. Theory is assimilated to practice. My choice of myself and my world order is at the same time my discovery of the world. Awareness and choice are really one.[43] This pragmatic conception determines the existentialist attitude towards the discipline of logic, which we shall now briefly consider.

LOGIC AS GROUNDED ON BEING

We have already considered that formal or symbolic logic which in certain parts of the world has now become the central philosophical discipline. The decadent logic of the late Middle Ages began to think of logical entities as separate things having a formal structure of their own, independent of all intentional reference to reality. Modern logic, as we have noted, has carried this reifying process to further extremes. Conceptual meaning has been ignored and sometimes reduced to the instrumental symbols of language. The syntactic structure of these symbols has been cut off from their referential functions. As a result of these prevailing trends, logic has been completely isolated from ontology and even from epistemology, without which its basic structures cannot be intelligibly understood. In many schools, it has lost all contact with living thought, and has become the private play-thing of individual technicians, each playing an arbitrary game of his own.

In *Sein und Zeit,* Heidegger makes several critical comments on this tragic history. He is clearly aware of the fact that Greek logic was intentional,[44] which radically separates it from every variety of symbolic logic. The Greeks saw clearly that subject and predicate were tools by which the mind analyzes and then re-synthesizes the confused original data of sense.[45] Heidegger accepts this subject-predicate analysis, as any intentional logician must.* He criticizes the Aristotelian analysis on another score. He thinks that it was ontologically unsound in being too insensitive to possibility. Being was conceived primarily as what is actually there and can be seen. Even logical entities were regarded in this way as things.[46] This helped to bring about the tragic separation of logic from being, and even from intelligibility, which is characteristic of modern subjectivism. According to Heidegger, the judgment is logistically dissolved into a system of rules, and becomes the object of a sort of reckoning rather than the theme for ontological interpretation.[47]

The logic of science and of all living discourse is referential. Our terms bear sense; they mean something existent. If logic is to be preserved as a humane discipline, we must revive something like the classical conception of intentionality. Heidegger's prejudice against theoretical reflection, however, leads him to think that this conception must be modified in a practical or pragmatic direction. He believes that our primordial insight into existence is achieved only in terms of our active projects. What we intend, therefore, is not primarily the pattern of things as they are in themselves, but rather the pattern of things as they are arranged in the light of some chosen project. In his account of insight and interpretation, Heidegger has made many interesting suggestions concerning the way in which such a logic of practice may be developed.[48] He has given less attention to the logic of theory, and

* Thus x is always understood *as* y. Cf. *Sein und Zeit,* p. 159.

on the whole regards it as a derived and even an unauthentic mode of reflection.[49]

Heidegger's major works have not been translated into English.* Until recently they have not been carefully studied and interpreted by Anglo-Saxon writers. Hence he has been bitterly attacked as anti-rational and anti-logical. Any careful reader of his works, however, can see that this is based on a serious misunderstanding. Heidegger and other existentialists are attacking modern logic, it is true. But except to a provincially-minded fanatic knowing little of the history of philosophy, this will not be interpreted as an attack on logic as such. What he is trying to do is to rescue logic from the hands of minute technicians, and to restore it to the position it once had as the interpreter and guide of meaningful discourse.

As Heidegger himself puts it: "What is going on here? . . . With the help of this widely heralded logic and *ratio,* one argues that whatever is not positive is necessarily negative, and is therefore advocating the abandonment of reason. . . . One is so filled with 'logic' that everything running counter to the prevailing lethargy of thought is judged without discrimination to be a. worthless negation." [50] Instead of becoming obsessed with minor details of mathematics, it is the function of logic to inquire into the structure of human meaning as such. "What will all these widely known systems of logic do for us, when without even reflecting on the matter, they simply dismiss the task of inquiring about the *logos* itself?" [51] Here Heidegger speaks for most existentialists. Whatever else it may have done, mathematical logic has certainly not shed much light on the Logos.

Logic may be turned into the theory of calculating machines. No doubt this is interesting and important. But there is another task that is even more important, no matter what we name it. This is to study the intentional structure of living discourse, and to devise a humane discipline for its guidance. This is not only

* A summary and commentary on *Sein und Zeit* together with a translation of four essays by Heidegger was published by Werner Brock, *Existence and Being,* Regnery, Chicago, 1949. It is to be hoped that a complete translation of *Sein und Zeit* may soon be available.

an aim of Heidegger, it must be the aim of all those now seriously concerned with the revival of philosophy.

Heidegger and other existentialists have made valuable suggestions concerning the practical branches of such a humane discipline. To the logic of theory they have given far less attention, as we have seen. This is because of their strong tendency to identify human awareness with action. In the end, as Sartre explicitly states, consciousness and choice are the same. As the existentialists see it, the study of awareness must lead us to action. Let us then follow them and turn to this basic topic.

HUMAN ACTION

The existentialists reject all attempts to explain human action in terms of blind tendencies or drives. They are interested in hard facts that can be verified by direct observation, not in tempting theoretical constructions. Their exhaustive empirical studies have made it clear that mature action is always *to* something which is disclosed in some way. This does not mean that all human action is directed by rational concepts alone. Mood and feeling play a most important role. But as we have seen, they are modes of disclosure, and cannot be reduced to purely subjective disturbances within the physiological organism. All the existentialists follow Kierkegaard in holding that among these feelings dread plays a peculiarly important role.

THE FEELING OF DREAD

In the main, Heidegger accepts the Kierkegaardian interpretation of dread, but he gives a more disciplined analysis which clarifies certain points.[52] Like Kierkegaard, he approaches dread by way of the feeling of fear with which it is ordinarily confused. Such active feelings have an innerworldly object and a reference to some tendency with which they are closely conjoined. I fear this sickness because of its possible influence on some project in which I am engaged. The object is different from the activity it threatens. This object is some being approaching from a definite region. What is threatened is my factual being, or some phase of this.[53] Such dangers can be more or less clearly defined, and practical steps may be taken to avoid them unless the situation is quite hopeless.

The structure of dread is quite different. Its object is indefinite. I cannot say precisely what it is that I dread. When asked, I say *it is nothing*. It cannot be localized. It is nowhere. Heidegger interprets this as meaning that it is my whole being-in-the-world which is the object of dread.[54] All objects, and everything that I already am, sink into a cloud of meaninglessness and indifference. What is left? Is there any phase of my existence which lies beyond this factuality? There is. It is I myself and my own real possibilities. All else has become suddenly alien and uncanny. Dread singles me out, and leaves me alone to face what I still might be. It also touches the whole structure of my being in the world, but with a poignant emphasis on those real possibilities which I really am, though they lie ahead of me. It is for them that I dread.[55] Because of them, I dread the facticity into which I have been thrown and the self that I already am.

This explains the awakening power of this strange feeling, which arouses the self to decisive choice and action.[56] As I remain lost in the world of everyday objects, manipulating myself and others along obvious lines that anyone understands, the best that is in me remains hidden. Before I can act with the whole of my being, I must break with this world of everyday into which I have fallen. The feeling of dread discloses this lostness to me. My world becomes meaningless and foreign. In the light of my real possibilities, I am revealed as something strange and uncanny to myself.

Fears are derived and debased forms of anxiety, which is their purest and most original form. These derived emotions are characteristic of lost existence. They reveal those particular objects in the world which threaten this or that determinate phase of my being. These fears can usually be met by shrewd precautions and counteracting measures that leave my existence untouched. But dread reveals my entire being-in-the-world as a deeper threat to me, leading me to choice of genuine existence, and freeing me from derived forms of fear. One who is stirred by the sense of dread has little time for these.

This feeling is hard to bear.

The impersonal one (*das Man*) who, for the most part, governs our daily lives, cannot stand this grueling experience. He runs away from it to lose himself in the world of things, artifacts, and the fears that always go with them.[57] As Heidegger sees it, this fallen state is a universal characteristic of human existence, in which all men first find themselves. The existentialists have given us vivid descriptions of its contemporary manifestations. But before we turn to these, we must first consider that care or commitment which characterizes all specifically human action, whether it be authentic or unauthentic.

CARE

We are apt to think of our inner life as a stream of psychic events arising in the past, then flowing down to the present, and next into the future. Amongst these, there are some which have an active character and which we call *willing* or *wishing*. No existentialist thinker would accept this widespread conception as being even approximately true. Heidegger's criticism of it is sharply and concisely expressed. My whole existence is active or conative in character.[58] There are no non-conative events in human life as it is lived. He uses the term care (*Sorge*) to express this conative structure. The image of a stream is wholly inadequate to convey its nature.

My life does not flow down from the past to occupy a punctual present, and then to enter a non-existent future. This is a radical distortion of the real phenomena which show that my activity is always to a future which I have already projected ahead of myself by understanding and mood. Human being is always ahead of itself, and this projective phase is primary and original.[59] My life does not so much evenly flow from the past into the future as break from the future into the past and present. Furthermore, the past and future are not separated from each other by a punctual present. They are held together in a certain unity which can be clearly seen in the structure of care.[60] This care is always ahead of itself, and never confined to the present. I am concerned primarily with what will be, a possibility that I understand. It is this envisaged future which directs my care. But I myself, and that which I care for, already exist in the world. As I exist with this being and care for it, I am thus both ahead of myself in some possibility and already in the factual world. This threefold order of human existing is the structure of care: ahead of itself . . . as already in the world . . . as being with. . . .[61]

Co-presence is not the same as care, not even active co-presence. To act on a thing is not the same as to care for it or to be careless of it. The future phase is absent, and the past being taken over by the future. Care is a special kind of being-with that is peculiar to man. One human being cannot merely act on another with whom he is co-present. Something resembling this, of course, does occur. But we recognize the difference. It is not the *sheer absence* of care. This is impossible in man. It is a *lack* or privation of care. The person is not merely acting. We say that he does not care.

This concern is not a property of man that comes and goes. It is an existential character that lies at the very core of his being. Whatever one is doing, he is always caring or not caring for something. I am a center of care. Of course it appears in a vast variety of forms, as drive, urge, desire, wish, or will.[62] But in all of these, we find the same projective structure that is the sign of care. According to Heidegger, even thinking and theorizing has this structure.[63] There is a possibility of attaining a truth I do not know. I am already in the world. When this possibility ahead of me arouses my concern, it takes over my factual existence and directs it to the necessary procedures and acts. Care may be authentic or unauthentic, as we shall see. But even the latter has the same threefold structure. The difference lies in the kind of possibilities to which existence is open. Everyday feeling and understanding are narrow in range. They accept what is given as basically fixed, and are blind to deeper and more far-reaching possibilities. They elicit a kind of care that is absorbed in the things that lie around us and is content to devise manipulations and changes that leave them essentially as they were. Such depersonalized existence understands itself as a thing that is simply there like other objects, and cares for itself by feeding, dressing, maintaining and operating itself, as though it were a delicate and complex artifact.

There are many different levels of care. The most significant difference concerns the weight of the futurity factor. The more rudimentary and commonplace ones are dominated by the object present before them. That to which they are moving is hardly focused at all. Drives and urges belong to this category.[64] They seem to flow out of the past. Hence the image of the stream is less inappropriate to describe them. Desires and interests are at a higher level. They are lost in what is present before them, and their futurity is dim. What we call *wishes* are characterized by a limited view of real possibilities.[65] The only capacities recognized are wholly inadequate to bring forth what is wished. So the wisher clings to this object as though it were really there. The more authentic kinds of care are manifested in those acts of purposive choice where basic possibilities are clearly grasped. They take over the whole personality in decisive commitment. All of these are divergent manifestations of the same existential structure of care—ahead of itself . . . as already in the world . . . as being with.

The only original feature of this formula is its generality and exactitude. Men have always had a concrete sense of themselves as creatures of care. To show this, Heidegger quotes an ancient Latin myth,[66] which may be translated into English as follows:

> Once when Care was crossing a river she saw a sounding piece of earth. Taking it up thoughtfully she began to form it. As she was wondering what she would make, Jupiter appeared. Care asked him to bestow spirit upon it, and he readily agreed. But when Care wished to have her name given the creature, Jupiter forbade this and said that his name should be used. While Care and Jupiter were arguing over this, Earth also arose and sought to have her name imposed, since she had given it a piece of her body. They turned to Saturn to judge between them, and he rendered the following judgment in all fairness: "You, Jupiter, because you have given the spirit, shall take his spirit at death. You, Earth, since you have given the body, shall have the body returned. But Care, since she first formed this being, shall possess him as long as he lives. Now since there is disagreement over the name, let him be called 'homo' because he is made out of 'earth' (humus)."

Heidegger makes several interesting comments on this myth.[67] Care first formed this entity; she is the source of his being. Care will possess him as long as he lives. His name has nothing to do with his existence, but merely expresses that from which he was made. What his essential being really is, this Saturn (Time) will decide. Here in concrete, pre-scientific language is the unmistakable statement of a truth that is now accepted by most of the existentialist philosophers. All the manifestations of human existence are filled with care. In whatever he does, man is led by a devotion to something. He is a center of care.

The threefold structure of this pervasive datum suggests a possible connection with the future, past, and present phases of time. Is it possible that a careful analysis of human action as it is given may shed some light on this obscure and complex topic? Heidegger believes that it can.[68] Indeed, his anthropological studies have culminated in a novel conception of time which has already exerted a profound influence on existentialist thought.

A NEW THEORY OF TIME

Heidegger's new approach to the problem of time is guided by penetrating phenomenological observations. Though his theory is sometimes obscured by the use of idiomatic German expressions, its general outline is clear, and in certain respects so original as to be of interest to all empirically-minded students of philosophy. We shall try to summarize this theory, and the phenomenological evidence on which it rests, by considering first of all the accepted view of time, then certain criticisms to which it is subject, and finally the opposed view to which Heidegger thinks any disciplined observer must be led.

Time as a Now-succession

We ordinarily think of time as a succession of present nows.[69] We image it as a flowing stream in which one now rises out of the past, is momentarily present, and is then replaced by another.[70] Each moment can be dated and assigned its fixed position in the order of before and after which makes up the "dimension" of time. The flow of time is even and regular,[71] and always proceeds irreversibly in one direction: [72] first the past, then the present, and finally the future. These temporal phases succeed each other in this order. But the present alone is real at any given moment, the past and the future being non-existent. The past was once a now, but at this moment is no longer. Here and now it is past and gone. The future will be a now when it really is. But at this moment it is a not-yet-now, and therefore non-existent.[73] This now-succession has no limit.[74] Whatever happens, it will go on and on indefinitely. Everything that happens, including myself, is a happening *in* this time.[75] I can examine these occurrences as objects there before me, and analyze their structure. I can observe present events with the aid of my senses. The past I can remember. The future I can predict and await. Such is roughly the common view of time with which we are all familiar.

According to Heidegger, it certainly contains an element of truth.[76] But is it intelligible standing alone by itself? Does it do justice to the phenomena of human existence? According to Heidegger, these questions cannot be answered affirmatively, as we may see if we ask the following questions with our concrete experience in mind.

First of all, the theory proceeds ostensively. It merely points at examples of what we call time, without telling us what time itself is. This event succeeds that. But the event is *in* time; it is not time itself. Perhaps time is the succession; first this, then something else. But this succession is not wholly discontinuous. What holds the two together? Is this objective or subjective? The theory by itself does not tell us.[77] We may say that something in the event remains and stays. Is this the continuity of time? It cannot be, for that which remains is *in* time just as that which changes. What is that unity of time in which both the permanent and the impermanent take place?[78] What is time itself? What kind of being is it? The theory does not tell us.[79]

Why is the flow irreversible?[80] This is an evident fact. Time never goes backwards. But the notion of time as a spatial dimension sheds no light on this. The order of spatial extension can be read either way. It does not proceed in one direction only. It does not proceed at all. Why does the past come first, then the present, and then the future? Is this the real order? If so, it is not made intelligible.

Does it really make sense to speak of the present succeeding the past, and the future succeeding the present? Do these phases of time come after each other in this way? Is this not a confusion of time with something *in* time? One event may be separated from another in time. But can the phases of time itself be thus separated? Can the present ever be separated from the past or from the future? Does it not then lose all meaning? Do not future, present, and past belong together in an integrated structure, each phase of which requires the other? [81] Can we make any sense out of the notion that one phase occurs all alone by itself, to be then succeeded by another?

This leads us to an even more critical difficulty that has puzzled many thinkers. The theory places a heavy emphasis on the present now.[82] Only this is real. At a given moment, therefore, the whole of the past and the whole of the future are completely non-existent. What, then, do we mean by these non-existent phases? If only the present is real, how can they mean anything at all? Without the past and the future, how much meaning can the present retain? In what sense is a point-instant surrounded by nothingness a present? Is not time itself dissolved with the dissolution of the past and future?

One often attempts to avoid this difficulty by supposing a present that is speciously extended into the past and the future. Such a specious present, as it is called, would thus include within itself a tiny piece of the past, and a small bit of the future. But does this not rather weigh us down with further monstrous problems? How can any bit of the future be actually present and still remain future? Is this not a downright contradiction? Furthermore, if some part of the future can thus be present, what is to prevent this from happening to the rest? How do we draw the line between that which is really present and that which is not? Is this an advance or a retrogression into confusion worse confounded?

Are we not similarly mixing the past and the future with the present when we think of the former as a punctual now that was once but is no longer, and of the latter as a now that will be but is not yet? [83] Is it not true that the past and the future have distinctive traits of their own that must stand in the way of any such attempt to reduce them to a now? For one thing, is it not evident that the past and the future are both specious in the sense that they seem to include a large number of nows, while the present is not specious at all, but is restricted to a single now? To think of the future as a now-not-yet is to confuse it with a present, and to ignore its genuine futurity. Is this in any way preferable to the reverse fallacy we have just considered, which makes the present specious by futurizing it, and thus ignoring its unique and genuine presence?

If time is without limit and is going on and on without end, why then do we speak as we do of time as passing? [84] Why do we not think of it as always coming, more and more without any end? If time is infinite, as the theory supposes, this is equally true. But we do not speak or think about time in this way. We feel it as something slipping away and vanishing. This is a hard fact of common experience which the theory does not explain.

It tells me that I remember part of my past, and await my future. It tells me that these very acts of remembering and expecting, together with the whole of my being, are all unrolling in time. But here we return to the original question, which may now be raised with perhaps a deeper sense of urgency and significance: What is this time that I am in? How is it to be described and explained?

Time as Ecstatic Existence

Heidegger's existential anthropology enables him to develop a new approach to these questions. It would certainly be an exaggeration to claim that he has answered them all with perfect clarity and coherence. But he has made a genuine advance. Let us now examine his answers to these problems in the order in which they have just been raised.*

According to Heidegger, time lies at the root of the structure of human care. [85] Time is an existential structure which pervades man's being-in-the-world. The human person is not a thing or a set of events *in* time. His being is stretched out into a future, past, and present which Heidegger calls the *ecstasies* of time. [86] He is

* These answers are most clearly suggested in *Sein und Zeit*, Secs. 79-81.

not something first confined to a given moment, and *then*
stretched out into a past and future. From the very beginning, his
being is stretched out into possibilities ahead of himself, and a
past which he must take over if he is to be with things at a factual
present. Thus in existing, he temporalizes himself in ways that
are authentic or unauthentic.[87] But in either case, the three
ecstasies of time are integrated in the unity of his being. He is
not *in* time, but rather he *is* it, and exists it. To have time for
something is to have self-devotion to it. To lose time, or to waste
it, is to waste the self.[88]

I am not confined to a present moment nor to a specious present. I am the future I have projected ahead of myself, and I still
am the past that I have been. But in this ecstatic being it is the
future that has precedence.[89] It is the future that must take hold
of the past, and guide it in present action. It is not an accidental
addition to my substantial being which is already there. I am
never all there. As long as I am, I am these possibilities. It is from
my station in this projected future that I guide and criticize my
action. It is from this being ahead of myself that I regard the flow
of my being out of the past, through the present, towards where
I am primarily, at my end in the future. This is why time is irreversible. Whether I merely wait for myself to happen and drift
on, or whether I decisively intervene in the process, I am always
stationed at the end towards which my being is surging.[90]

But this being is not exclusively futuristic. It is also stretched
out over the past I have been, and is concerned with things in the
present. These ecstasies are interdependent and inseparable. One
cannot exist without the others. Hence it is incorrect to think of
the present as merely succeeding the past, and the future after the
present. It is existential laziness and indecision that is responsible
for this delusion. The future that thinks in this way is a mere
detached observer, so lost in what it is seeing as to forget itself
and its station. The ecstasies of time are inseparable phases of a
single integrated structure. But this unity must be maintained by
resolute choice that holds them tightly together with the future,
not after but *before* the present. It may be lost by irresolution.[91]
Such lapsed existence fails to see its real possibilities, and never

takes over the past. Then the ecstasies fall apart, and the existing person is disintegrated.

The accepted view is wrong in giving absolute priority to the present now, and in thinking of past and future as non-existent.[92] We fall into this error because of the theoretical pan-objectivism to which we are so susceptible. Heidegger explains it ultimately as a flight from that decisive choice to which dread arouses us. Such action is full of risk and danger. It is more comforting to let ourselves drift with the current, and gape at the finished results. There may be some truth in this moral explanation. But theoretical confusions are also involved. Being is not restricted to the kind of being-there that belongs to a thing-object lying before me. Human existence cannot be reduced to this level. In their own peculiar way, the future and past are also existent. As long as I am, I am the unfinished possibilities projected ahead of me, and the unfinished past that I have been.[93] A present without past or future would certainly lose all human significance.

We do not really understand the integrated structure of future, past, and present by imagining them to be mixed together in a fantastic brew of specious contradiction. This future is in the mode of possibility. No part of it can become actually present without altering its mode of existence. The past is already there; its factual content fixed, and not open to choice. The present moment is not yet *there* to be forgotten or taken over. It is still indeterminate and open to choice. The ecstasies of time fit into an integrated union. But each has peculiar characters of its own. One cannot be reduced to another.[94]

My past is not a punctual now that was once but is finished and gone. As long as I am, I *have* my past as that which I *have* been. It is not something once there, but now finished. It is not finished, because it never was all there. Even when I try to forget and evade it, it still weighs on me and limits my action. Past possibilities may be maintained and repeated by choice in this moment. So far as personal integrity is achieved, it is achieved in this way.[95] The future is more than a not-yet-now that will be. This would suggest that until then, the future is nothing. But this is clearly false. Right now I am this future which stretches ahead of me in the mode of possibility. It profoundly affects the other phases, and determines the sense of my existence. It is from this future that I interpret the past, and direct my present action. To reduce the future to a set of nows is as great a mistake as to futurize the present. The three ecstasies temporalize themselves all together, but each in its own peculiar way.

The time that I am is not infinite, but certainly limited and, indeed, known to be so. A man may try to escape from the thought of his death, but he never succeeds in this completely. Every man at least dimly knows that he is about to die, and knows that his time is limited by this ultimate and inexorable barrier. This is why men speak of time as passing away.[96] They run away from the dread that arouses them to decisive choice. They stand outside as their lives drift by, and wait for the moment that never comes. It is this self-abandonment that elicits the poignant sense of passage.

At last we can give an intelligible answer to the question of why I cannot gain a vantage point from where I can stare at time from the outside, as an object. I can know it only subjectively and practically from within. I am not located at a moment *in* time like a thing. Time is the basic structure of my existing, which temporalizes itself first as a future ahead of myself, as a past I have already been, and a present I am with. The present lies between the other two, and divides them from one another. But it offers me *the moment* for choice.[97] If I take this opportunity to grasp my real possibilities, and in their light to take over the past that I already am, leading it to decisive action, then the present becomes a binding link, and the process holds its integrity. If not, the whole structure splinters apart, and the mind is filled with confusions. Among the more serious of these are the common misconceptions of time we have been discussing.

Explanation of the Accepted View

Heidegger offers a coherent explanation of these accepted views of time in terms of unauthentic existence. Such existence tries to escape from itself. Instead of making the active choices which the moment offers, one forgets himself and becomes absorbed in the manipulation of artifacts, or in the contemplation of things that are there before him. He even regards himself as an object compressed within a present now. Time is thus dissolved into a succession of things or events, and is readily reduced to the level of a spatial dimension.[98] Deprived of binding decision, the empty moment separates the future from the past, and the ecstasies lose their unity. Time is visualized as a piecemeal succession in which the past is followed by the present, and the present by the future.

I can see neither past nor future—nor, indeed, time itself. But the object at which I gaze is here before me now. So the pan-objectivist gives an absolute priority to this now, and reads it into the past and the future, ignoring their peculiar differences.[99] Evading the austere thought of death, he soothes himself with the image of time as a flux of nows that will never end.[100] This makes genuine decision unnecessary and even fanatical. There is abundant time for all things in the now-succession. Here are the main features of that vulgar view of time with which we are all familiar. It is a distorted and debased shadow of the real time that we glimpse in moments of rare but decisive clarity.

HISTORY

Heidegger has made a similar study of the notion of history, with results that are equally striking.[101] Here also he criticizes the commonly accepted view, which he then explains as the unauthentic version of another more in keeping with evident data accessible to all.

History as a Stream

By history, we ordinarily refer to a succession of events in the past. This emphasis on the past is so strong that we sometimes define the discipline having the same name as the study of the past.[102] We recognize causal factors at work in these past events, and refer to some of them as epoch-making or of historic importance. By *past* we generally mean a now no longer existent. But we recognize that implements once used in the past may survive in the present. Such past relics are of special historical interest, and are sometimes placed in museums. We also recognize that past events may in some way work on the present and determine it.[103] But these events are now over and gone. Nothing can now be done to change them, though our interpretation may change. They involve great numbers of individuals interacting together. History is always social.

We often imagine it as a great stream flowing down from the past to the present, and finally into the future. In agreement with a conception derived from naturalistic philosophy, we sometimes think of this flow as an advance. The past is something stable and sure which has carried us down to the living present. It is on this "basis" that we must advance further. A great man is one who makes such a contribution. His work will meet some general need, and be assimilated. New events and new forms are constantly recurring. History never repeats itself. Our own lives take place in this on-going flow.

The science of these events, as has often been noted, has the same name.[104] Its function is to work out an adequate interpretation. As to what this would be, there is, however, an interesting division. Some say that the historian should try to get outside of history and study it from a detached point of view, in order to get at the facts as they actually happened. Others say that this is impossible. The historian himself is in history.[105] Hence any interpretation is relative to the period. Each age devises its own history, or even creates it. Some sort of compromise between the two views is often thought to be reasonable. These views doubtless express many isolated truths. But they do not fit into a coherent account of the facts, which can be thought through without confusion and contradiction.

If the past no longer is, how can it survive in the present? The article in the museum may be scarred and worm-eaten, but these properties exist in the present, and may be analyzed like any others.[106] What, then, is the pastness of this article? Furthermore, if the past is dead and gone, how can it work in the present? What is the nature of this working? Indeed, the whole notion of "the past" seems unclear. If this is the essence of history, the more ancient a time, the more historical it should be.[107] But this is evidently absurd. What, then, is meant by the historic past?

The whole image of the stream seems quite inaccurate. At a given moment, the whole stream actually exists in all its parts from beginning to end. But according to the theory itself, this is not true of history. The past is a now-no-longer, and the future a now-not-yet. If the past is thus non-existent, how can it be stable? How can it function as a firm foundation for further achievements? Instead of helping, does it not often hamper and restrict us? Instead of allowing it to assimilate us and carry us on, should we not rather struggle with it and redirect it? Is this not a more accurate characterization of those who were really great? A stream does not struggle with its past. The future is uncertain and obscure. In all probability, history will finally come to an end. What, then, does the naturalist mean by this advance of history? If something new is always emerging, what, then, is responsible for the continuity of history?

If this unity and order is given with the facts, why can it not be more clearly seen by trained observers? On the other hand, if there is no unity and order, what, then, can be meant by world-history, and even by history itself? If a trained observer can get outside of history to examine it, why, then, does it not have the same structure as other sciences that are sharply distinguished (as biology and geology) from the facts they study (life and earth)? But the discipline is not called *historiology*. It is named by the name of the facts themselves. This would fit with the opposite view that history itself is a creative fact of history. How, then, would such creative interpretation be distinguished from what we call fiction? Is any combination of these two reasonable? Can a little bit of science with a bit of fiction constitute a unique discipline? Can history as such be intelligibly conceived as either in or out of history? These are some questions that the prevailing view does not clearly answer. They are important questions. Can any real light be shed on them by an empirical study of human ontology? Heidegger believes that it can, and in the last pages of *Sein und Zeit,* he has sketched out an existentialist theory of human history.

Human Existence as History

Heidegger says very little about human communication in its authentic forms.* But this is presupposed by his view of history as the way man (i.e., social man) exists in the world.[108] Men are

---

* This is mentioned in passing (*Sein und Zeit,* p. 264) as involving a respect for the self-surpassing possibilities of others. But no analysis is given.

not in a stream of history. They *are* their history. As a social mode of time, it is divided into the three ecstatic phases of future, past, and present, no one of which can be without the others. Social man is always ahead of himself, but he cannot remain lost in the possibilities which his understanding projects. If he is to act, he must take over his factual past and commit it to present action. Hence the concern for the historic past. This past, however, is not dead and gone. It is something we still have, and need to hold. It is not a now that was once all there but is no longer. It is our past that we have been. It is not all gone, because it never was all there.[109] It never occurred as a mere event, but as ahead of itself in the future. We cannot really understand a so-called historic fact without understanding its future. Possibility is the very heart of human history, as it is the guiding center of human care. The past that is the object of historical study is a past with a human future, and a future that we may share and repeat.[110]

The image of the stream is inadequate, not because all of its parts exist together—this is also true of the phases of time—but because they all exist in the same mode as being *there*. History exists as an integration of the diverse modes of possibility, already-thereness, and being-with. Hence the past event was no floating futurity. It had its own past, which it took over in acts of chosen determination. These acts now belong to us as part of the past we have already been. They are fully determinate and limited. Hence the passion of history for facts. If we are to act, we must take them over and struggle with them to fit them with real possibility. In this sense, history is always in tension with the determinate past, which weighs upon it and restricts its fluency of action.

But the past also gives us its possibilities, and some of these are "real." * These are always hidden in mists of ambiguity which must be resolved by insight. The unity of history is not a fact to be simply accepted. It is a struggle to be maintained by decisive choice, if it is to be at all. It is a struggle that is also constantly lost by confusion and indecision. The artifacts and things of history are always new. But its real possibilities may be maintained

* Heidegger uses this term without explaining its meaning. (*Sein und Zeit*, p. 349.)

and repeated by fidelity, love, devotion, and choice.[111] With respect to these basic existential categories, there is no advance. In the face of their ultimate human possibilities, all men are equal and contemporary, as Kierkegaard pointed out.

Men are neither *in* history, like things and artifacts, nor can they free themselves from history and become detached from it. They are their history.[112] Their being in the world is historical. Thus the world is not a number of things that were once all there in a certain form, but which have had a history so that our things are now quite different. The world itself is historical.[113] What was once *in* the world was different. But the world itself was never all there. It was always temporalizing itself as a past, a present, and future. This future is still ahead of us now in the world of today, our future as well as that of the past. In this sense, and to this degree, our world is the same as that of the Greeks.

The unity of history is maintained by decisively clinging to the essential possibilities of man. To this task, the professional historian can make a vital contribution. He is studying the being of man. His duty is to clarify such insights as we already possess, and to show how these real possibilities have been won or lost in the past. By helping us to understand more clearly those that still remain to us, he is participating in the actual process of history.[114] This understanding is the most primordial part of history. Without the relating of real possibility to brute fact, there would be no process of history. In this sense, the science of "history" is history itself, and the single name is not only appropriate but required.

The Accepted View as Unauthentic

This account also enables us to explain the accepted view as an unauthentic distortion, supported by personal weakness and lassitude. The most striking feature of this view is its neglect of futurity. The thought of death as an ultimate boundary, and the dread that this elicits are hard to bear. Men therefore try to evade the idea of possibility by misunderstanding themselves as things which are all there now, and whose possibilities, so far as they have them, are fixed and inflexible.

In history, this attitude expresses itself by an exaggerated em-

phasis on hard, determinate facts which are simply *there*. Instead
of trying to understand the past as it was and is being actually
temporalized with danger, risk, and ultimate uncertainty, one
looks at the past as an *ex post facto thing* that is simply *there*.
The present is objectified. Even the future is turned into a future
perfect, and regarded as what it will have been, *after* it has once
occurred. Futurity is thus ignored, everything being reduced to
the mode of pastness. History is viewed as a stream whose main
course is already fixed, and down which the waters are ever advancing—towards what, nobody knows. Still some sort of progress
is achieved, for new forms are constantly appearing. Freedom is
even confused with this inevitable and omnipresent novelty, and
the real freedom which enables us to stand firm and to resist the
flux is misconceived as uncreative rigidity. The historian is
viewed as a detached observer, merely recording facts and laws, or
as a novel fact in history, determined by his time, or by caprice,
to devise creative constructions. In either case, he is freed from
the hard responsibility of choice.

Such is Heidegger's theory of human time and history. It is certainly one of the most profound and original expressions of existentialist phenomenology. He has taken certain implicit suggestions of Kierkegaard and turned them into a rich and coherent
theory. Though subject to many minor variations, this theory is
now a common feature of existentialist thought.

In explaining it, as well as in dealing with other topics of major importance, we have been forced to use the terms *authentic*
and *unauthentic*. We have noted the essential role that they play
in the thought of Kierkegaard. But this moral motif has been
richly developed and applied to contemporary problems by
thinkers living today. It is now time for us to examine more carefully these ethical implications of existentialist philosophy. .

Existentialist Ethics: Integrity and Decision

In the two preceding chapters, we described certain common conditions which belong to our being as such. These omnipresent factors of experience have to be explained, or at least explained away, by any type of philosophy. They are dimly grasped by every human being. Even though they lack precise concepts for the clear expression of their awareness, all men know that they exist in-the-world with-others, and that this existence is restricted by inescapable limitations. They realize that they have been thrown into situations not of their own choosing, that they are subject to chance and mischance, that they are in some sense guilty, and that they finally face the ultimate limit of death. These factors are always found with human being and restrict it from the outside. In Chapter Four we turned to the internal structure of human existence and analyzed certain factors—awareness, care, and time—which are commonly recognized as essential. Men are not distinguished from one another by these structures. They are found in everyone. An existence lacking them would simply not be human.

We must now consider another group of factors which are not essential in this sense. They center around an obscure and complex phenomenon to which we refer by such words as *choice* and *decision*. Modern moral philosophy has tried to separate itself from ontology. At the same time, as we have noted, it has over-simplified or ignored the problem of human freedom. According to the existentialist analysis, there is a connection here. Freedom is not to be approached as a kind of thing, or a kind of change, or even as a kind of possibility. It is a way of existing, and a sound analysis must take us far beyond sociology and psychology to the basic categories of ontology. If any light is to come, it can come only from these regions that are still obscure. At the core of human freedom lies the phenomenon of decision.

This is a basic existential, a way of being-in-the-world that affects all the conditions we have been describing. But unlike them, it is not necessary. Men cannot exist without time. They can exist without being free. Decision divides us from one another. We are in the field of ethics. In agreement with Kierkegaard, the existentialists hold that the major division, in relation to which all others fade into insignificance, is the difference between those who really decide with authenticity and integrity, and those who may seem to decide but really do not. This difference affects every necessary aspect of being-in-the-world, the way we are-with-others, our guilt, our death, our awareness, and even our time. The existentialists have given us many penetrating descriptions of these differences as they are manifested in contemporary life. Hence after a discussion of the central factor of human decision, we shall present a brief summary of this contrast between authentic and unauthentic existence.

HUMAN DECISION AND FREEDOM

Men may fear their freedom and throw it away. This is not true of the other animals. We speak of certain species as being domesticated, but not as being enslaved. To lose something implies at least an original access to it. Human being has access to freedom that is gained by decision, and there is abundant evidence to show that this sometimes occurs. The existentialists go farther than this. According to them, decision is no accident added on to something stable already existent. It lies rather at the very center of man, from where it determines the basic texture of his existence. In the words of Jaspers: "So far as I choose, I am; if I am not, I do not choose." [1] According to Sartre: "I am my liberty." [2] Much has been written recently on this topic. Divergent accounts have been given. But the analysis of Heidegger in *Sein und Zeit* still remains the clearest in structural disclosure, and the nearest to evident fact. We shall, therefore, follow his analysis, omitting its more peculiar features, and sticking to the central core which is representative of existentialist thought in general. It consists of three parts: death and human integrity, conscience and guilt, and projective decision.

DEATH AND HUMAN INTEGRITY

We often speak of moral integrity with a sense of its basic importance. There are few things worse than moral disintegration and the loss of personal wholeness. But if we question ourselves concerning the real meaning of such phrases, we shall soon see that they are plunged in mists of obscurity. What do I mean by the whole of myself? Is it not clear that as long as I am, I am incomplete? This would certainly seem to follow from the analysis of care given in the preceding chapter. I am the future that I have projected ahead of myself. But this future exists only as possibility. Hence I am incomplete. It is death that ends my existence. Human wholeness or integrity demands the limit of death. But as we have already seen, this concept also is far from clear. I am apt to confuse it with the death of someone else whose last breaths and movements I can observe from the outside, or with death in general. But it is my own death that terminates my life, and this I shall not be observing from the outside. Furthermore, I am not humanity in general, but an individual here and now, existing in flesh and blood. Death is not the ripening of determinate potentialities, for many die in senility long after any such process has been completed. It does not seem to be the realization of my life in the sense of its being all *there*. When this can be said, I shall no longer be *there* at all. What kind of an end is this, whose presence involves the non-existence of that which it is ending?

According to Heidegger, the difficulty arises from confusing existence with *being there*.[3] My existence is never all there in this sense, and neither is my death. When understood existentially as it really is, my death cannot be regarded as a fact that is already there for me to see. Like everything else that I really am, it shares in the structure of care. It is not behind me as an object of sight. It is rather ahead of me in the future, as the object of a special kind of care.[4] The death that I die is not a finished fact, but a possible mode of existing endfully with death in view. This is possible for me here and now. It is, in fact, the only way to an existential wholeness or integrity. What is this way, and how is it to be exactly analyzed? Heidegger's analysis of this being unto death (*Sein zum Tode*) is obscure at certain points, but its general structure is clear.

The real death that lies ahead of me is the possibility of myself as not being at all.[5] This means not only the end of my factual being, but the end of my guiding futurity as well. Death is the possibility of my not being able to be. Now, our minds gain insight into something only by contrasting it with its negation. Thus we understand being only through the concept of nothing, the rational through the non-rational, etc. This is even more true of what we know through feeling. Such knowledge becomes more sharply etched and poignant by contrast with that of its absence or its opposite. Thus our feeling for health becomes more intense when we have experienced sickness, our sense for freedom sharper and clearer when we have seen something of slavery at first hand. It is in this way, according to Heidegger, that the thought of my non-existence brings into sharp relief the essential meaning of my existence. More especially, the absolute end of my futurity reveals the structure of my own real possibilities.[6] In the light of death, I am brought before myself in an integral perspective where all may be seen. Three things about this perspective are especially important.

Many things that I do, many functions that I perform, are replaceable. They also can be performed by others. These will survive my death. What will not survive is the way in which I perform them, and the things that only I can do. The thought of death individuates me, and brings me back to the self that is my very own.[7] Kierkegaard intuitively recognized this when he said that each man must die his own death alone.

What I can do as a banker, as a teacher, in this respect or in that, until one year or ten years are over, has limits and can be exceeded. But what I can devote myself to with the whole of my being-unto-death, is the last unsurpassable limit of my possibilities. It is the utmost I can do; the farthest I can go. These *last* limits of my existence are revealed only in the light of death.[8]

Finally, it is this mode of futurity alone that reaches the ultimate end, and reveals my being in its limited entirety. If I think of myself as a technician, a citizen, a husband, a father, a child, an adult, or even as an old man, something is left out. It is only with death before me that I can see myself as a whole.

This final perspective, therefore, reveals my own essential being, but it does not cut me off from my interest in things, and my care for other persons. These, of course, belong to my being-in-the-world. Without them, I could not be at all. But the thought of death prevents me from losing myself in them, and enables me to choose finally between them. In revealing the last futurity that lies ahead of me, it also prevents me from resting satisfied with the past that I have become. Knowing its finitude, however, I am protected from the danger of misunderstanding the possibilities of others exceeding it, or of trying to bend them to my own limited projects.

I know that my death is certain, but the "when" is undetermined. As Heidegger points out, this certainty cannot be explained by any counting of finished cases, which would justify only a high degree of probability. To regard *Dasein* in this way is a mistake, for as he exists, he is never a finished case. This is not a theoretical certainty at all, but belongs to another order. Certainty in general refers to the way in which a disclosure of truth is maintained or "held." [9] In this case, it is my own last possibilities that are disclosed. As we shall see, I hold these before me by a final decision that I maintain to the bitter end. But this leaves me free and open to the possibilities of any given situation. At such a moment, I may hold and repeat myself, or I may become lost in indecision. This possibility is also certain. The bounded future is ever before me, but *when* it may end is indeterminate. This indeterminacy of death is revealed by the feeling of dread which urges me to cut myself off from the functions and processes in which I am lost, and to hold myself in a final decision.[10]

It is through dread, therefore, that I am brought before myself in the final perspective of death. This reveals the last possibilities which are my very own, unsupported by external agencies. It is through this that I am able to project myself to the very end, and to see the possibility of maintaining my integrity.

Heidegger's description of this being unto death is highly abstract and often obscure.[11] Is this anything more than the expression of a personal ideal? Is there any factual evidence to bear out the claim that this being-to-death really belongs to the universal structure of human existence? Heidegger believes that there is such evidence.[12] It is to be found in those confused experiences to which we refer by the word conscience.

CONSCIENCE AND GUILT

We often think of conscience as a review and a negative criticism of our acts after they have been performed. We accept the Kantian picture of conscience as a courtroom scene in which a cold and austere reason passes judgment on what we have done.[13] This judgment is usually negative, but sometimes we are reluctantly acquitted with specific recommendations for better conduct next time. According to Heidegger, this is an artificially intellectualistic picture which is far from any close agreement with the primordial given facts.[14]

First of all, the gist of conscience is not exclusively or even primarily negative. We experience it rather as an appeal for positive action.[15] It is true that the recognition of something "wrong" in an act is often the occasion on which we hear such an appeal. But the message of conscience is never restricted to mere condemnation of a specific action once performed, nor warning against one that is contemplated. There is always at the same time an urge to something positive. Thus we speak of the goads and pricks of conscience. We do not spur on our steed when we merely wish him to stand quite still. Furthermore, conscience is not primarily concerned, like a court, with the impersonal judgment of specific acts in terms of fixed norms. It speaks to me personally and touches me to the depths of my being, including all my fixed norms. That its message is not determined by fixed norms is indicated by the incessant controversy concerning the precise nature of what it is that conscience says.[16]

Most of all, the whole courtroom picture is quite inaccurate in suggesting that what is at issue is a finished act already there to be examined by abstract judgment. It is true that part of my being is factual. But this is not yet finished. Conscience is concerned with the whole of my being, and therefore especially with that guiding part which is already projected ahead of me. This is clearly indicated by the language of the spurs and pricks. Let us try to refrain from biased interpretation, and try simply to describe the experience as it occurs in the concrete. In attempting to do this, we must be guided by what men actually say about it.

We find them speaking of it as a voice, or even as a call (*Ruf*). This suggests that it comes from a distance, remote from the factual present. It is certainly neither arranged nor controlled by me as I am. We refer to it rather in language that suggests something foreign and strange, and yet at the same time interior to our personal being. It comes out of me from beyond me.[17] Hence the many mythical explanations in terms of superhuman forces far above us with intimate access to our souls. What, then, does the voice of conscience say? Here we are given many answers, and the path of interpretation is more confused. Nevertheless, we notice among the more accurate descriptions some convergence with respect to *how* it speaks.

There is at least the strong suggestion of a sharp contrast with the impersonal talk of one's everyday life, with its constant argument, insatiable curiosity, and underlying ambiguity.[18] My conscience, on the other hand, speaks to me personally. It is not directed to anyone but myself alone. It is never loquacious and disputatious.[19] There is no arguing with my conscience. It speaks to me in silence without any wasting of words. Nevertheless, its message is unambiguous. I may dread this message. But its meaning is quite plain. In spite of the many things that it seems to say, there is one thing that is always present and underlies all the rest. It tells me that I am guilty, and calls me from my evasions to take over my guilt and struggle with it.[20] How, then, does Heidegger interpret these facts of common experience as thus suggested in common speech?

There is no need to seek for remote and superhuman forces. Human existence is always ahead of itself. To some degree it is aware of those last extreme possibilities, which are far away from the factual being into which it has already been thrown, and in which it has become lost by derivative modes of care. Conscience is the voice of care speaking to one's self from this last projected future, and calling one really to care.[21] But man is not a wraith of pure possibility. He exists in the world with a factual being already there. If he is to approach his own real possibilities, he must return to this being as it already is, shot through with the nothingness of imperfection.

Heidegger's account of this nothingness is hard to follow.[22] He rejects the notion of privation because he thinks this would imply that human existence might be somehow realized as a given fact completely present. And yet he uses negative language in referring to the factual state in which man is lost and always guilty.

This guilt can never be overcome. Wherever he is, whatever he does, man is always behind his last possibilities, and therefore guilty. Any other view is dismissed as Phariseeism and egregious self-content.[23] Nevertheless, it seems also to be implied that in some sense men may listen to the voice of conscience, take over their guilt, and at least approach a final integrity. It remains a fact, however, that conscience always says *Guilty*. This guilt is not conceived as something that may be added to or subtracted from man. It attaches to his finite being as such. He is inevitably guilty, not because he has violated some law, but because his existence is necessarily pervaded with negation.[24] This is what my conscience tells me. The answer cannot be found in talk, but only in silent decision—to take over my guilt, and by decision to cut myself off from lost factuality in integral devotion, or being-unto-death.[25]

PROJECTIVE DECISION

The self that seems to govern our everyday life has never really chosen. What it calls *choices* are merely adjustments to the *status quo* into which it has been thrown. Genuine choice means to come to one's self, to be responsible not merely for this or for that, but for the whole of one's personality. It is the voice of conscience that calls us to take ourselves over in this way. To hear this voice is to project our real possibilities to their final end, and to decide ourselves by accepting guilt and cutting ourselves away from the given factuality.[26] The self is not a *thing* that underlies a succession of mental states. The self is a way of existing, a wringing of pure possibility from the jaws of the guilty facts. This self does not take us into another realm. It exists here and now in the moment, or it does not exist at all. But it is a pervasive existential category which affects everything that we do and say, every phase of our being-in-the-world.

It is only in decision that I become sure of myself as a whole, and actually face the ultimate boundaries that limit my existence.[27] It is only through decision that we find ourselves not merely on hand, but in a situation confronted by threatening and friendly forces. It is by the light of decision that we take our bearings and find a way through these.[28] It is only such a being who can endure chance and accident,[29] live out a destiny, and be capable of tragedy. It is through decision that we learn the meaning of guilt, and really face the final limit of death by existing in its light.

Decision vitally affects the constitutive phases of my inner awareness, care, and time. Decisive existence is conscious being-to-the-end. It means pushing my awareness to its last horizons, where I achieve the most inclusive perspective on my being-in-the-world that is open to me.[30] It means expanding my devotion to its final limits in those ultimate possibilities which are really mine.[31] Finally, it means gathering the three ecstasies of time together out of their confused disunity, and concentrating them all at once in the openness of a single moment.[32] This is human integrity, the whole of a human person concentrated in a single moment by a decision towards those final possibilities which are really his. Such existence is sure of itself, because it is grasping itself in its entirety. At the same time, it is free from all routine commitments, and is open to any possibility in a given situation, including that of self-reversal.[33] This is what the existentialists mean by choice and decision. It is not a new accident or event, but a new way of existing that pervades every phase of the being of man.

Freedom in this sense of choice or commitment is a constant existentialist theme. Certain details of Heidegger's analysis would not be accepted by other thinkers. But its major outlines would

be. According to Marcel, ". . . there is an enormous and con-
cealed intellectualist element" in the "Kantian type of ethical
system." [34] He says that "to will is in some way to commit oneself; by which I mean to commit or bring into play one's own
reality; to throw oneself into what one wills." [35] This is close to
Heidegger's analysis of final decision.

Marcel distrusts any reduction of ethics to abstract principles
and norms that will involve us in "Phariseeism," [36] the word used
by Heidegger in rejecting any possibility of escaping guilt. He
feels intensely the "insufficiency" of our objective categories for
dealing with personal existence. "All that is deepest in me falls
outside this mode of thinking." [37] Freedom is not objective. "It is
only conceivable in the measure in which I have in me the means
whereby I can transcend the order of the him." [38]

For Jaspers also, human existence is constituted by choice. The
mass man is lost in indecisiveness.[39] There are no fixed moral
rules, but nevertheless all men are inevitably guilty. * Sartre has
not yet written his *Ethics*. But in spite of verbal differences, his
views of choice and action are essentially the same. He says that
death is a pure absurdity, and disagrees with Heidegger on this
point. But Heidegger says nothing about it, one way or the other.
Sartre seems to reject the notion of authenticity.[40] But he certainly defends the value of freedom, whatever he may call it, and
condemns his *bêtes noires,* the "serious people," who think of
themselves as objects.[41] He rejects stable moral rules and norms,[42]
and holds that all human existence (*pour soi*) is guilty, at least
in the sense that it is committed to the hopeless project of becoming complete and divine, which can never be achieved.[43] Freedom, nevertheless, is worthy. In spite of the fact that it can never
be realized, it constitutes the fluid and negative essence of man.[44]
Jaspers' and Sartre's analyses are often less clear and coherent
than that of Heidegger, but they do not differ from his in major
respects.

The contrast between the decisive and the indecisive modes of
existing, first suggested by Kierkegaard, though it be called by
various names, such as free *vs.* determined, personal *vs.* objective,

* "Also ob ich handle oder nicht handle, beides hat folgen, in jedem Falle
gerate ich unvermeidlich in Schuld." (*Philosophie,* Vol. II, p. 247.)

or authentic *vs.* unauthentic, is also stressed by these authors. Following Kierkegaard and Heidegger, they have given us many concrete studies of this contrast, which stands at the center of what we may call the existentialist ethics. It is to this central moral or existential contrast that we shall now turn our attention.

AUTHENTIC VS. UNAUTHENTIC EXISTENCE

All the existentialists accept authentic *vs.* unauthentic modes of existing as a basic distinction which divides men at the root of their very being, and is manifested at every level of their concrete existence. Though many of them would not like the term authentic because of its associations with nineteenth-century idealism, it expresses a moral ideal that is founded on human ontology, and is therefore capable of being checked by evidence accessible to all. Under different names, the contrast between authentic and unauthentic human existence is a recurrent theme in the existentialist literature, to which many different thinkers have contributed. In the following pages, we shall continue to follow the exposition of Heidegger fairly closely because of its disciplined precision. But at relevant points we shall try to show how the contributions of Jaspers, Marcel, and Sartre also fit into this analysis.

Since decision is not something incidental to man, but affects the very core of his being, we shall show how it is manifested in all the necessary existential structures we have studied—being-in-the-world; with-others; the ultimate limits of situationality, chance, guilt, and death; and finally the internal phases of awareness, care, and time. In each case, we shall first of all consider the unauthentic, and then more briefly the authentic mode we have already tried to clarify. This should enable us to understand the ontologically grounded ethics that is the crowning phase of this metaphysical doctrine, and at the same time an illuminating approach to the moral problems of our time.

BEING-IN-THE-WORLD

The unauthentic person is undecided and unsure of himself. This affects his being-in-the-world. He is not only unsure of himself, but unsure of the world he inhabits. This uncertainty is clearly reflected in those peculiar philosophic doctrines which question the existence of a so-called external world, and which have emanated from idealistic sources since the time of Descartes. They are still defended by eminent critical epistemologists in our own day. Such theorists pay little attention to ontology, and conceive of a human being as an isolated mind-thing whose only access to external beings and persons is in detached reflection on his own sense data. From such peculiar premises it is quite natural, indeed inevitable, that the existence of any world should be subject to doubt. Such doubt is often regarded as a sign of philosophical acumen, or even as that narrow gate through which alone one may enter into the subjective regions of modern epistemology. As the existentialist sees it, however, it is rather a sign of grotesque confusion and radical unauthenticity in the being of those who spread such doctrines.

The common man, of course, is saved by his active life from falling into such fantastic errors. Nevertheless, he also is uncertain and susceptible to such errors, if given the time and interest to think. He tends to confuse the world with the things and artifacts in the world, which are the constant object of his practical attention. The world for him is a vast collection of things. When he thinks of the world at all, he makes no clear distinction between the human world and the unfathomed universe around it. In the humanly ordered world, each thing has its given place and purpose. Even the largely uncontrolled entities of inorganic nature are thought of in this way, since we have technological ways of meeting their blind and brute resistance.

Thus a storm is something to be met in technical ways; a mountain something to be climbed or crossed; an ocean to be navigated. This is even more true of the instruments and artifacts which surround us in our everyday lives. Each of these is *for* a certain purpose. It is *in* a certain place. The road is there as a means of conducting me to my office. The office is there for the sake of doing business. Economic activities have their place within the process of human life as a whole, which has wider horizons, including a vast number of instrumental structures. What is the ultimate end-for-the-sake-of-which that determines the place of all subordinate structures? What is the last horizon of the world within which all subordinate places lie?

Our minds are apt to become quite unclear in facing this question. We are dimly aware that all instrumental purposes are justified only by some ultimate end. We know that our lives are lived within a last horizon we call the world. When one tries to give an answer, one becomes confused and is apt to say that it is to achieve the goals of an all-enveloping life-stream, or to realize all human desires so far as this is possible. According to the existentialist, this is an unauthentic and untrustworthy answer.

In the first place, what one calls the world is only a tiny little island carved out of a vast and mysterious context which really engulfs it. We know little or nothing of this enveloping ocean. We do not know what it is, where it came from, nor what it is for. We do not know our place in it, nor the real place of what we call "places." This is the real world, not the fragment we have reduced to partial subservience to our wishes. Is this an ordered whole, or is it rather a purposeless waste? Scientific and technological procedures are too restricted to help us in answering these questions. But the transcendent world really surrounds our little island. We know that it is there. To confuse it with this realm of ours, to assume that it is governed by our purposes, or even that it is governed by any *purpose,* is therefore to fall into a childish subjectivism. Who are we, to think that the whole surrounding universe is ordered to our ends, to any ends resembling these, or to any ends at all? This raises another question.

Who are we? It is we who have established the instruments and places within the human world. But who are we? One thinks of himself and of others in the same general way as he thinks of instruments and artifacts. Each of us has a certain place in the world, an allotted time, and certain functions to perform. This is even true of myself. I am a peculiar thing in the world, to be used in this way or in that; I hope for a useful purpose. But this is based on a gross distortion. What one calls the world is not completely independent of him and of his purposes. One has ordered it in accordance with his wishes. Then I cannot be included within a world that I have helped to make. Man cannot be one of his artifacts, something at hand to be used for an extrinsic goal. Neither can he be truly conceived as a mere theoretical object, just there to be observed from a detached point of view. Can man become detached from himself? Can he be used as an instrument for the sake of himself? Can the same being *be* both means and end?

These questions suggest certain human perversions which, according to the existentialists, are characteristic of our time. They are exemplified in that impersonal oneness which is everywhere and nowhere, and whose unauthentic confusions and reflections are a constant threat to our real existence.

It is not merely that one does not understand the world in which he exists. No man ever will do this. One is confused about the world, and is not aware of his confusion. One thinks of it as a vast collection. He mixes the vast enveloping world with the world of human contrivance. But even concerning this world of his own, he is confused and uncertain. He is not aware that its order is not fixed and inalterable, but belongs rather to his finite and transient being. This confusion and uncertainty are the marks of unauthentic being.

The authentic person has really decided. He is sure of the whole of himself as revealed in the light of his last possibilities. He knows that his being is not circumscribed like that of a thing, nor locked up inside a mind container. He knows that this being is stretched out ahead of himself, and is aware of its relational structure. Hence he is sure of the human world that he inhabits. But he also knows that there are broader horizons beyond in the ultimate world of reality, which he does not confuse with the human island. This, he recognizes, is ordered to an apex determined by human choice, and he is aware of its varying forms and manifestations. He has decided the structure of his own world, and is aware of the risks he has taken in so deciding. Whether this world is at peace or at odds with that of his friends and neighbors, he is ready to bear the responsibility and to defend it. If occasion should demand, he is ready to change it, and even retract it. But the last decision rests with him. As Sartre portrays him, he knows that in making this decision he is responsible for the whole of mankind, and dreads this heavy burden.[45] But, nevertheless, he makes it and holds to it, for he knows that it is only by this that he can really be.

BEING-WITH-OTHERS

The clearest and most penetrating description of the impersonal aloofness which dominates our daily life with others is Heidegger's famous account of *das Man,* oneness, in *Sein und Zeit.*[46] We do not discover other human beings by an elaborate process of sensation and inference. Our being makes us open to them from the very start. Caring for others is an essential phase of our existence, which, of course, has many possible forms.[47] Like all manifestations of existence, it is guided by a mode of understanding.

For the most part in our everyday life, we understand others from what they do, the functions they perform.[48] I also understand myself primarily in terms of the things I deal with, the house I live in, the clothes I wear, the professional operations I perform. I am also a center of functions. These functions are replaceable. Someone else might perform them. It matters little precisely who the person is. He is someone doing a thing that one does.[49] As Kierkegaard saw, this impersonal anonymity pervades the daily press.[50] Here we are presented not with a person expressing insights of his own, but rather with someone speaking from a detached point of view, and expressing what anyone might have seen. We often refer to this as objectivity. It is a depersonalized mode of existing which dominates the open public world.

In this world, one does not commit himself beyond the position that one tends to take. One does not decide for himself, and shies away from personal responsibility.[51] We do not know exactly who decided; it was someone who performed the act. New and divergent insights are discounted as already long familiar. One knows it already. The exceptional is always leveled down towards the average.[52] In this world, one is always master of the situation, confident and self-assured. One knows everything already, and all is essentially in order. One shies away from hard burdens and tries to make them easy. One is reassured by finding himself supported by widely prevailing opinion. One tries to escape in a refuge of nameless indecision from what is really and authentically his. This impersonal mode of existing is unauthentic because deprived of personal freedom. It is, however, an omnipresent fact. This is the world to which we are all first introduced. If one is ever to find himself, one must do so in the everyday world of *das Man*.

One communicates with others in a characteristic manner which is suggested by the English word *talk* (*Gerede*).[53] This mode of speech is distinguished by three predominant traits: an emphasis on linguistic symbols rather than intentional meaning, curiosity, and existential ambiguity.

Meaning, of course, can never be wholly suppressed. Nevertheless, in everyday discourse, the being which is talked about is suppressed. The emphasis is on the saying. One assumes that when more words are uttered, more actually is being said. Something is so because it is said so.[54] Pointed questions tend to be disregarded. Real understanding has been already achieved. The only problem lies in the saying. This emphasis on the symbolic tools of understanding, which are subject to technical manipulation, has been given philosophical expression in the analytic or linguistic philosophy of our day. The theory is here defended that many problems concerning being can be clarified or even solved by the proper manipulation of linguistic symbols. The structure of language determines not only thought but even reality.

Our pragmatic control of instruments and things is guided primarily by sight. Hence everyday talk is dominated by an emphasis on sight as against the other senses, and even by a tendency to confuse sight with genuine insight. Being is what can be *seen* by someone. To see is to understand. Hence it is not necessary to dwell on the object. To see it is sufficient. Then turn to something else. The point is to *see* as much as possible.[55] This incessant lust for vision is what we call curiosity. It never stops to ponder an object, but rushes on to further views. It has no firm position, but ceaselessly changes its point of view. It is everywhere and nowhere, and never comes to rest.

Heidegger is concerned to bring out the sharp contrast between everyday talk and the voice of conscience, which conveys its message without argument, idle proliferation of words, and restless curiosity.[56] One cannot talk to one's conscience. Nevertheless, I know what it says, and my conscience means it. This is not true of our everyday talk. In spite of the profusion of words, we are not clear as to precisely what has been said. Even when this may be surmised, we are not sure as to whether it was really meant by the speaker. We are left to swim in a haze of references only half fulfilled.[57] When something talked about really happens, this quenches the interest. It was already known before. One is not concerned with being as it really is, but rather with one's average glimpses and reactions.

This impersonal mode of being-with is unauthentic. One misunderstands and confuses himself with the things that he manipulates. So far as he feels the real possibility of something else, he runs away from it and, concealing his dread by a mask of self-assurance, loses himself in the public world of *das Man*.

This penetrating analysis, first suggested by Kierkegaard, has been descriptively confirmed and applied to further data by other existentialist authors. The ontological confusion of the human person with a thing or artifact is a constant theme of this literature. Many manifestations of it in our contemporary life have been described with great accuracy. These manifestations have been intensified and spread widely over the world by the influence of the Industrial Revolution.

Thus in his *The Philosophy of Existence,* Gabriel Marcel says of the mass-production worker:

> Surely everything both within him and outside him conspires to identify this man with his functions—meaning not only with his functions as worker, as trade union member or as voter, but with his vital functions as well. The rather horrible expression 'time table' perfectly describes his life. So many hours for each function. Sleep too is a function which must be discharged, so that the other functions may be exercised in their turn. The same with pleasure, with relaxation; it is logical that the weekly allowance of recreation should be determined by an expert on hygiene. . . . It is true that certain disorderly elements—sickness, accidents of every sort—will break in on the smooth working of the sys-

tem. It is therefore natural that the individual should be overhauled at regular intervals like a watch. . . . The hospital plays the part of the inspection bench or the repair shop. . . . As for death, it becomes objectively and functionally, the scrapping of what has ceased to be of use and must be written off as a total loss.[58]

The depersonalization of human existence is a constant threat. But its manifestations may vary in form and intensity in different periods of history. In our own time, the Industrial Revolution has fostered and accentuated them in a number of ways that have been described by Jaspers in his influential book, *Die Geistige Situation der Zeit,* translated as *Man in the Modern Age.*

He begins his analysis by referring to the development of modern technology, which has so radically altered the material conditions of human life.[59] In 1800 the total population of the world was about 850 million. In 1930 it was roughly 1,800 million, having more than doubled in one and a third centuries. This unprecedented increase was made possible by technical advances, a new basis for mass production, the organization of enterprises, an increase in the productivity of labor, an enormous improvement in the means of transport and communication, the codification of law, and the establishment of effective police systems by which public order is ensured. Our life is now dominated by a vast web of apparatus in which millions of human individuals must perform regular and machine-like functions.

Since our very existence now depends on the smooth working of this great web of interlocking mechanism, there has been a strong tendency to mechanize and to standardize not only those routine acts which are essential to maintain the apparatus, but human thought and life itself. The more men are encouraged to look upon themselves in materialistic terms, as complex aggregates of matter, the more easy it will be to fit them into the great machine, without running the risk of individual rebellion, chaos, and disruption. Hence there has arisen that unique phenomenon of the massive conditioning of thought and life by the control of propaganda, streamlined, standardized modes of life, and the so-called rule of the masses. These tendencies carry with them an unprecedented threat to human freedom and even to the possibility of genuine human existence. To reveal the complex nature of this threat, and that mode of personal sacrifice and action by which alone it may be overcome, is the purpose of the existential analysis.

> The masses are our masters; and for everyone who looks facts in the face, his existence has become dependent on them, so that the thought of them must control his doings, his cares, and his duties. . . . He belongs to the masses, though they threaten to let him founder amid rhetoric and the commotions of the multitude. Even an articulated mass always tends to become unspiritual and inhuman. It is life without existence, superstition without faith. It may stamp all flat; it is disinclined to tolerate independence and greatness, and prone to constrain people to become as automatic as ants. When the titanic apparatus of the mass order has been consolidated, the individual has to serve it. . . . If he wants to make his livelihood by intellectual activity, he will find it very difficult to do this except by satisfying the need of the many. He must give currency to something that will please the crowd. They seek satisfaction in the pleasures of the table, eroticism, self-assertion; they find no joy in life if one of these gratifications be curtailed. They also desire some means of self-knowledge. They desire to be led in such a way that they can fancy themselves to be leaders. Without wishing to be really free, they would fain be accounted free. . . .[60]

Human existence itself is conceived on the analogy of a beautiful, well-geared machine as the regular performance of routinized, repetitive functions—even rest and recreation being regularized as in the timetable of an efficient shop.

> In becoming a mere function, life forfeits its historical particularity to the extreme of a levelling of the various stages of life. Youth as the period of highest vital efficiency and of erotic exaltation, becomes the desired type of life in general. Where the human being is regarded only as a func-

tion he must be young; and if youth is over, he will still strive to show its semblance. . . . Since a human being no longer has any specific age, he is always simultaneously at the beginning and at the end; he can do now this now that and now the other; everything seems at any moment possible, and yet nothing truly real. The individual is no more than one instance among millions; why then should he think that his doings are of any importance? What happens happens quickly and is soon forgotten. People therefore tend to behave as if they were all of the same age. Children become like grown-ups as soon as they can . . . and the old pretend to be young. . . .[61]

Like Heidegger, Jaspers notes the emphasis on words and language as such—an unmistakable sign of the unauthentic flight from being.

The mass-diffusion of knowledge and of its expression leads to a wearing out of words and phrases. In the cultural chaos that now exists, anything can be said, but only in such a way that it signifies nothing. . . . When language is used without true significance, it loses its real purpose as a means of communication, and becomes an end in itself. Should I look at a landscape through a pane of glass, and should this pane of glass become clouded, I cease to see the landscape, if my attention is directed towards the glass itself. Today no attempt is made to use language as a means of contemplating being, language being substituted for being. . . . This concentration upon words for their own sake is the outcome of a convulsive endeavor to discover form in cultural chaos. The upshot is that today the manifestation of culture is either imperfectly understood and watered-down chatter in which any words you like are used; or else it is verbosity in place of reality. . . .[62]

Although what statisticians call the expectation of life is considerably increased, we all have a growing sense of vital insecurity. As Jaspers sees it, this dread is really due to the resignation of our existential freedom before the encroachments of the titanic mass-order. It is cloaked under various disguises such as the fear of old age, sickness, and biological death. Nevertheless, in general, life seems full of dread.

> This increases to such a pitch that the sufferer may feel himself to be nothing more than a lost point in empty space, inasmuch as all human relationships appear to have no more than a temporary validity. The work that binds human beings into a community is of fleeting duration. In erotic relationships the question of duty is not even raised. The sufferer from anxiety has confidence in no one; he will not enter into absolute ties with any other person. One who fails to participate in what others are doing is left alone. The threat of being sacrificed arouses the sense of having been utterly forsaken, and this drives the sufferer out of his frivolous ephemeralness into cynical hardness and then into anxiety.[63]

This is a threat to the smooth functioning of the mass mechanism. So, many institutions have arisen whose function is to tranquillize people, and to make them forget their fragile personal existence.

> The organizations in question are designed to arouse a sense of membership. The apparatus promises safety to its members. Doctors try to talk the sick or those who believe themselves sick out of the fear of death. But these institutions function effectively only when things are going well with the individual. The life-order cannot dispel the dread that is part of every individual's lot.[64]

The answer is not to be found in soothing opiates. When existence is paralyzed, the dread of life cannot fail to grow. It must be faced and overcome by the actual exercise of personal freedom. As Jaspers puts it: ". . . this anxiety can only be controlled by the more exalted dread felt by existence threatened with the loss of its selfhood, which induces an overriding religious or philosophical exaltation." [65]

Philosophy especially is seen as the essential prerequisite for a real awakening of minds to the problems of mass standardization, and for arousing them to the genuine exercise of existential freedom. But this must no longer take the form of pretentious system-building in the modern manner. In these systems Jaspers sees only temporary, ineffective anodynes. It must rather take the form of a ruthless tearing aside of all veils, with a genuine intensification of self-consciousness on the part of physically weak individuals. Mass uniformity must be resisted in every walk of life. Individuals must be encouraged to think for themselves, and to understand themselves *not as things* but as free persons. A real contact with the great classics of philosophical and religious thought may give great aid. But philosophy in this sense must be torn from the seclusion of academic walls. It is an essential component of human freedom which is now at stake.

Existential philosophy is an attempt to meet this need. "Man torn from the sheltering substantiality of stable conditions and cast into the apparatus of mass life, deprived of his faith . . . is devoting more decisive thought to the nature of his being." [66] Aroused to genuine questioning and reflection, free men may infuse the routine performance of some repetitive function with the light of freedom. Being ever ready to make themselves available for the personal communication of others, they may help them to understand. Thus free associations of persons may spontaneously arise with the hope of subordinating machines to men, rather than men to machines. But the issue can never be sure. The freedom of men cannot be predicted.

The basic problem of our time is whether an independent, human being in his self-comprehended destiny is still possible. Indeed it has become a general problem whether man can be free—and this is a problem which, as clearly formulated and understood, tends to annul itself; for only he who is capable of being free can sincerely and comprehendingly moot the problem of freedom. . . . [But] perhaps freedom has only existed for a real but passing moment between two immeasurably long periods of sleep, of which the first period was that of the life of nature, and the second period was that of the life of technology. If so, human existence must die out . . . in a more radical sense than ever before. . . . [67]

At this stage of our history, the authentic person will refuse to be lost in the world of public functions without a struggle. He will try to understand his real possibilities, and to make up his own mind in the light of these. Aware of himself as a center of freedom, he will sharply distinguish between persons and things. In caring for others, he will direct his attention not so much to their replaceable functions as to themselves in projecting their own futures and following them, even though they be opposed to his.[68] He will wonder at things he does not understand, and ask questions of himself and others. Above all, he will not be afraid to stand alone.

Heidegger maintains that decisive existence will be open to genuine communication with others. From his discussion of talk, we can infer that such communication must use symbols lightly with an emphasis on intentional meaning, that it must dwell on each item of subject matter until it is analyzed, and finally that it must unambiguously disclose being as it is. But beyond a few passing references, he says very little about it.

Jaspers has gone into the problems of communication more thoroughly.[69] In addition to the verbose discourse of everyday, he distinguishes the objective language of abstract science. He does not deny all validity to this. It is all right in its place, but it is wholly inadequate for the communication of living existence. Its concepts are universal. But existence is individual. It is concerned with abstract fixities. Existence is concrete and always unfinished. Finally, scientific discourse is detached and objective. But existence is concerned with itself and subjective. Can this free existence be communicated to another?

Jaspers gives an affirmative answer, and devotes considerable attention to what he calls existential communication.[70] This makes no use of universal concepts and judgments. It cannot be planned or controlled, but must spring up, so to speak, on the spur of the moment. It has no stable structure, but passes beyond all fixed limits. It is ever unfinished, and cannot be confined within any comprehensive system. It is a friendly struggle between two alien ways of ordering the world, or indeed, between two different worlds. Any final agreement will kill it. In spite of these negations, which also apply to philosophy as Jaspers conceives it, he nevertheless thinks that free existence can be communicated in such a way as to arouse and strengthen the freedom of others. Every person should be ready to open himself to such discussion. To prepare men for this is a primary function of philosophy.

In spite of Jaspers' suggestive remarks, this conception nevertheless elicits many questions. All communication must use concepts of some kind. How, then, can my lived existence be communicated to another, if all concepts are abstract and therefore inadequate? This "other" does not possess my lived existence. What are the instruments of such discourse? If it has no stable structure, how does it differ from chaos? Can two persons differ in friendly argument, unless they differ concerning the same? But in what sense can two subjective existences be the same? How, then, is even difference possible? If no agreement is possible, what, then, is the use of argument? How can the freedom of one arouse freedom in the other, unless the meaning of freedom is the same? Jaspers often suggests these questions himself. He never goes far in answering them. Other existentialists have asserted that authentic existential communication is possible. But they have not presented us with any coherent analysis.

The problem remains where Kierkegaard left it. My existence is subjectively mine. It is due to my own decision. How, then, can it be transmitted to another? Their unqualified attack on theoretical apprehension has made it impossible for existentialists to deal adequately with this question. The absence of any clear account of authentic communication remains a major weakness in the doctrine. As we shall see,[71] it has had an important effect on the theory as a whole.

BOUNDARY SITUATIONS

Jaspers' doctrine of the boundary situations is now very widely accepted amongst existentialist thinkers. The most important of these, situationality, chance, guilt, and death, we have already considered. These are inescapable conditions of human existence. They are limits in the sense that we can do nothing to alter or transcend them. Nevertheless, they are always present and must be faced. There is an authentic and an unauthentic way of facing them. The difference is sharp and clear.

Situationality

Situation is a practical or existential category. Events or things are never in a situation. The brain has spatial surroundings. It is not in a situation. The living organism may interact with an environment. But to be-in-a-situation is grounded on decision. This is, in fact, a necessary limit of human existence. Whether fully aware of it or not, one is always in a situation.[72] Nevertheless, there are two ways of facing this limit of situationality.

One suddenly finds himself in a situation, or falls into one. He views this at first as a rather exceptional occurrence, a special problem to be solved by shrewd calculation and scientific techniques. After *solving* it in some way, he soon finds himself in another situation which has to be *solved*. In the intervals between, he is forgetful, and looks on these as periods of peace where aesthetic fulfilment takes place. His aim is to escape from the situation, for which he finds science the most efficient instrument. If he is asked why he thinks these situations have arisen, he will give an objective answer: This is the way things are, he will say. These problems are simply given. It is part of life to have problems. His job is to *solve* them once they arise. When he is asked what, then, is the use of solving one, only to fall into another, he may be disconcerted. But he will soon find an impersonal answer: One is made that way. One must seek adjustment, even though it is never attained. He is unaware of the basic decisions which are responsible for his being in any situation at all. The structure of his world is confused. He is unaware of his ultimate end.

Having made no decision on basic issues, his attitudes are fixed and inflexible. When something really startling arises, he is lost and easily guided by those using an objective type of analysis. Such an analysis thinks of a situation in general terms. It is not yours nor mine, but is made up of objective conditions and circumstances which can be met by clever devices.[73] Basic decisions are postponed as long as possible. When they can no longer be avoided, a reasonable compromise is made that will meet the immediate problem. Long-range commitment is viewed as unsound and hazardous.

There is, however, another responsible way of facing this limit of situationality.[74] The authentic person has decided himself in the light of his last possibilities. He does not fall into situations, but brings himself into them. He knows that in taking over his factuality, he has committed himself to situationality as well. He is aware that no escape is possible. Rest and peace are always in situations. He has made up his mind about what he is seeking. He knows that it is *this* decision which has brought him to where he is. Holding fast to his last possibilities, he is open and flexible in finding his bearings, wherever he is. He is ready for anything, and hard to bewilder. He recognizes the situation as his, and interprets the friendly and opposing forces in relation to his ultimate end. He does not postpone his decisions, because the structure of his world is clear. Basically they have already been made. They must now be sustained and repeated. Very flexible in most affairs, on ultimate issues he is uncompromising. On such issues he is not easily led, but makes up his own mind.

Other Boundary Situations

Different lists of boundary situations are given by different writers. Chance, suffering, and conflict are analyzed by Jaspers.[75] The existentialist rejects all attempts to justify these hard facts rationally. Chance is sometimes presented as a necessary condition for freedom. Suffering and conflict are interpreted by the idealist as necessary stages in the acquisition of mature knowledge. But this is a gross distortion. Chance wrecks our purposes. Suffering and warfare shatter us. Behind them all is death. These things are not good.

Another approach is to admit that they are evil, but then to explain them away or to minimize them. Thus determinist theories try to explain away chance as a manifestation of ignorance. Optimistic minds may try to explain suffering and conflict as minor aspects of a providential scheme, and blind themselves to the pain and misery around them. Accidents constantly break in upon us and snuff out our possibilities. Physical and mental suffering must be borne by every man. The very fact that we exist is a result of military victories by those who preceded us. Every day that I live has been taken from the possible existence of others. These are hard facts that cannot be explained away or minimized.

A last approach is to dream of Utopian schemes where these evils may be eliminated, or at least sharply reduced by skilful management. Thus with sufficient scientific knowledge, we might perhaps plan for accidents of every variety and reduce them to a minimum. With the growth of medicine we might eliminate suffering, prolong life, and even reduce death to the painless, fearless quenching of a flickering light.[76] But these are only fantasies by which I try to escape from the facts—to my own damage. This supposed escape is false and unauthentic.

These facts are neither good, nor are they avoidable evils. Certainly they are present; not present, however, as facts which are good or evil, but rather as inescapable limits which hem me in and restrict my being. They are boundaries. The authentic attitude, therefore, is to push back the boundaries, so far as this is possible. It is right to try to avoid accidents, to allay suffering, and to strive for peace. But these endeavors have inexorable limits beyond which they cannot go. Authentic existence, therefore, will not try to escape from them. It will rather accept and bear them.

Guilt

A similar attitude of escape and evasion underlies one's attitude towards guilt. According to the existentialists, this running away from the facts is always unauthentic, and results in a loss of the self. Thus one may imagine fixed norms or standards that one may at least approximate. In this way one may partially abrogate the guilt. On the existentialist view, however, there are no fixed standards. All those so far suggested have been riddled with criticism, and conclusively shown to be mere rationalizations of personal decision. This is another attempt to escape from an unavoidable limit of our existence. In the end, what person can honestly say that he is not guilty? This boundary is inescapable, and applies to every man. Some have dreamed of escaping it by refraining from all action. If strictly adhered to, this would lead them to a quietistic suicide.[77] But this, too, is a delusion. Even non-action has consequences. Whether we act or do not act, in either case we are guilty.

The authentic man will take over his guilt, and admit his responsibility. Jaspers, in fact, defines responsibility as an acceptance of guilt.[78] This again does not mean that the free person welcomes it as a good, or that he is indifferent to it. He tries to stay within the boundary, and to escape such guilt as is avoidable. But there is a last profound guilt that he cannot escape. This is neither good nor evil, but a limit whose ultimate nature we cannot understand. We can only face it and bear it.

Death

The last of these inscrutable limits is the ultimate boundary of death, which has been strikingly neglected in the literature of modern ethics, but which is a constant theme of existentialist literature. This has strengthened the impression that there is something gloomy and morbid about this philosophy. But it all depends on the attitude we take towards everyday life. If this life is sound and healthy, there is something in this objection. But the existentialist thinkers do not agree. They offer evidence to show that this life is governed by ambiguity and confusion. These are manifested in a loss of self and a distracted care for things. This everyday life misunderstands its limits and evades its real responsibilities. It is not sound and healthy. The existentialists find this judgment strikingly confirmed by a close study of the common attitude towards death.[79]

Death is an evident limit that every person must face. But in everyday life, we find ourselves constantly evading and suppressing the thought of death. It is not a subject for polite conversation. When unavoidable, it is referred to in indirect and euphemistic ways. Great pains are taken to conceal his approaching death from the stricken person. Many devices are used to evade this inescapable fact.[80] Tolstoi has given us a penetrating description of these in his story, *The Death of Ivan Ilyitch*. We have already noted certain theoretical manifestations of this flight from death: its objectification as the death of another, its interpretation as a ripening or harvesting of vegetative life, the universalized and abstract version of it as the death of someone in general.[81] None of these views can withstand careful examination. They are all evasions of the death which is of greatest concern to me—which I must die by myself alone.

One admits that this death is certain, but when it will come is indeterminate. These are the clear-cut facts. But one introduces an interesting qualification. He says: *Yes, it is certain sometime, but not right away.* This is a significant dilution of the facts.[82] His immediate cares and plans are safeguarded. His life is not projected to the very end, but only up to a certain point. This segment is perhaps exempt from death. The rest is vague and confused. Up to a certain point, uncertainty is similarly excluded. After a while, yes, uncertainty. But not for a little while. This is clearly an evasion, for the evident truth is that death may come at *any* moment, including the next. Certain moments must be protected from this future. One thinks of his life as a series of successive events, one following after another. Death itself is a last event which will finally be there, but may be for some time postponed. These equivocations are false and unauthentic—a flight from the boundary of death.

The authentic person does not run away from this fact.[83] He meditates upon it—not as a finished event that will sometime be there, but as the end that lies ahead of him in terms of which he can project his existence as a whole. He knows that it is certain, and that it may strike at any moment, even the next. He does not try to dilute these facts. How will this influence him? Will it not drive him away from all postponement, and lead him to recognize the importance of this very moment? Must he not act now in such a way that should death strike, his whole life may have some total significance? Will he not, then, try to gather himself together, and strive to concentrate the whole of his being in decisive action here and now? [84] As the existentialist sees it, this is not morbid, but rather the way of integrity and freedom.

So far we have considered certain external phases of human being: being-in-the-world, with-others, and the final limits that restrict this being. Now we must turn again to the constitutive phases of this being: awareness, care, time, and history. These also may be maintained in an unauthentic and an authentic manner.

AWARENESS

According to the existentialists, unauthentic awareness is dominated by a circumscribed object there before me at which I gaze with little clear consciousness of the noetic act. The seeing which guides our practical manipulations has this structure.[85] Hence all data, including consciousness itself, are interpreted in this way. This also is usually conceived as a thing or mind-container within which lie atomic experiences. Since physical objects or events dominate our senses, there is a strong tendency to think of awareness as consisting of such events—electrical changes in the cortex, vibrations in the central nervous system, etc. Awareness is a set of processes going on within the brain, or within the living organism.[86] No attention is paid to the intentional structure that is peculiar to mind, and is never found in physical things or relations. Awareness is not of something which it reveals. It is what it is, a process or field, lying within its spatial boundaries. This oversimplified ontological view is responsible for the subjectivism which has so persistently dominated the history of modern epistemology.

Language is reduced to the physical symbols of discourse, which have a formal structure and order of their own. The task of logic is primarily concerned with this symbolic structure. Sense data are objects present "in" the organism. They have physical causes, and are thus related to the external public world. In spite of the fact that being-the-effect-of is clearly not the same as being-the-manifestation-of, sensation is taken to be the chief source of information about reality. It reveals facts, that is, *objects* like visual patterns, sounds, flavors, and smells. This at least gives us a basis for inferring how things really are. Other feelings, like fear and dread, may have external causes, but they depend more on internal changes, and therefore reveal our own subjective states rather than anything external.

The unauthentic person suppresses feelings like dread and its allied emotions as too vague and indefinite to mean anything.[87] Instead of this, he is subject to many fears for the "real" things and artifacts with which he is mainly concerned, and which, as he thinks, his senses reveal as hard facts. He discounts what is called conscience and has plausible theories to explain it away.

Reason, as he sees it, manifests nothing. It is a constructive power which makes up guesses and interpretations. When its operations are governed by the strict rules of logic and its premises are taken from sense, it may be very useful, as in science, in expanding information by valid inference. Otherwise it is very dangerous, and ensnares us in a web of fiction. The awareness of such a person is dominated by physical objects and artifacts.[88] All other data, if recognized at all, are fitted into this frame. The frame itself is divided into loosely joined segments which lack any overarching unity. Philosophic reflection alone can provide such unity. This is ignored and dismissed as unreliable speculation.

Authentic awareness is more self-conscious. It realizes that any object must involve a subject and acts of awareness of some kind. It resists the idea that mind is a container, and thinks of it rather as a lantern or a light, which, though intermittent and flickering, may penetrate to being. The authentic person realizes that physical things do not act in this way; hence, even though he may be unable to refute it, he resists both physicalism and the subjectivism that always attends it.

In his discourse, he pays more attention to what he is saying than to the words by which he says it. He uses words and symbols flexibly and lightly, trying to make them vanish as soon as possible after they have performed their signifying function. He respects sensory evidence, but does not believe that it is exhaustive. He attends to the dread that sometimes stirs within him, and listens to his conscience. He sometimes reflects on the last possibilities that he might realize, and knows that all is not in order. As a result of this, he is less subject to fear and terror of the forces that constantly threaten his things and implements. His mind is open to possibilities, and he constantly wonders why things are not otherwise than they are. He knows that sense is vague and confused, and respects the revealing power of rational insight. He has made up his mind about basic issues, but is always ready to examine new evidence. His world has structure and overarching unity, and if he has escaped academic books (and has ever heard of it) he has a feeling for philosophy.

CARE

Unauthentic care is focused on present things and artifacts. It is aware of their determinate possibilities, and tries to manipulate them towards useful goals. These are judged to be useful in terms of serving everyone as he already is, or, as it is often put, keeping things as they are. The unauthentic person accepts the everyday world as basically sound, and thinks of himself as a relatively stable object within this world. He accepts himself as he already is, and conceives of his moral function as keeping it going for a segment of time which he says he can foresee. He thinks very little about his death, and does not care for his conscience. He knows theoretically that people are not quite the same as things, but he thinks of them primarily in terms of the functions they perform.

These replaceable habits are needed to keep things going. They are a part of life. So all men need to be trained in them. Sometimes, however, they break down. The way to help others when this happens, is to perform their function for them until they are rested and cured.[89] This is genuine love and devotion. Unauthentic existence is dominated by drives or interests guided largely by sense and imagination, and therefore having a restricted range of objects and a truncated future. The interest is to get its object, possess it, and then be satisfied. In this way, the problem will be solved and another can take its place. If such interests are blocked, the mind is closed to other possibilities, and takes refuge in wishful thinking.

Authentic care, too, is concerned with present things and artifacts. But it is also aware of its own last possibilities, and is open to those of others. The authentic person accepts the everyday world, but not as basically sound. He gives himself to his dread, and feels the strangeness of things as they are. He knows that they might have been very different, and wonders why they were not. He also realizes that he himself might have been very different, and that even now he might become so. He thinks of his own death and the real possibilities still before him. Such existence accepts guilt, and does not try to dilute it or explain it away. The authentic person thus becomes responsible, that is, ready to com-

municate, and to answer questions, complaints, and charges, not
only those raised by others but also those raised by himself. He
respects the decisions of his associates, and is aware that the greatest help is to aid them in understanding and realizing their human freedom.[90] He is aware of himself as a whole, and cares for
his integrity. His drives and interests are subordinated to final
purposes that he cares for up to death.

TIME

The existentialist ethics is founded on ontology. So closely
are the two related that the way in which our lives are temporalized is dependent on moral decision. There is an unauthentic and
an authentic way of existing through time. Unauthentic existence
cannot hold the three ecstasies of time together in an integrated
structure, but allows them to slip from its grasp into separated
fragments which merely go on in discontinuous succession.[91]
The past is no longer *held,* but fades away into something already over and gone. The future becomes a non-existent now not
yet there. Only the objective present is real, as separating the
past from the future. No longer held together, the ecstasies fall
apart and succeed each other: first the past, then the present, and
finally the future. But the present alone is actual. The past and
the future are real only by becoming present, and thus by losing
their distinctive character.

Thus leveled down to a bare succession of nows, it is easy for
one to regard time as a peculiar type of spatial "dimension" all
of whose parts are actually present. The distinctive temporality
is thus squeezed out of time. This view now claims the support of
relativity theory, and of science in general. It has influenced
common sense, and has recently been given philosophical expression by Donald Williams.[92] Unauthentic time is held to go on
indefinitely with no determinate limit.[93] The self is viewed as an
object lying in this temporal dimension.

The authentic person feels that time is close to his inner
being.[94] He knows that to give time to something is to give himself; to lose time is to lose himself. His care is dominated by
futurity. Having thought this through to the end, he is able to
bring it to bear on a final decision in the moment. Making this

decision, he takes over the past and repeats its last possibilities. Instead of separating a non-existent past from a non-existent future, the moment of decision holds them together in an order of wholeness and integrity. This future is no longer a non-existent present not yet there, but the guiding phase of his being. The past is not a non-existent present that once was, but is sustained as the past that he has been. Each ecstasy retains its distinctive character, but is held together with the others in a structure that is now integrated from beginning to end.

These phases are brought together and concentrated all at once in the moment, but not in the mode of a spatial dimension. The existential structure is not all there to be stared at. It is in transition—temporalizing itself. Indeterminacy and projected futurity sharply distinguish it from a mere expanse of space, and even from a physical process whose successive phases are determined by the past rather than the future. Human being exists in a different way. Its future does not succeed the present. This present is already ahead of itself with a future that is holding and guiding it. This future, however, is not an infinite succession of nows. It is strictly limited by the ultimate boundary of death. The authentic person knows that his time is ending. He cannot postpone existing. Unless he fills this moment with the significant content of final choice, he will lose himself in a chaos of successive fragments. He knows that this self is not merely an object in time but is its temporality.

HISTORY

Unauthentic existence thinks of history as a vast succession of events in which life is placed, and compares it with a stream whose channel is largely fixed in spite of meandering here and there.[95] The past is already set and stable, and provides us with a firm foundation in the present for creative contributions to an ever-advancing future. In order to make such contributions, we must first fit into the past. We may be ignorant of this past, but it is already finished and gone. What is most important is to be original and new. History as a study is primarily concerned with the past. We watch the great flux of events as they unroll in a present that now exists no longer, and try to understand the laws of their unfolding, so that we may perhaps carry them further. To be free is to produce something novel and creative that one will some day recognize as a genuine advance. History never repeats herself.

The authentic person realizes that he is not merely a set of events in history, but that his own existence is historical. He is skeptical of spatial metaphors, and doubts the theory of automatic progress. The past may be factually determinate, but its meaning is still uncertain. It is not so much a firm foundation for new achievement as a burden that presses upon us and restricts our field of action. The future is dark and mysterious. It is not a mere now that has not yet happened but lies ahead of us, as at great moments in the past. At these decisive moments, different final futures become apparent in history. Their meanings may be described, analyzed, and compared in a disciplined way. This is a major task of the study of history. But the future itself is still unfinished. Hence between these opposed possibilities, a final decision must be made. Whether he knows it or not, each human person is making such a decision by directing his life in a certain way. Even not deciding at all is the making of a decision with a strange disintegrated future of its own.

The study of history may shed light on the meaning of these different futures, and the nature of the factual past that each of them may take over. It can help us decide which of them is most worthy of decisive repetition. It is by such repetition alone that historic unity may be freely held and sustained. History has no automatic unity. Such unity as it has is constantly being lost by lassitude and irresponsibility. Such unity as it may possess will depend upon personal fidelity and final decision.

Freedom must not be confused with novelty. If this were its nature, freedom would be easy and automatic, for all that happens is novel. True freedom is hard and precious. It is open only to persons who have understood something of those final but still unfinished possibilities which here and there have brought meaning into the past. It is brought into being again at a present moment only by those who have decided between them with finality, and who exist with integrity up to the end.

– 6 –

Existentialism as a Philosophy

WE HAVE now examined the central core of existentialist thought, its phenomenological method and the view of experience to which this method has led, its ontology, its theory of human knowledge and action, and finally its ethics. In making this survey, we have occasionally drawn from the work of other writers, but in the main we have followed the exposition of Heidegger in *Sein und Zeit* because of its systematic clarity and widespread influence. We have tried in this way to gain an understanding of those basic doctrines which are shared by most existentialist philosophers. These doctrines, however, are not complete. To give us an integral view of being, they must be supplemented by further elements contributed by individual inference and speculative power. Hence in this chapter, we shall try to summarize briefly the philosophical positions of four existentialist thinkers: Karl Jaspers, Jean-Paul Sartre, Gabriel Marcel, and Martin Heidegger. After gaining some conception of those views of the world to which existentialism leads, we shall turn our attention to a critical estimate of this philosophy.

KARL JASPERS

Jaspers has been deeply influenced by Kant, especially in his view of human awareness. But in other respects, his thought exemplifies those central existentialist conceptions which we have been considering in the preceding chapters.

According to Jaspers, awareness always involves acts of constructive interpretation. The experience of each individual has already been interpreted by him, and therefore differs from the experience of others.[1] There is no basic empirical structure which can be verified by all observers. Certain facts can be measured and analyzed by the sciences. At this level, universal agreement can be achieved. But the facts are indefinitely numerous, so that the task of science is never completed. Furthermore, these facts can be given different philosophical interpretations which are not subject to conclusive verification. No universal phenomenology is possible. Philosophical theories are only plausible constructions. Each individual must think for himself out of his own concrete situation, appealing to others for possible agreement and aid.[2] This skepticism is strongly emphasized by Jaspers throughout his works.

If taken literally, it would seem to be inconsistent with the whole phenomenological trend of existentialist thought. But he does not take it literally without qualification. Human existence and its situation may be clarified and illumined in such a way as to exercise a universal appeal, and to elicit widespread agreement on the part of careful observers. Jaspers is a keen observer and has devoted himself persistently to the task of phenomenological description.[3] He often seems to think that he has attained verifiable results. How this is to be reconciled with his epistemological skepticism is never made clear.

Jaspers rejects any universal ontology, or theory of being, as binding on all.[4] Nevertheless, he believes that human existence in general, and certain recurrent aspects of the human situation, may be illumined and clarified.[5] All the entities of experience are caught up in a ceaseless flux. There is no lasting structure anywhere. Everything passes finally into destruction.[6] Man is no exception to this general principle. Everything in him is transitory. Each individual, and the species as a whole, is destined to annihilation.[7] There is no stable essence or nature of man. Nevertheless, we can regard him in two different ways which reveal two distinct but inseparable phases of his being. Jaspers calls these *Dasein* and *Existenz*.[8]

Dasein is myself regarded as an object, the whole of my empirical reality. *Existenz* is my very self. It cannot be known as an object. To think it, in fact, is to kill it. But neither can it be grasped as a subject behind the phenomena. Here the analysis departs from that of Kant. My *Existenz* is not something in general. It is my very own. *Dasein* has traits and characters. Its possibilities are fixed. *Existenz* is infinitely open to new possibilities. The traits of *Dasein* are infinitely rich, but they can be understood up to a given point by theoretical reflection. *Existenz* is wholly opaque to such theoretical investigation. It cannot be defined and delineated in any way. *Dasein* is determined. *Existenz* is free. These two phases of my being are opposed. There is a constant struggle between them. But they are also inseparably connected. My *Existenz* is in my *Dasein,* and all the acts of the former are manifested in the latter. Even though it can never be observed nor theoretically understood, *Existenz* can be illumined by philosophical reflection, as Jaspers calls it, and communicated to other *Existenz*.

Dasein is in the world with others and inseparably related to them. *Existenz* also cannot be adequately conceived as a Leibnizian monad.[9] I also am in the world, as the field where my choices must be manifested in action. I *am* my relations to transcendence and to other *Existenz*. This *Existenz* is finite and strictly limited by the boundary situations of suffering, conflict, chance, guilt, and death. These are neither good nor evil. I can neither understand them, nor do anything about them. They can neither be surmounted nor evaded by clever schemes and plans. They constantly restrict all human action. We cannot see through them nor over them. They stand like inescapable barriers of life. I cannot understand them except as limits which hem me in. *Dasein* in its attempts to prolong its being in the world, becomes lost in the objects of its desires. It evades the ultimate limits, and is often unconscious of them. But they are always present. It is *Existenz* that becomes aware of them. By this awareness I am stirred to express myself freely and authentically.

I am also aware of an all-encompassing being possessed by both *Existenz* and *Dasein* which surrounds and pervades the worlds.[10] Jaspers calls this the *Umgreifende* (all-including). This being is possessed by all things whatsoever, and is itself wholly indeterminate. It has no specific traits of its own, and cannot be defined or characterized in any way. Jaspers seems to think of it as a vast continuum out of which all specific entities are somehow shaped or carved.

A unique feature of Jaspers' metaphysics is his theory of transcendence. He holds that Kant's arguments in the *Critique of Pure Reason* have finally disposed of the classical arguments for the existence of God, though he grants them some importance in having shown the non-self-sufficiency of the world.[11]Both the pantheistic conception of God as an immanent power, and the theistic conception of God as an eternal person are rejected as too "ontological" and "objective." [12] This transcendent is wholly other, and above all Gods. It is accessible in certain peculiar ways to all men, but is entirely ineffable and opaque to human intelligence. No positive traits can be attributed to it. Any definite picture or doctrine is a distortion. It is beyond all form and does not change. As the "ultimate *Umgreifende*," it has no defects, but is never seen or known. How then is it accessible?

Jaspers tries to answer this question by his theory of the cipher writing, a term which he has taken from Pascal.[13] Transcendence is never directly revealed to me, but only through certain enigmatic signs or ciphers in the world. Metaphysics, as Jaspers conceives it, is the attempt to interpret these ciphers which fall into three classes. First, any empirical fact, for example the sea, can become a cipher. In such an experience, transcendence may suddenly shine forth in an uncertain light, only to vanish again before it can be clearly fixed or identified. Second, there is the less direct language of art and mythology. These images can also be deciphered. Finally, there is the language of metaphysical systems. It is a mistake to take these literally. But as thought symbols, they may often lead certain individuals in different ways to the presence of transcendence.

This transcendence, however, is most poignantly revealed to me in my own free acts. True freedom always dimly knows that it cannot stand alone, that it depends on something beyond. When cut off from transcendence, it fades away and disappears. Freedom exists only in a certain closeness to transcendence. But when closest, it is ever restless and in doubt. Transcendence is apt to loom before me when I am in solitude, or suddenly plunged into concrete boundary situations. It always appears *in* the cipher, and never as something wholly distinct. In this respect, the cipher differs from a sign, which is always distinct from the *signatum* that can be independently known. This reading of the ciphers is free and cannot be forced. I may refuse to listen and turn away. Even when I pay attention, the presence is always ambiguous and unsustained.

Jaspers' view of human awareness never strays far from Kantian conceptions.[14] Reason is bound up with human action, and is incapable of manifesting things as they really are. All fixed theories and concepts are relative to a certain purpose. What we call *the world* is only a flickering appearance, distorted by subjective aims and biases. The subject, as we have seen, is wholly opaque to conceptual reflection. Kantian subjectivism of this kind is peculiar to Jaspers, and not characteristic of existentialist thought. In other respects, his analysis of man does not differ markedly from that of Heidegger.

Human life is dominated by practical interests, though these are always guided by a projective intelligence. Man is ever ahead of himself in the pursuit of possibilities which are never finally achieved. Two basic paths are open. He may give himself over to the inner-worldly interests of *Dasein,* in which case he sacrifices everything to the ultimately futile aims of extending and prolonging his life.[15] Or he may see the fleeting and foreign character of the world and give himself over to his existential possibilities.[16] In either case, his existence is ever unfinished and necessarily historical. Decisive choice occurs at a moment, and binds the future together with the past. Such choices must be maintained and repeatedly taken over.[17]

In thus accepting his own responsibility for the past, authentic *Existenz* finds itself necessarily tainted with guilt. When this guilt is accepted and directed to the future by decisive action in the present moment, the interval which we call a human life may be filled with a consistent and even timeless content. This content may be transmitted to others by that unplanned, and nonconceptual existential communication which we have already studied.[18] Jaspers' detailed descriptions and analyses of different levels of communication, while open to certain objections, as we have seen, are an important and original contribution to existentialist philosophy. Aside from this, and the intense irrationalism which breaks out at frequent intervals, Jaspers' theory of man does not differ radically from that of Heidegger.

Existenz may give itself to *Dasein* and the love of life, or to its own open possibilities in the face of transcendence. We are presented again with the two pathways, the unauthentic and the authentic, which are a constant theme of existentialist thought. Here and there in the vast flux of human history, we find traces of genuine *Existenz* whose possibilities we can still understand and take over. These personalities can arouse us to our own *Existenz*. We can understand their choices and communicate with them. But for the most part, history has been dominated by successive efforts to realize the determinate capacities of life in fleeting situations which have passed and cannot be repeated. Divergent cultures, kingdoms, and empires rise on the scene, grapple with vital problems, expand and contract, and then, like all that is living, sink into oblivion.

In this historic sequence, Jaspers distinguishes four periods of paramount importance.[19] First there was the *Promethean Age* of foundational history when language was first used, fire discovered, and tools invented. Second, the ancient civilizations grew up like islands of light in Egypt, Mesopotamia, on the Indus, and later in China. Third, there was a brief formative period from 800-200 B.C. when most of the globe was inhabited and men became aware of history. Many radical questions were asked, and the horror of life in the world was discovered. Human existence was in a turmoil of exploration and discovery. Philosophical reflection began, and the great world religions were founded. In the next period of almost two thousand years, we find human history frozen and congealed in fixed patterns of life and thought. The fourth, in which we exist, began with the rise of modern science and technology. So far, it has been characterized by the discovery of new types of vital realization, and the tumult and revolution that these must bring. Now it seems to have lost its creative fire, and is beginning to congeal into an all-inclusive technological pattern which may persist indefinitely and finally extinguish every spark of personal freedom.

In this novel situation, we are confronted by: (1) the mastery of science and the web of technology it has brought forth; (2) the unity of the globe and the interdependence of nations and peoples; (3) a vast increase of world population; (4) the appearance of inert masses of men, subject to control by irrational propaganda; (5) the breakdown of all past ideals of order and the questioning of all traditional values; (6) the appearance of two world powers engaged in mortal combat, each possessing weapons of sufficient power to destroy all civilization; (7) a universal sense of menace and impending catastrophe; (8) the domination of human thought by objective, quantitative categories, and the view of man as a complex object; (9) the application of this materialistic viewpoint to social policy, the passive acceptance of mass death in mechanized total warfare, and the fanatical willingness to kill whole peoples with indifference; and (10) the reduction of religion to a period of Sunday rest and relaxation.[20] Is there any way of arousing personal existence to meet this dreadful challenge?

Jaspers has devoted many pages to the consideration of this problem. It cannot be met by mass organization and technological equipment of any kind. The only hope lies in the individual person and his sacrificial expression of freedom. The revival of philosophy might play a vital role in helping to arouse this human freedom.[21] It cannot be produced on the assembly line. It requires personal reflection. By the radical questions it raises, it can show us the limits of science, the inadequacy of technological values, and the genuine possibilities of man. By leading us to reflect upon our existence and the implacable boundary situations that hem it in, philosophy may deflate our absurd fanaticism, and arouse us to authentic existence. It is in this way that most existentialists now think of their function as philosophers struggling in our present tragic situation.

This way of freedom, however, is neither easy to understand nor easy to realize in action. My acts are always limited by certain conditions, forces, and moral principles. Nevertheless, the free act is not exhaustively determined by these. It is able to respond creatively to these forces and principles by choosing between them, and subordinating one to another. I am not determined by my motives and reasons. I have chosen them to be mine.[22] As Jaspers sees it, freedom is a spontaneous act of autocreation. Its reason is simply that I willed it to be so. It is a mystery quite opaque to theoretical understanding. As Kant saw, it cannot be demonstrated. Nor can it be observed as an objective fact. It is the very heart of personal existence.

I *am* the free choices I make. The actual making of them, however, is always full of uncertainty and risk. I must be ready to accept the consequences of my choices. But I can never know just what they will be. Hence the exercise of freedom is pervaded by dread.[23] Such action is never arbitrary. It is also pervaded by a sense of existential necessity. It is the only thing I could do. Since my real possibilities are open, even up to transcendence, I cannot avoid willing an absolute fulfilment that is never achieved. Hence freedom is always a failure, and its maintenance necessarily means the acceptance of guilt. To live and to struggle unceasingly in such failure and risk is to exist as a man.

Such existence will be guided by five principles of philosophic faith: (1) there is something transcending the world; (2) there is an unconditional imperative—at all times and at all places personal freedom is to be respected and maintained; (3) man is not perfectible—always weak, dependent, and inadequate; (4) but he need not rely exclusively on himself; he has access to something transcendent which can guide him; and (5) the world subsists ephemerally between God and existence.[24]

This philosophic faith is opposed by five principles of nonfaith which guide all unauthentic practice: (1) only the world exists; there is nothing transcendent; (2) all moral imperatives are variable in time, and determined by habit and cultural conditioning; there is no unconditional imperative; (3) man is perfectible; he is strong through his science and technological power, independent, and adequate to himself; (4) he needs no guidance from God; this is dope for the people; he can and should rely on himself; and (5) while everything in the world is transient, the world itself is absolute and all inclusive.[25]

The affirmative faith of philosophy is not atheism, for it holds to the transcendent. But neither is it theism, for it rejects all "sectarian" interpretations, and any sort of attribution of personality or positive properties. This raises certain questions as to how this transcendent can be distinguished from nothingness. Is such an alternative between religion and atheism really possible? * But Jaspers defends it as a real possibility, open to all men, whatever their cultural background may be. He is certainly right in pointing out that it is violently opposed to the materialistic faith that rules contemporary thought. It will lead those who guide their lives by it to shipwreck and shattering.[26]

But according to Jaspers, this has a peculiar value of its own, and should be freely embraced and even welcomed. The truth is what dies. Duration is really an inverse measure of value. The more degraded existence is, the longer it lasts. Thus matter lasts longer than life; life longer than spirit; and the mass much longer than the individual. For the human person, stable and sheltered duration is existential death. Physical death and destruction are the last cipher which may help us to see transcendence more clearly. It shines through the debris and ruin. Our own non-being manifests what lies beyond it. In passing away into nothing, our existence becomes transparent, and suddenly reveals the transcendent which remains. In this way, death may become the support of a living philosophic faith.

Jaspers is constantly hampered by his Kantian commitments. But in spite of this, he is a penetrating phenomenologist whose keen observations of human life break through the haze of subjectivist dialectic with which he often surrounds them. He is also a moral philosopher with genuine insight, who clearly understands the basic moral issues of our time.

We now turn to a different type of thinker, Jean-Paul Sartre, who is not only a phenomenologist and psychologist of penetrating power, but a systematic philosopher with an incisive grasp of ontological problems and great dialectical ability as well.

* An enlightening discussion of this question will be found in M. Dufrenne and P. Ricoeur, *Karl Jaspers et la Philosophie de l'Existence*, pp. 389-394.

JEAN-PAUL SARTRE

Of all the existentialist thinkers, Sartre has gone the farthest in trying to clarify his basic ontological principles, and to relate them together in a coherent manner. In trying to perform this difficult task, he has sometimes made dubious assumptions of his own. But his thought is existentialist in the sense that he accepts the central ideas we have been tracing. Furthermore, he is thoroughly familiar with the work of Heidegger, the most disciplined of all the existentialist writers and the sharpest observer of empirical evidence. His attempt to clarify the basic concepts presupposed by this body of fact and doctrine, and to fit them together into a systematic structure is, therefore, of great interest. Strong points as well as basic weaknesses are bound to be revealed in a much brighter light. What sort of total view of being and man is implied by the central core of existentialism? Sartre has devoted his energies to giving us precisely such a total view.

Like other existentialists, Sartre is primarily interested in the concrete data of experience as they actually appear. Like them, he claims to follow a purely descriptive or phenomenological method. His major work bears the sub-title, *Essai d'Ontologie Phénoménologique,* an *Essay on Phenomenological Ontology.* This descriptive method is common to all members of the school. But he has gone farther in trying to clarify what this description must involve, and what *phenomena* really are. We may characterize his explanation as an extreme reaction to idealism.

As we have already noted, Sartre is especially anxious to reject the Kantian conception of a thing in itself behind the phenomena, and separated from them by an impassable gulf. This is correct, for it is surely the thing which appears. But he goes too far when he asserts not only that the phenomena are real but that they exhaust *all* positive reality. The appearance is an aspect of reality, not all there is. It does not distort being. But neither does it comprehend this being in its totality. Other aspects are also there to be revealed in other ways. This identification of being with the succession of its finished appearances has important consequences in the Sartrian ontology.

For one thing, it leads to the strange conception of the *en soi* as an absolute plenum with no potency, and indeed no real relations to anything beyond. In itself, the appearance is complete. It is supplemented only by other appearances, each of which is fixed and finished. The way is thus prepared for a view of being in itself (*en soi*) as a finished continuum fully in act, and lacking all power and potency. Heidegger suggests such a view by his conception of sub-human existence as a determinate being-on-hand (*Vorhandensein*), something finished and simply there, in violent contrast to the unfinished potentiality of *Dasein*. In Sartre, this contrast between a sub-human *en soi* that is fully in act, and a human *pour soi* that is a purely potential nothingness, is magnified to an exaggerated opposition that warps his whole ontology.

If being is a dense field without distinction, there is no place in it for determinate structure or finite difference. One thing cannot be distinguished from another. All such distinctions then have to be referred to the projects of the *pour soi* which literally makes its world. If this expanse of being is fully in act, it cannot be deprived of anything it requires. Hence negation and privation have no ground in reality. They, too, must be referred to the negativity of human existence. Sartre does not use his phenomenological method to test these basic principles. He simply assumes them without argument.* Had he tried to examine them in the light of the evidence, he could hardly have failed to see their empirical inadequacy. The cloud in the sky before me is not an airplane. Each finite structure has limits which are the ontological ground for negative judgments. Nor is the cloud fully in act. It can pass away, or turn into rain. These potencies are not nothing, but they are marked by an absence of realization. Without a recognition of them, the fact of physical change becomes unintelligible.

This denial of physical potency also leads him to follow Heidegger in adopting an even more subjective interpretation of the principle of sufficient reason. The *en soi* has no internal structure nor causal powers. Hence it cannot act nor be the *ground* of anything. Action seems to be restricted to man. In fact, the

* For an illuminating discussion of Sartre's procedure, Cf. Régis Jolivet, *Les Doctrines Existentialistes*, pp. 155-156, including note 20, and p. 165, n. 37.

whole idea of a ground lacks any real basis beyond the processes of human freedom. Things cannot be otherwise than they are. But the *pour soi* is free. It always might choose otherwise. This is the meaning of the question *why*. But the only answer is to be found in an arbitrary choice of some kind, which has no intelligible grounds. Hence in the last analysis, everything, both the *en soi* which is simply there, and the *pour soi* with its caprices, is ungrounded.

Sartre recognizes this consequence, and emphasizes what he calls the radical contingency of our world, which lacks any reason for being. Everything is absurd. This he states as a truth that really holds of all being.[27] At this point, he recognizes the principle of sufficient reason as something more than a peculiar habit of the *pour soi*. Things really need a ground, but such grounds are absent. This is inconsistent with subjectivism. On the other hand, if sufficient reason is not really required, to assert that the universe is absurd is quite meaningless. Sartre's views here are either inconsistent or unintelligible.

His account of the constitutive structure of human existence is full of interesting and often penetrating psychological observations, though the question is legitimately raised as to whether these observations have anything more than a limited personal significance. His analysis follows Heidegger very closely, but differs from it in one fundamental respect. Sartre complains that his predecessor has restricted himself too much to the level of pure description, and has failed to give an intelligible ontological explanation of these phenomena.[28] This objection is certainly striking, coming as it does from a thinker who also asserts that everything is ultimately absurd and inexplicable. Nevertheless, it does express a weakness in Heidegger's anthropology, which is admittedly only a descriptive fragment rather than a full-fledged theory of being. Sartre's attempt to complete this theory is important not only as an exercise in basic ontology, but also as revealing certain further weaknesses in the structure of existentialist thought.

We have already noted the characteristic tendency to minimize theoretical reflection and the determinate structure (essence) which is its object. In Sartre, this baldly emerges in the statement that man has no common nature or essence. He makes himself into what he is by the projects which he chooses. Heidegger is somewhat vague on this issue, but the drift of his thought is in the same direction. Sartre states it in such a way that the error becomes quite clear.[29] It is so clear, in fact, that Sartre himself is forced to correct it at certain points where he refers to common "conditions" which always apply to human life.[30] Man, for example, is condemned to freedom. Whether he likes it or not, he must choose. He also desires to be *en soi*. Such statements certainly imply the presence of that common structure which has previously been called *essence* or *nature*. Existence is never found without such structure. To slur over its presence in man is to commit a serious error.

Heidegger gives no ontological explanation of the basic cognitive act to which he refers descriptively as *disclosing*. He gives us no careful analysis of this intentional outstretching of the mind towards its object. On the other hand, as we have seen, he devotes many pages to the temporal ecstasies, or ways in which our *practical* activities are stretched out into the future and the past. He finally seems to conclude that the former is reducible to the latter, and that all cognition is, therefore, subjectively centered and practical. Sartre follows this in the main. But there are certain points at which he makes significant departures.

First of all, he insists that cognitive disclosure must be carefully analyzed and explained, and devotes many pages to this topic. The cognitive act of disclosing is itself ecstatic, stretched out towards something other that transcends it. His explanation in terms of the *pour soi* as *nothing* is indefensible if taken literally. But, as we have seen, if taken as a capacity first empty but then reaching objective fulfilment, it is suggestive and probably sound.[31]

In the second place, while he follows Heidegger's illuminating account of the ecstasies of time,[32] he never tries to explain cognition in terms of these. Both modes of stretching are characteristic of the *pour soi,* but they are clearly distinguished.[33] This is an important modification which shows at least some recognition of the independence of theory from practice. The fact that cognition is dealt with first of all, as necessarily involved in the whole phenomenological method, would seem to suggest a certain priority of the theoretical over the practical, though this is more dubious.

In his analysis of action, Sartre follows Heidegger quite closely. I *am* the past that I have been, and I am always projected ahead of myself in the future. The ecstasies cannot be separated. They constitute an integrated order of transformation. The future is ever becoming the future perfect; this is becoming present; and the present is turning into the past. Human care always follows this pattern, and cannot be divided into an authentic and an unauthentic mode of temporalization. Human action is not a mode of being at all, but rather a mode of negativity. It is a totality always pursuing itself, but never achieving unity.[34] Instead of being filled with final choice, the moment is always refused. Choice itself is viewed as a flight from the present into the future. No sooner is any aim realized, than it must be rejected to preserve the fluid negativity of the *pour soi,* which can never rest. This doctrine of personal nothingness is a basic departure from Heidegger and other existentialists, certainly for the worse both systematically and phenomenologically. Whatever he may be, the human self, with its knowledge and acts, is not literally annihilating nothingness.

Nevertheless, Sartre's analysis reveals three weaknesses of the existentialist theory of man in striking clarity. The first of these is the supposed arbitrariness of human choice, and the lack of any firm grounds. For Sartre, the whole effort to justify an act is a cowardly abandonment of freedom and responsibility, the turning of myself into a thing. Whether I decide to die for justice or drink at a bar, the matter is indifferent. As Heidegger also maintains, in either case I am necessarily and equally guilty. This may be an account of something we may call metaphysical guilt. But the phenomena of moral guilt and justification are never focused.

The second weakness is an almost exclusive emphasis on what we may call *subjective time.* It may be true that human existence temporalizes itself through an integral order of the ecstasies. But surely this is not the only time with which we are concerned. There is a flux of world-time also which is sweeping the stars, the planets, and my own life in a single irreversible direction. Sartre recognizes this more clearly than Heidegger. According to him, my past sinks back into this world-time, but not my present and future.[35] This answer is not satisfactory. Unless it is wholly fantastic, my projected future must take account of world-time, and my very act of projecting it must occur within this universal flux. We cannot follow Heidegger in dismissing it as an unauthentic expression of human time.

Finally, the third and most evident phenomenological weakness of the existentialist theory of man is its failure to account for human communication. According to Heidegger, my ordinary mode of being with others is impersonal, debased, and unauthentic. He briefly refers to the possibility of authentic communication between persons, but nowhere explains how this is possible or even reconcilable with his picture of the genuine person who has broken from his fellows to live alone with himself in a world of his own choice. The more authentic we become, the more isolated we seem to be. Jaspers has struggled with this problem, but his rejection of universal concepts and judgments makes an intelligible solution impossible. In Sartre, this weakness emerges with brutal clarity.[36] When two persons meet, each tries to absorb the other as an object into his world. Communication is thus restricted to conflict. Love, friendship, and devoted cooperation for common ends are excluded *a priori*. This must seem dubious to any careful empiricist.

Sartre has not yet written his book on man and human ethics.[37] But what men ought to do depends on what they are. My ethics will be determined by my view of human existence. This is clear to all the existentialist thinkers. The basic value is really to exist. Hence their anthropological descriptions are constantly passing over into moral suggestions and recommendations. This is also true of Sartre. Unless he changes his whole philosophy, the existentialist ethics he must defend is already clear in outline.

We may describe this as an ethics of pure freedom: man has no stable nature; he possesses no constant tendencies. There are no changeless norms to which he can look for the guidance of his conduct. To set up such norms is merely to rationalize choices that have already been made. Liberty itself is the only stable norm. To maintain this is always good. To stifle it, especially in myself, is always evil. What is this freedom? For Heidegger, with his positive view of human existence, it is a freedom *for* final commitment-unto-death. For Sartre, with his negative view, it is rather a freedom *from* any such commitment, save to the principle of having no final commitments at all.

Accordingly, the free man chooses his motives and reasons as the situation demands. But he never gives himself wholly to any of them. Retaining the negative mobility that he essentially is, he constantly places his past behind him, and steps into a creative future. No sooner does this appear on the scene than it too is rejected. Men cannot help but imagine stable states of realization in which they might stay satisfied with their mobility intact. But such a union of the *pour soi* with the *en soi* is impossible. Those only become maximally free who train themselves to dispense with such illusions. They therefore flow lightly (with no viscosity or hardening) over the surface of things and retain their negativity. On such an individualistic basis, there is no place for social ethics at all. Sartre has flirted with many political theories and movements, last of all Marxism. But the connection between existentialist thought and any definite political philosophy, as it is now presented to us, is wholly arbitrary and unstable.

Sartre does not care for the terms authentic and unauthentic. But the same notion appears in other language, and underlies all those moral suggestions and insinuations with which his works are filled. The free man lives out his existential nothingness, and becomes what he really is, i.e., what he is not. He is dynamic, fluid, and ever creative. The non-free person, on the other hand, is ceaselessly trying in bad faith to become something fixed and affirmative which he is not. Such people adopt fixed principles, and have a firm and serious sense of duty. They are the conformists who make up the masses. Above all they are the serious people who move slowly and heavily,[38] giving many reasons for the immediate policies to which they rigidly adhere, but falling into mythical Utopianism when questioned concerning the ultimate end.

Such bad faith takes two distinguishable forms—*les lâches*, the cowards who hide themselves behind their norms and reasons, and the *salauds* (an untranslatable term), who use them as weapons for aggressive self-assertion.[39] They never succeed in making themselves into solid things, for the restless negativity, which they are, turns every achievement into bitter ashes. They never remain satisfied. The most they can achieve is to become viscous and sticky, like a slimy stream, or a smile that, as we say, becomes frozen on the lips.[40]

This cannot be identified with the ethics of existentialism. Nevertheless, it singles out a dominant note of this ethics, the note of pure freedom, and thinks it through with a wealth of concrete illustration and a ruthless consistency. Sartre is profoundly sensitive to ontological problems, a master of dialectic, and a really great psychologist.

GABRIEL MARCEL

Like Heidegger himself, Marcel does not care for the term existentialism, and does not use it in connection with his own work.[41] His philosophical development has been dominated by a radical rebellion against the subjectivistic and idealistic conceptions of modern philosophy, and he often refers to the sense in which his thought has been steadily moving in a realistic direction.[42] For him, this has meant primarily a sharp rejection of the notion that mind is a constructive or creative power, and a defense of the descriptive or phenomenological function of philosophy.[43] The world of immediate experience is rich with mysterious and pervasive data from which the various restricted sciences must abstract. Philosophy is an empirical discipline whose primary obligation is to the concrete data. It is ceaselessly threatened by reductive abstractions and the supposedly comprehensive systems built on these.

Those who lose themselves in such constructions, and who finally feel that the demands of systematic clarity and consistency must take precedence over the concrete data, are betraying philosophy. Marcel finds that such abstractions have been his worst enemies, and speaks of himself as always seeking for a concrete and phenomenological mode of approach.[44] Under the influence of modern science, the study of the world of experience, as directly perceived, has been neglected. To describe the structure of this world in a disciplined way, and thus to inaugurate a genuinely empirical mode of philosophizing is the greatest intellectual need of our time. Throughout his whole career, Marcel has striven to meet this need, and has already contributed many penetrating observations and descriptive analyses to the growing discipline of phenomenology.

According to him, experience is always divided into a subjective and an objective pole, but there are certain data, like existence, which are not restricted to either one alone. He emphasizes the fact that existence is an absolute presence.[45] This presence pervades all other data, and the task of describing it and of making it more intelligible is the primary function of philosophy. The idealist conceives of thought as a creative construction. It is just as serious a mistake to regard it as a mere passive registry or transcription of sensory data. These sensory data are always originally vague and confused. The task of discovering their real order and structure, therefore, is neither wholly active nor wholly passive.[46] It is rather best described as a "responsiveness." [47] But the task is to find out, to discover. The worst of all errors is to think of the mind as a thing fixed once and for all, with an *a priori* structure which it must impose on alien data impinging on it from the outside. Understanding is an act, but not an act of construction.

Marcel distinguishes sharply between a problem and a mystery.[48] A problem is objective and abstract. It is there before me, rather than inside me. The acts by which I deal with it are not themselves part of the problem. They may, of course, become problematic, but this is another matter. Problems, as we say, have to be solved one at a time. The focusing that lies back of the problem is not focused. This is presupposed but excluded. My own inner being must be dealt with in another way. For the most part, this means that it is not dealt with at all. Indeed, it cannot be dealt with, unless we broaden the meaning of this phrase. It confronts us with a different situation requiring a different method of approach. According to Marcel, this is what we mean by mystery. The mystery refuses to be isolated and marked off. It is not only objective but subjective as well. I cannot get outside it to work out a solution, for it pervades my own inner acts. My very attempt to deal with it is part of the mystery.[49] Such a "problem" I must live.

This does not mean, however, that I must fall back on blind action. The insoluble and the unintelligible also belong to the field of the problematic. Hence it is a major error to think of a mystery as totally unintelligible or ineffable. To see it as a mystery, is already to begin to see. The task of philosophical reflection is to extend and to clarify this vision so far as possible for each individual. It is a task which he alone can perform by the concentration of all his powers, theoretical and practical. The philosopher lives or exists with his mysteries. The most basic of these is existence itself.

Marcel has not attempted to order his reflections on being in a systematic way. Nevertheless, his writings are full of interesting hints and suggestions. When carefully read from an ontological point of view, they clearly reveal the realistic trend of his thought. Being is actually present in us and around us. It is by the act of existing, and other such acts, that things and persons make themselves *present* in various ways. Marcel has given us many penetrating descriptions of these modes of presence, and has lifted them from the obscurity of neglect into which modern essentialism has let them fall.[50] On the other hand, he has not followed Sartre and other existentialists in denying the real co-presence of order and structure in the world.

Essence and existence are correlative, and one is never found without the other, though the two can be separated in thought. But experience presents us with determinate existence, and active, flowing essence. Both factors must be recognized.[51] To suppose a separate "realm of essences" is to reify abstractions. Structure is never found apart from existential action of some kind. This is true even of thought, which bestows a certain mode of being on its determinate objects. But being is said in many senses, which must be clearly distinguished if basic confusion is to be avoided. The relational existence, which is given to the entity as an object of reflection, is different from the subjective existence of the entity itself. But in none of these modes do we ever find being without structure.

The act of existing is always of some kind. Marcel uses the

phrase "active essence" in referring to this union of essence and existence.[52] It is as dangerous to forget the one as to forget the other. He believes that the doctrine of real essence needs to be critically re-examined, but he has consistently defended it in his writings.[53] He has also recognized the important corollary, sometimes denied by other existentialists, that contemplation has its rights as well as human action.[54]

The world cannot be reductively analyzed into a number of atomic units which are externally juxtaposed in space and time. Marcel is constantly calling our attention to relational structure. Thus there are real relations which really make a difference to their terms. "When I put the table *beside* the chair, I do not make any difference to the table or the chair, and I can take one or the other away without making any difference; but my relationship *with* you makes a difference to both of us, and so does any interruption of the relationship make a difference." [55] Relational structure also enters into my intrinsic being. Marcel notes that this has been neglected by past analysis, and refers to the "outrageous oversimplification . . . of the relationships which bind me to myself." [56] He strongly emphasizes the intentional or relational structure of noetic activity, and the way in which it has been neglected "by the psychologists of the past who, in fact, considered only states of consciousness." [57] With Heidegger, he finds that the basic human existentials are relational in structure. Thus human existence is in-the-world,[58] with-others, or intersubjective,[59] and always in a dynamic situation.[60]

At one point, however, he makes an important distinction, not found in Heidegger, between "our own historic human world" and "the universe taken as a whole." [61] It is regrettable that he does not develop it further, but the fact that he makes it shows that he has rejected the non-mental but pragmatic subjectivism towards which their exclusive emphasis on practical reason has led both Heidegger and Sartre. We understand the world first of all in relation to our action. These relations really exist. But the universe itself is more comprehensive. We have access to this not by action but by theory and pure contemplation.

Marcel has not ordered his views of man and human action into any systematic form. Both his strictly phenomenological method and its results are close to those of Heidegger. He is, of course, concerned with the study of human awareness and feeling, and as we have seen, clearly recognizes its intentional structure. As long as he exists, man is unfinished and open to further being. He is concerned with his existence. Marcel distrusts broad generalizations, but he would probably accept Heidegger's judgment that man is a creature of care, if certain qualifications were introduced. Man is a wayfarer (*homo viator*) whose very existence is temporal and historical.[62] These cardinal phases of Heidegger's analysis would probably be accepted. But Marcel has supplemented them in two important respects.

Heidegger's analysis of human existence (*Dasein*) implies that it is situated at a particular here and now, but he has not devoted any careful attention to the human body and its status.

Marcel's studies of my relation to my body are often illuminating, and at least partially fill an important gap in existentialist theory.[63] He points out that one of the most serious obstacles to existentialist thought is our tendency to reduce the human body to the level of a mere mental object. Though it is certainly possible for me to regard my body as one extended object among others, this certainly does not exhaust the whole phenomenon. I find that all my activities, even that of thought, are in some sense localized within my body. I feel my body internally as I cannot feel other things. I can separate myself from all other objects, but my body is always with me, and I find myself in grave difficulties when I attempt to conceive of myself apart from it. Hence it is not correct to think of my body as an instrument, like a saw or a pencil, which I may accept or refuse at will.

It is rather a necessary condition for the employment of any such instrument. My body as such is reducible neither to an object nor an instrument. It is a part of my being. I do not merely observe my body nor use it. I *am* my body, and exist it, though this must not be taken in a crude, materialistic sense. I am also something more than this.[64] But it is not an object which I own or possess. I may try to achieve a perfect identity with such objects. But these attempts are always vain, and lead only to the loss of myself. As objects, they are separate from me. But my body is not merely an object. It belongs to my subjective being. I do not have it or own it; I *am* it. Marcel's account of this peculiar phenomenon is filled with penetrating insight.[65]

His remarks on contemplation are not so thoroughly developed, but as we have already pointed out, they are concerned with an important human phenomenon which Heidegger, as well as most existentialists, have so far neglected because of their emphatic rejection of idealism. It may be a mistake to disregard practical insight. But it is also a mistake to disregard theory. According to Heidegger, pure theory is a derivative and on the whole unreliable form of care, ever ahead of itself in the future, lost in its object, and lacking in self-consciousness. Marcel offers cogent empirical evidence for questioning all these assertions. As he says, ". . . contemplation is not oriented towards the future. . . . Time for contemplation is nothing if it is not present time." [66] Certain theoretical attitudes are lost in their objects, but certainly not all. There is a philosophic contemplation that "is a turning inwards of our awareness." [67]

In fact, is it not precisely such a purely theoretical examination of inner states and activities that the existentialist phenomenologists have been cultivating so assiduously since the time of Kierkegaard? Far from being an unfortunate perversion of practical awareness, is it not rather a discipline that must be cultivated and realized to some degree if practice is ever to be soundly understood and guided? It is strangely absent from modern life. But is this not a tragedy? Marcel asks "whether this almost complete vanishing away of the contemplative activity in the modern world has not something at least to do with the terrible evils from which mankind is suffering." [68] This abandonment of the recurrent existentialist polemic against theory is a most welcome deviation.

Marcel is a clear and penetrating moral philosopher. Like other existentialist thinkers, he is deeply concerned with the unauthentic existence of modern mass society. His account of what he calls "the broken world" of modern life in Chapter II of the *Mystery of Being,* and of "the fanaticized consciousness" in Part II of *Man Against Mass Society,* are rich in descriptive insight and sharp analysis. In recent generations, many men have gradually fallen into oversimplified modes of reductive materialism without acting in accordance with these doctrines. In our own generation, however, this cultural lag has caught up with us, and we are now witnessing materialism in action. Men are not only regarded as physical complexes reducible to their objective functions, subject to external manipulation and control; they are now being actually treated in this way, and for anyone who still understands the nature of human awareness and freedom the spectacle is terrible.[69]

But the way to attack a false theory is not to abandon theory altogether. As Marcel sees it, the problem now confronting us is primarily philosophical. Old authorities have broken down. Can men's minds be turned to a serious study of their own existence and its distinctive character? Can enough minds be sufficiently illumined in time to save us from disaster? No one knows the answer to this question, though the clouds seem ever blacker. Marcel counsels those who discern the coming of night to strengthen their faith, not as an escape, but rather as a means of standing firm and of rallying those with philosophic vision. He rejects the traditional arguments for the existence of God, but believes that a careful analysis of moral feeling and moral action are capable of showing men that their own best acts presuppose a faith in something transcendent. One of the most interesting of these descriptive analyses is that of hope in Chapter IX of the *Mystery of Being*.

Marcel is not a coherent, systematic thinker. But he is a keen observer whose wandering descriptions often lead him to suggestive insights, independent of any affiliation with a particular school. He dislikes the term *existentialism,* but his thought, which is largely derived from Christian sources, has much in common with the common core we have traced in the preceding chapters. He is a peripheral figure whose phenomenological insights are constantly leading him in a realistic direction.

MARTIN HEIDEGGER

Heidegger published *Sein und Zeit* in 1927 while he was still at Marburg. This is still the most important and influential work that is accessible to the public. So far as existentialist thought is

concerned, it is a text of authoritative weight. Hence in our exposition of the central core of existentialist doctrine we have followed the analyses of being-in-the-world, the unauthentic condition of *das Man,* disclosure and interpretation, care, temporality,
and historicity as Heidegger presents them in this text. This
work, however, is only a fragment of a larger treatise on being as
such, which has never been published. More recently, in shorter
written statements and personal conferences, Heidegger himself has
shed some light on the basic ontological position within which his
anthropology must be placed. He has been especially anxious to
disavow certain interpretations of *Sein und Zeit* which have become widely known. It is hard to determine the extent to which
these disavowals reject actual misunderstandings of the published
doctrine of *Sein und Zeit,* or rather signify growth in his own
point of view. We shall hazard a few suggestions on this matter.
But our major aim in these following pages will be to summarize
the views which Heidegger now holds on fundamental ontology,
and which we have not been able to consider before.

There is no question that Heidegger originally conceived *Sein
und Zeit* as a sort of anthropological introduction for a new approach to the study of being as such. His reasons for believing
that a radically new approach is necessary are clearly given in
Sein und Zeit.[70] He has consistently maintained this attitude, and
still holds it. The Greeks clearly recognized the basic importance
of the problem of being, and made real progress in formulating
it. But they became absorbed in the study of surrounding things
and their properties, and confused being itself with the entities
that exist in this way, as simply there in the flux of time (*Vorhandensein*). They clarified the categories by which such things
can be understood. But their attempt to apply these categories
uncritically to man prevented them from seeing the most unique
features of human existence and temporality. Since that time,
being as such has never been clearly focused, but constantly confused with the structure of things that are (essence).

According to Heidegger, no real progress was made in the Middle Ages. The failure to distinguish being from things that are
was correlated with a continued tendency to regard man as a
thing or a substance with fixed properties unfolding *in* time. But

human existence cannot be adequately understood except in relation to being. These errors were magnified by the tendencies of modern philosophy to regard the human person rationalistically as an isolated mind whose only contact with the world was in detached cognition, and to take the subject-object relation as basic. As a result, the problem of being is hardly ever raised. Being itself is taken for granted as a comman predicate more abstract and less informative than any other. It indicates a certain instantiation or thereness that is obvious. Nothing more needs to be said.[71]

This view is a tissue of falsehood and evasion. Aristotle showed conclusively that being is not an abstract genus.[72] The things that lie before us may share in being. But they cannot be identified with being as such. After freeing our minds from these provincial prejudices, the problem of being must be raised again. A new approach is necessary. In *Sein und Zeit,* the approach was made from a phenomenological study of man, who is open to being, and Heidegger shows this by his raising of the question.[73] As he has recently emphasized, this was the point of view of *Sein und Zeit.* Hence he is right in distinguishing his position from that of Jaspers, who despairs of ever arriving at a general ontology, and from that of Sartre who denies any being transcending man. Heidegger is interested in being as such, and has been consistently so interested. There is no reason to doubt that this has always been the mainspring of his thought.

In *Sein und Zeit,* understanding and interpretation are said to rest primarily on projects of *Dasein.* These possibilities are not grounded in known facts. They become possible only through the decision that projects them.[74] Since theory is constantly disparaged, this would seem to imply a man-centered and pragmatic theory of truth. But in his recent *Letter on Humanism* Heidegger now clearly rejects such an interpretation, and holds that the truth about being is anterior to both theory and practice.[75] Even without *Dasein,* that which is would still be. But being itself would be hidden. Truth is the wresting of being from its hiddenness, and man is the mysterious agent of such revelation. In this sense, he is the guardian of being, not its creator. No further light is shed on the nature of this revealing power in man. "Man him-

self has been thrown into the truth of being; ek-sisting outside
of himself in this way, he may guard the truth of being so that
each being may appear in the light of being as exactly the being
it is." [76] He is the revealer, not the creator, of being.[77]

We have noted the important role assigned in *Sein und Zeit*
to the feeling of dread as manifesting the real condition of man.
It shows me that I am alone in a world that is strange and uncanny. My existence is foreign to the objects of this world into
which I have been thrown without rhyme or reason by something
alien and wholly negative. My future is bounded by a barrier of
nothingness, and my freedom can be expressed only in a final
being-unto-death. I try to suppress and evade these harsh facts,
but dread calls them to my attention. As Heidegger says, it reveals
the uncanny nothingness that encompasses me before and behind.[78] It is not surprising, therefore, that these statements have
been interpreted as an expression of philosophic nihilism. Man
comes from a senseless nothingness, and to nothing he returns.
His very existence is a flux of negation.[79] But in his *Letter on
Humanism* Heidegger has clearly rejected this nihilistic interpretation.

Being is not to be identified with *that which* is.[80] It is neither a
single entity, nor a set, nor the whole collection.[81] But these are
the objects with which we are most familiar. We are constantly
confusing them with being itself. Hence it is not astonishing that
being must appear to us first of all as an alien nothingness
transcending all that we know, and yet surrounding us everywhere, and very close to us. It is only by the thought of nothing
that being can be revealed to us. * Nothing is not the term but
the pathway to this term. It is with the mystery of being that we
are secretly linked. We may cut this link, and plunge into the
world of things which seem to exhaust reality. But to do this is
precisely to gain nothing—to lose ourselves. Our free existence is
the dwelling place of being.[82] According to the *Letter on Humanism,* our authentic function is to make room for it in ourselves,
and to manifest it in our thoughts and deeds. Man is "the Shep-
herd of being." [83] Here also we have been given new light on

* Heidegger makes it clear in *Sein und Zeit* (p. 187) that the *nothing* revealed
by dread is "no total nothingness." It is rather human *being*-in-the-world.

Heidegger's conception of what he calls fundamental ontology.

Why then has he not developed it further? Why has the whole project to which *Sein und Zeit* is only an introduction never been completed? Heidegger's answer seems to rest not only on the supreme difficulties of the task, but also on those of language. We live in a time of transition when older tools of expressing the truth have been found to be inadequate, and new tools have not yet been forged. In the cultural chaos surrounding us, this leads many to nihilistic views. There is no being as such, or if so, it is wholly inaccessible. This is a subjective delusion that must be resisted. It is we who have cut ourselves off from being, the holy, and the divine, which are the objects of philosophical, poetic, and religious aspiration.[84]

In one of the essays of *Forest Paths*, Heidegger suggests that this may be the real meaning of Zarathustra's famous statement, "God is dead" *—that is, strange, and remote, and dead-to-us. In a time of loss and transition, there is no point in repeating ancient mistakes, or in manipulating ancient instruments that can no longer meet the tests we must apply to them. What is called for is rather silent concentration in the forging of new tools, hesitant and patient waiting rather than confident display. Heidegger finds this attitude exemplified in the German poet, Hölderlin, who, early in the nineteenth century, foresaw the anguish and dereliction of our own time, but who maintained an attitude of expectant reverence, in spite of the remoteness and "failure" of God.[85]

Heidegger thinks that this offers us a worthy example of how we should act in a time of transition when old ideals have disintegrated and new ones have not been born. So far as his own work is concerned, he denies the atheistic implications which many interpreters found in *Sein und Zeit*, and claims that this question lay entirely beyond the introductory scope of his work.[86] In his *Letter on Humanism*, he goes even farther than this, rejecting all traditional versions of natural theology, and maintaining that God is entirely inaccessible to philosophical investigation, whose object is being as such.[87] This opens up horizons in which the problem of theism can be raised, but philosophy is in no position

* "Nietzsche's Wort 'Gott ist tot,' " Holzwege, pp. 193-248.

to establish the existence of God as a world-ground, or as possessing any distinctively religious attributes. Its duty is rather to arrive at "an adequate conception of human being with reference to which it may once more be possible to ask concerning the relation of this being to God." [88]

Heidegger's philosophy will probably never achieve a final formulation. His thought is still growing and groping for exact and unequivocal ways of expressing and stating his ideas concerning being. Of all the existentialist thinkers, his method is the most exact, his ideas the most revolutionary, and his ontological insight the most profound.

SOME WEAKNESSES OF EXISTENTIALIST THOUGHT

We have now considered the existentialist rebellion against certain sterile trends of modern thought, and the new insights concerning descriptive method, ontology, theory of knowledge, and ethics. These insights constitute a standing appeal for the revival of philosophy, which in Europe is being heeded not only by professors but by intelligent men and women everywhere. In this sense, existentialism is certainly a challenge to all of us to rekindle these insights in ourselves and to bring them to bear on our decisions.

So far we have tried to understand this way of thought, and the truth that it bears within it. But the task of philosophy includes something more—not only to understand but also to criticize. Reality is very rich; our cognitive powers feeble and flickering. It is hard for us to discern certain truths without neglecting others equally important. This is apt to introduce partiality, bias, and finally serious error into our total world-view, if left uncriticized. Unfortunately, the existentialist insights are marked by such partiality at every one of the four levels we have considered. We have had occasion here and there to refer to these omissions and mistakes. It is now time to focus them more sharply. They constitute another sort of challenge to philosophy—for answer and correction.

To help us in performing this part of our task we shall turn briefly again to the chief sources of existentialist thought for a critical review. Then we shall try to suggest a philosophic program that may do justice to the genuine insights of this living philosophy, and at the same time avoid its more serious errors.

We shall consider these as they affect the four major aspects of existentialist thought: its method, its metaphysics, its view of knowledge, and finally its ethics. In each of these phases, we shall find that it suffers from omission, exaggeration, and sometimes from positive error.

METHOD

Without direct evidence by which theories can be checked, there can be no knowledge worthy of the name; no data, no discipline. Here the existentialists are right. But so far they have applied this method to *human* existence alone, and have paid relatively little attention to other levels and manifestations of being. They have given us no philosophy of nature, but only an anthropological fragment. So far, the broader speculations which they have based on this limited foundation, like those of Sartre and Jaspers, lack discipline and coherence.

Brute facts, of course, must be described as they are given. This is a necessary first step, but it does not complete the work of understanding. Causes and reasons must also be given. The data must be explained in the light of these. Here the existentialists are very weak. Many of them have rebelled so violently against inadequate, *a priori* explanations that they have rejected the notion altogether. They accept the law of contradiction but apparently deny the principle of sufficient reason. *That* something is there must be accepted on the basis of the evidence. But to raise the question *why* is to indulge an anthropomorphic bias. We ourselves and the world are simply given. Each fact may be described as it is. There is no cause or reason.

This is pressing the phenomenological attitude too far, to a position which contradicts the given evidence. There are many data which show that things depend on one another. The denial of any causal principle is an extremely dubious metaphysical assumption lacking empirical support, and implying the ultimate unintelligibility of the universe.

The first impact of such a negativistic view on our practical feelings and endeavors is vividly expressed in certain passages of Sartre. If events merely happen without a reason, there is no moral justification. One aim is as arbitrary as another. "Human being is a useless passion . . . and to intoxicate yourself alone in a bar or to conduct the nations is equally vain." [89] Life itself is absurd. More than this, existence itself is absurd. It is orderless, structureless, simply there to be gaped at and accepted. As Sartre expresses it in his book entitled *Nausea:* "All these existents which bustled about . . . came from nowhere and were going nowhere. Existence everywhere infinitely in excess (*de trop*) forever and everywhere: existence, which is limited only by existence. I sank down on the bench, stupefied, stunned by this profusion of beings without source . . ." [90]

It cannot be denied that the thought of uncomprehended chaos does elicit that feeling of nausea for which the book is rightly named. But the thought itself, the concept of reasonless chaos, lacks all empirical foundation. In a world entirely lacking in structure, we could not distinguish chaos from order, nor anything from anything else. Knowing would be impossible, and we could not even gape and stare. To take such a concept seriously is to misread the data of experience and, as we shall see, to fall into metaphysical error.

METAPHYSICS

The essentialist trends of modern philosophy have led it to exaggerate the importance of inactive, timeless structure which is more readily grasped by the human mind. Hence it has had difficulty in focusing the existential categories of tendency, causal efficacy, and temporal dynamism. The existentialists have performed a vital service for philosophy in calling attention to these essentialist trends. In addition to the essential traits that determine a thing and mark it off from others, there is also the act of existing which separates it from nothing. This is correct. But unfortunately, in many cases, the reaction has been so extreme that essence has been unduly slurred over, and sometimes openly denied. This leads to a one-sided existentialist extreme as dangerous as its opposite.

Thus we find Jaspers defending a fluxist view of reality which reminds us of Heraclitus and of his modern disciple, Bergson. Reality is exclusively identified with an active *élan* which is not only distinct from, but radically opposed to, determinate structure. To understand it in terms of any fixed concepts, is to misunderstand it. What is stable and immutable stifles it. As Jaspers says, for this existence to be achieved, is to cease to be.[91]

Such a view as this, as is well known, is not only self-contradictory in being asserted; it is also false to the empirical data. Existence is certainly opposed to non-existence. Change must be understood by a stable concept, if it is to be understood at all. Concrete experience never presents us with a structureless flux, but always with tendency of a certain kind, moving in a certain constant direction, determined by stable and intelligible traits. Realization does not stifle and kill; it is fitting and good for the entity. Essence is coordinate with existence; one is never given without the other. To ignore either is to commit a grievous metaphysical mistake. To deny or even to neglect this ubiquitous factor of form, which is found in all existence, is to fall into serious error. In dealing with man, and especially with human freedom, the existentialists in various ways and to various degrees have fallen into it.

EPISTEMOLOGY

Modern philosophy has placed too great an emphasis on theoretical awareness of objects, and has ignored the practical knowledge which is manifested in deliberation about concrete situations and in our moods and feelings. The existentialists are right in calling attention to this. In describing the feeling of dread, and the world as it is revealed by such emotions, they have made important contributions to phenomenology. But here again their intense reaction to a detached intellectualism has led them to an indefensible opposite extreme of anti-intellectualism which unfortunately began with Kierkegaard himself.

If we took his attacks on theoretical reason seriously, we would have to reject his own writings, which are a triumph of theoretical analysis, for the first time describing and illumining obscure regions of practical experience. Kierkegaard is a great phenomenologist, bringing into the light of accurate analysis forms of personal existence and consciousness that had long been hidden.

Why did he not recognize this fact?

Partly because of his bitter attack on Hegel, the theoretical philosopher and system builder, the ruling philosopher of the time. Hegel failed, however, not because he formulated theories, but because his theories were not exhaustive and sensitive enough. As is so often true of rebels, Kierkegaard became so annoyed with Hegel that he threw out the baby with the bath. In rebelling against him, he seemed to feel that he was rebelling against human reason itself. This, of course, was a mistake, which unfortunately has influenced many of his successors.

Thought is held to be a kind of action, and the detached apprehension of anything as it really is becomes impossible. Such a voluntaristic view is expressed by Jaspers in the following passage from *Vernunft und Existenz*, where he identifies philosophizing with a mode of acting: "Though it proceeds by setting up rational ends, it passes beyond all such determinate ends. It turns every answer to what I am seeking into a new question, which is never there before me as something definitively known." [92]

Similar passages are found also in the writings of Sartre. Pure theory is impossible. Consciousness and choice are one and the same. "Man is nothing else than the ensemble of his acts, nothing else than his life." [93] If this were true, I should never be able to observe my acts, and to describe them as they actually proceed. As has been pointed out by discerning critics, Sartre himself is constantly employing this method of self-reflection.

Many existentialists now seem to hold, however, that as soon as we adopt a theoretical point of view and regard ourselves, or indeed anything else, as an object of thought, we relativize and distort it. Such objects are fixed, determined, and abstract. Subjective existence, on the other hand, is creative, free, and concrete. To think objectively is to mutilate being. This is a vice which leads to human slavery. Thus according to Berdiaev, the Russian existentialist thinker: "Personality is not an object among other objects, and not a thing among other things. It is a subject among subjects, and the turning of it into an object or a thing means death. The object is always evil; only the subject can be good." [94]

A little further on he says that: "The source of slavery is objectivization." [95]

There is some truth in these remarks, but also dangerous exaggeration. Personality is not a thing. This is correct. It is also true that we possess an awareness of our own activity which is non-theoretical and non-objective. But this practical apprehension is dim and hazy. Unless it is supplemented and clarified by objective insight, it may lead us into irrational bias and fanaticism. Impartial observation and description also have their place, as witness the existentialist literature itself! It is dangerous to neglect any mode of cognition to which we have access. Each has its contribution to make.

ETHICS

The existentialists have performed an important service in calling our attention to the direct, empirical evidence that human beings are in some sense free, and in thus reviving the interest in ethics as a central discipline, which has long been on the wane. But sometimes they press their assertion of freedom to such lengths that it becomes fantastic and unbelievable. Thus, according to Sartre, man cannot be at times free and at other times a slave; either he is always and entirely free or he is not free at all.[96] For any critical mind, such exaggerated statements tend rather to discredit the notion than to confirm it.

Even those who reject this extreme view are very skeptical of universal moral principles. The germs of this skepticism are found in Kierkegaard, though he does not hold to it consistently. Thus, in his influential work on the Abraham story, *Fear and Trembling,* he seems to hold that all moral laws are abrogated by religion. This conception has been taken over by our contemporary *Neo-Orthodox* theology. In *Either/Or,* he says that what we choose to do is of little importance so long as we choose it with serious intensity. This anarchistic notion has been further developed and emphasized by Kierkegaard's philosophical disciples.

According to Sartre, anyone who tries to justify his action on the basis of stable moral principles is guilty of bad faith, the attempt to evade responsibility for what he does. Jaspers holds that

184 *The Challenge of Existentialism*

existence is opposed to lifeless law and rebels against all rigid determination.⁹⁷ This would seem to imply a moral relativism and irrationalism as dangerous in its way as the denial of human freedom. Are there no norms which are valid for all men as such? Is there no stable hierarchy of values? Are not certain kinds of action really better than others? Does all choice rest upon an arbitrary preference? If so, it is the end of ethics as a responsible discipline.

This irrationalism is connected with the strange moral solipsism which runs through Kierkegaard's writings. It is only through the exercise of reason in forming universal concepts and judgments that I may escape from the cosmic loneliness which my physical existence imposes on me. When this phase of my being is slurred over, I am left alone with my own peculiar choices and acts. I cannot communicate with others, and cooperative action becomes impossible. Human love and friendship are inexplicable.

This morbid individualism is often expressed in the writings of Sartre. "Hell is other people." For him, social experience is apparently epitomized by the image of being stared at suddenly by a pair of alien eyes as he eavesdrops through a keyhole. Shame and conflict seem to be the normal social emotions. His major work, *L'Être et le Néant,* ends with an account of the inevitable tension between alien individuals, each a world in himself, and each attempting to absorb and to transcend the other. As he puts it finally: "The essence of the relations between awarenesses is not *Mitsein;* it is conflict." ⁹⁸ He is here expressing a one-sided moral solipsism.

Kierkegaard was conscious of this danger. "It is dangerous," he says, "to isolate oneself too much, to evade the bonds of society." ⁹⁹ He struggled with the problems of communication. Jaspers and others have made penetrating but disjointed observations and comments on this complex phenomenon. But their disparagement of theoretical reason has made it impossible for them to work out any coherent account of human communication. No adequate or even noteworthy *social* philosophy has as yet come from existentialist sources. This is a striking weakness. They are no doubt right in pointing to the human individual as the bearer of human freedom, and in rejecting the totalitarian theories of Hegel and Marx. But so far they have given us no plausible alternative to take their place.

CONCLUSION

Such are the major weaknesses of existentialist philosophy. It is a movement of rebellion, a challenge to the scientific idolatry, the easy-going optimism, the drowsy materialism of modern life and thought. It is a powerful stimulant, awakening us from many comforting illusions and arousing us to vigorous action. It is strong in moral fervor but weak in rational argument. It approaches us as we hustle about, like Sancho Panza, absorbed in our household tasks. Clothed in shining armor, and riding a noble steed, like Don Quixote, it sneers at our bourgeois comforts, and exhorts us to desperate action, little matter what or where. In spite of the penetrating shafts of criticism it hurls at us, however, it is not altogether clear whether, taken as a whole, it is divine truth or summer madness. Noble action and sacrificial devotion are no doubt important. But if they are to be used for the fighting of windmills, Sancho may be well advised in taking a second thought.

Let us then do this. Granting that the existentialist challenge to basic trends in modern thought is unanswerable, what of its challenge to philosophy itself? Are moral freedom and authentic human existence to be purchased only at the price of an ultimate irrationalism? Must disciplined description be restricted to human existence alone? Is existence itself absurd? Must we abandon the principle of sufficient reason and the hope for explanation? If we recognize practical reason, and its primordial levels of mood and feeling, must we then discard all theoretical insight as moral disease? Must we abandon all hope for the recognition of universal moral principles, and for the rational guidance of action? If we reject an organic theory of society, must we then accept an extreme individualism that condemns the individual to a cosmic loneliness, and leaves society to be organized, if at all, by force and tyranny? Is moral freedom to be purchased only at the price of an ultimate absurdity and irrationalism? These questions constitute a second and far more serious challenge to philosophy itself.

Is there any means by which the penetrating insights, the profound moral appeal, and the amazing contemporary relevance of this mode of thought can be preserved in a coherent philosophical synthesis which may avoid its weaknesses? I believe that there is. In the subsequent chapters I shall try to sketch briefly a realistic answer to this challenge.

-7-

Realistic Phenomenology
and Metaphysics

WE HAVE now examined the divergent interpretations of Jaspers, Sartre, Heidegger, and Marcel. We have noted the ranges of unfamiliar data which have been brought into view, and the way in which a study of these has enabled the new empiricism to correct many of those phenomenological errors in post-Cartesian subjectivism that have brought philosophy into an *a priori* reductionism and sterility. But we have also been forced to recognize certain weaknesses in existentialist philosophy that call for reinterpretation and correction. This is a movement of rebellion against the abstract intellectualism of post-Cartesian thought which, as is often the case with such movements, has sometimes been led into equally dangerous exaggerations of its own.

In these concluding chapters, we shall make a few suggestions concerning the way in which, as it seems to us, the genuine insights of this new philosophy may be sustained by bringing them into relation with the allied insights of realism. Limitations of time and of space will prevent us from undertaking a complete exposition. But we may perhaps be able to suggest enough so that the interest of the reader may be seriously turned towards the possibility of actually reviving philosophy again as a responsible and cooperative empirical discipline. In this chapter we shall deal first with phenomenology, and then with metaphysical protocols and ontology.

PHENOMENOLOGY

The method of this empirical discipline must be genuinely descriptive or phenomenological in character. The chief contribution of the existentialists has been to show that the practical existence of man, as it is lived, is open to such description. Their interest in these unfamiliar data has been so great that they have unduly disparaged data of other kinds to which we have access by the very same method of theoretical description. Thus Merleau-Ponty, for example, in his epoch-making *Phénoménologie de la Perception* [1] shows with great clarity how theoretical science is derived from and presupposes the primordial world of projective perception. But aside from this, his attention is exclusively directed to the formulation of a description of this primordial world which will avoid the more glaring reductions and distortions of so-called *empiricism*. This, of course, is defensible. One cannot do everything. But Merleau-Ponty says almost nothing of universal concepts and judgments, or of the logical structure of science. One is led to infer that all pure theory is necessarily a distortion, which raises serious questions concerning his own reflective method of pure description. [2]

The existentialists have shown that such theory, in spite of its abstractness and generality, may still be applied to the obscurest regions of inner experience, mood, and feeling, without undue distortion. The philosophy of the future will accept these results, so far as they are verified. But it will not assume *a priori* that man is the center of the actual world, nor that human action alone is subject to disciplined ontological investigation. It will attempt to describe the divergent manifestations of these pervasive data as they come, first analyzing them with painstaking care, and then devising explanatory theories which are not only internally consistent but also do justice to every kind of fact.

EXISTENTIAL DESCRIPTION

All human experience is intentional in structure—in its practical as well as in its theoretical phases. [3] I cannot do without doing something; I cannot think without thinking about something. Every phase of these relational structures, the objective as well as the subjective, is given with the same evidence. There is no more reason for denying the one than the other. Hence idealism, which attempts to reduce the object to a state of the subject, and pan-objectivism, which attempts to reduce the subject to an object, must be rejected. Both are always found together in an intentional structure of some type. This much has now been established by patient investigation. But what is the precise nature of this intentional relation? How is it to be explained? What does practical experience have in common with theoretical experience? What are the chief points of difference, and how are they to be explained? These questions as yet are far from having received any really exact or verified answers.

The subjective pole of practical experience is always mine. It is individual and concrete. This has led certain existentialist thinkers, like Jaspers, towards a subjective relativism which denies the abstractive capacity of reason to grasp what is invariable and essential in the concrete and unique. But this is refuted by the factual existence of science. It has led others, like Heidegger, to gloss over the distinction between the *existentielle* (which is individual and subjective) and the *existentiale* (which is universal) without adequate logical explanation.[4]

These weaknesses must be thoroughly corrected by the new philosophy, which must show that the very same methods of description, analysis, and explanation can be applied to the subjective pole as to the objective pole of human experience. This cannot be done, however, without a careful, critical examination of the realistic theory of logical abstraction, and a clarification of many points in this theory which still remain obscure. The importance of such investigations has already been seen by dialectical materialists,[5] as it must eventually be seen by all those who are now seriously committed to the defense of a disciplined empiricism. Only in this way, can we ever come to a clear understanding of those logical processes by which a thinker like Heidegger, for example, "leaps" from his personal existence, and his own world, to *Dasein* and worldliness in general.

PHENOMENOLOGY AS A THEORETICAL (NOT
A PRACTICAL) DISCIPLINE

Heidegger's notion of the phenomenological method as plunging into a supposedly non-vicious circle of practical presuppositions and assumptions which are then clarified and interpreted
must also be rejected. The aim of phenomenology, as the realist
conceives it, is to get rid of all uncriticized presuppositions, especially those derived from practical projects of any kind. The
struggle of human existence to achieve subjective fulfilment is an
extremely important and basic aspect of experience. It is rich in
both empirical content and obscurity. The existentialists have
shown that it is open to phenomenological description and clarification. But this rich field of experience is an object of investigation. It cannot itself function as a phenomenological norm, without introducing bias and confusion. It is true that awareness
belongs to our being, and that to complete and to clarify this
awareness must always operate as a basic existential aim. But the
aim of theoretical awareness is simply to understand existence, including the practical existence of man, as it really is, so far as this
is possible. Husserl's famous saying *zu den Sachen selbst* is a classic
statement of this purely theoretical aim. To understand the nature of human practice is not a practical endeavor. It is pure
theory, not practice, and as we have often had occasion to point
out, the insights of Kierkegaard and his living disciples cannot be
understood except as contributions to the discipline of theoretical phenomenology.

What, then, is the point of view of this peculiar discipline?
Who, then, is speaking to us when the phenomenologist speaks? *
Is it, then, some non-authentic no-one who is speaking—some impersonal person who is forgetting who he is? Is this a human
observer detached from his humanity, trying to be nowhere and
everywhere at once? Must we then follow after Husserl, and finally accept the doctrine of the idealists? Is it, then, the transcendental point of view of the absolute consciousness that we

---

* For a discussion of this important question from the standpoint of the
French phenomenologist, Merleau-Ponty, cf. De Waelhens, *Une Philosophie
de l'Ambiguité*, pp. 399 ff.

REALISTIC PHENOMENOLOGY   191

must try to approximate—the ultimate container within which
we ourselves, and everything else as it really is, must be ultimately included? These questions reveal serious difficulties that
have never been adequately dealt with. To the reader they may,
nevertheless, suggest the sort of realistic answer that may be further clarified in the future, and may act in a regulative capacity
to guide the investigations of a genuine, empirical philosophic
discipline.

Theoretical awareness, of course, is a capacity which belongs
to the being of man. It is not, however, a capacity for the making
or construction of projects. Man is constantly engaged in such
projective endeavors which, like all other phases of his being,
need to be clearly understood if they are to be brought under
proper guidance and adequately realized. But this awareness is
not a constructive power. It makes nothing up, so far as it functions adequately. It adds nothing to that which it really knows.
It does not project something new (not existing before), but
rather unites with an object that exists already, assimilating it
and revealing it as it already is.

In order to perform this manifesting function, awareness must
in itself be as nothing. At this point, the realist will find Sartre's
idea of the nothingness of consciousness quite suggestive. Any
positive determination will color its vision, and prevent it from
exercising its assimilative function. No physical power can achieve
this state of indeterminacy. Such a power to heat, to compress,
to dissolve, etc. has a nature of its own. Any influence received
into this will be warped and modified to become something new.
But as Aristotle long ago pointed out, the noetic power is non-
material. Free from all positive determination, it is stretched out,
ready to identify itself with anything as it is. But when it becomes permanently colored by some bias, we do not understand
things as they are in themselves, but only from a certain point of
view, as they are mixed with the demands elicited by a certain
fixed position.

In order to escape from this imprisonment in a world of our
own construction, we must first become detached from practical
assumptions and presuppositions. Taking nothing for granted, we
must learn to wonder at all things, and thus to regain that noetic

nothingness which is a necessary condition for the attainment of knowledge. To the materialist, of course, it seems as though this were an absolute nothingness. But such a view is quite mistaken. Absolute nothingness has no power of any kind; it does not unite with being; it has no relational structure. It simply is not. The power of reason is all of this. In its potential state, it is indeterminate but able to unite with the existence or non-existence of what is in question. If we are to be ready to examine any question in the light of the evidence alone, apart from all subjective prejudice, we must return to this noetic nothingness. Our minds must be ready to give one answer or the opposite.

All insight is conditioned by this ever-present nothingness. Every possible concept has its opposite. Even the human concept of being is opposed by that of nothing. As Sartre has pointed out, every question prepares the way for two possible and contrary answers. Is Peter there or not there? Is this the reason or is it not? That which is prepared for either being or nothing is not absolute nothingness, which is not prepared for anything. It simply is not. Knowing is a pure potency, unlike matter in lacking all determinacy, but ready to receive being as it is. In so far as this potency is actualized, we understand things simply as they are, not from this point of view or from that. We do not lock them up inside a finite or absolute container of any sort, but rather stretch out our minds to existence. To some degree, such knowledge is open to us, but only on the condition of long and grueling discipline.

A crucial part of such discipline is to become detached from every practical bias and interest. Do we then become detached from our humanity? Do we cease to speak as men? The answer, of course, is No. But what is the being of man? Does it restrict us to the pursuit of practical projects which we ourselves have fabricated? Is the whole of our existence exhausted in the ceaseless attempt to gain more entitative being for ourselves? The answer to this is also No. There is a radically different sort of project in which we all participate to some degree, and on which the success of our practical endeavors ultimately depends. This is the noetic enterprise of man, which seeks not for an entitative ownership or possession of things, but rather for intentional union with them.

This enterprise is eminently and distinctively human. But as long as it speaks only from a human point of view, its task is unfulfilled. As long as we see things only in the light of this project or that, we do not really understand them as they are, and we cannot judge our projects. The aim of pure theory is to understand our projects, ourselves, and all things from no point of view at all, but in the light of being. Practical projects differ from species to species, and from culture to culture. But theoretical truth is the same for all.[6] To utter such truth is to express at the highest level the peculiar being of man.

DESCRIPTION, INFERENCE, AND EXPLANATION
IN PHILOSOPHY

The first step in the attainment of such truth is the use of all our cognitive faculties—feeling, sense, and reason—in the description of objects as they are given. The next step is to analyze out the essential aspects of these complex data, and the relational forms in which they are united. These belong to what we call phenomenology. At every stage, our eyes are fixed on the object we are describing. No inference must be allowed to creep into the picture. No fixed interpretation should warp our view. Our attention is focused solely on the existing phenomena as they are present to us, and on the constitutive structure of this presence. When this has been accurately achieved, we have already embarked on the last phase of the process, the quest for explanation in terms of reasons and causes.

Any factor that is clearly grasped is a reason. Any structural phase or relation is a reason which makes something as it is. A general law of science is a reason which enables us to explain why a given instance is as it is. But the range of data which appear to us is very slight in comparison with the hidden riches of reality. From the laws of causal dependence which we find exemplified in experience, we may infer other entities and phases of being which do not appear. In this way, our view of the world is enormously broadened by an inferential theory that penetrates far beyond the horizons revealed by our practical activity. This expansion of theoretical horizons is the next step in the quest for truth.

The final step is the formulation of an integral theory which will be internally coherent, and at the same time take account of all known entities and phases of being, whether they are directly revealed or only inferred. At every stage of the process, the attainment of truth must depend on the priority and predominance of the data over explanation and interpretation. It may be wrecked at any point by the reversal of this noetic order. When some explanatory theory that has gained prestige is tenaciously held in priority to the data as a necessary *a priori* presupposition, empiricism is lost. Instead of allowing the data to suggest our interpretation, we allow an interpretation to suggest to us what the data must be. Instead of discovering an explanation, we invent one. Instead of clarifying the actual data, we merely clarify a theory. Instead of interpreting the facts as they are present, we merely interpret a theory we have already accepted. We are caught in the vicious circle that Heidegger tries to defend. This is not phenomenology—but rather its opposite.

METAPHYSICAL PROTOCOLS

It is reassuring to the realist to find that the existential phenomenologists, in their study of human being, have clearly focused many of the pervasive protocols which constitute the peculiar object of philosophical investigation. The greater adequacy of their suggestive analyses, as over against prevailing reductionist theories, is chiefly due to this striking fact. Thus they have shown beyond any shadow of doubt that the act of human existing is something more than a fixed determinate essence, and also that this act is characterized by many modes (Heidegger's *existentials*) which may be described and clarified. They have also shown that good and evil are not fixed qualities or properties at all, but rather existential modes of this type—an authentic way of existing in which real human possibilities are actualized, and an unauthentic or privative mode in which the person fails to be what he really is.

THE ONTOLOGY OF MAN

The existentialists have seen that the act of existing is something very different from the mere presence of an essence before the mind, and that non-existence is very different from the absence of such an essence in a faculty that is ready to receive it. Non-existence is not ready for anything, but is completely and radically opposed. This distinction has been slurred over by Sartre in some of his dialectical attempts to regard the *pour soi* as a sort of creative Hegelian nothingness. But aside from this ill-fated venture, the existentialists have recognized the full significance of the law of contradiction, and have revived the strong *either-or,* without which ontological thought sinks into an abyss of confusion and ambiguity.

They have clearly grasped the weakness and contingency of human nature and that potential futurity which is an essential phase of his being, distinguishing him radically from sub-cognitive things that merely develop through divergent phases succeeding one another in time. They have recognized change as a pervasive datum with many forms whose continuity and discontinuity require exact philosophical analysis. Heidegger's study of the ways in which human being temporalizes itself has resulted in new insights of great importance. The phenomenological studies of the existentialists have also forced them to recognize the vagueness which attaches to all incipient phases of awareness, and which therefore pervades experience of every kind until it is clarified by rational analysis and interpretation. In this way they have corrected certain reductive mistakes which have deflected the thought of post-Cartesian empiricism, and which have prevented it from arriving at a sound view of human being.

The so-called scientific theories of man, which are now so influential in the Anglo-Saxon world, are not wrong and misleading because of mistakes in quantitative measurement, or a failure to observe fixed properties. They are wrong for a much more fundamental reason. They have misunderstood the existence of this being. He exists in a manner quite different from that which they have supposed. This has now been shown with penetrating clarity in the light of evident facts to which all have access. Hence it is not surprising that the effects of this insight on anthropology are quite revolutionary. The philosophy of the future will no longer be able to look upon man either as a mind-thing locked up in itself, having access to a distant world only by devious processes of cognition, or as a complex organism-object interacting with its environment. These notions are now out of date. They will never be revived again by responsible empirical investigators.

Unfortunately, however, the existentialists have not turned their attention to the field of sub-human nature. They have not only neglected this field of investigation, as we have noted. They have also been guilty of reductive oversimplifications analogous to those which "scientific" anthropology has committed in the case of man. As examples of this, we need only refer again to Sartre's extraordinary notion of the *en soi* as deprived of all potentiality, and Heidegger's tendency to regard all sub-human entities as finished and simply there on hand (*Vorhandensein*). Such errors must be rejected by the new philosophy. There is indeed a gulf between human and sub-human being, but the existentialists have been so eager to correct the reductive mistakes of "scientific" anthropology that they have exaggerated the extent of this gulf, and have unduly oversimplified the structure of non-human existence.

Such existence, it is true, does not understand and noetically project its future. The existentialists have identified this special mode of noetic possibility with possibility as such. This is a mistake. Even the projected possibilities of man are founded on real possibilities which belong to him by nature, whether he clearly understands them or not. Unless such insight is achieved, his formulated projects will be distorted and even fantastic. Certain ranges of action are possible for man; other ranges are strictly impossible. This type of real possibility also belongs to all finite entities which are never complete and finished but always on the way towards further being not yet possessed. Unless this were true, they could not change. But the continuous change of all natural entities is an evident philosophic fact. The new philosophy will certainly study the complex structure of this natural change and its various forms and manifestations.

In his important work, *Philosophie der Natur,* Nicolai Hartmann has shed a good deal of light on many of the problems which lie at the border line between the natural sciences of physics, astronomy, biology, and ontology. But aside from a few introductory works, this field is now an unexplored wilderness. The philosophy of the future will not follow the existentialists in devoting attention exclusively to human being. It will most certainly attempt to proceed further in the task of gaining some clear light on being as such. In this light, it will then try to analyze and to compare all the different modes of being that are accessible to us, including the changing being of natural entities. It will also attempt to clarify the foundational concepts of the sciences, and to interpret their ever-changing results on the basis of the more stable insights of ontology.

WEAKNESSES IN THE EXISTENTIALIST ONTOLOGY

Even on the basis of the little that is already known, it is clear that certain gaps will have to be filled, and certain weaknesses corrected in the existentialist ontology of man. The most basic are three in number.

The Neglect of Theoretical Cognition and Essence

The most glaring of these weaknesses is a failure to recognize any stable structure or essence in the make-up of man, which we have had constant occasion to notice. The existentialist thinkers have been led into this by (1) their prejudice against theoretical reflection, and (2) their desire to emphasize the freedom of human existence, which has been so seriously neglected by modern schools of ethics.

But the first point is a sheer inconsistency, for their own phenomenological method is purely theoretical. The second point is a mistake. Man possesses no unlimited freedom, and determinate law is not opposed to the limited freedom he possesses. As Kierkegaard himself pointed out: ". . . without law freedom simply does not exist. . . . It is the law which gives freedom." [7] This truth will be clearly recognized by the new philosophy. Action and existence are never found without structure and essence. Loose tendencies cannot exist. They are always tendencies of a

198 The Challenge of Existentialism

certain kind, proceeding in a certain direction. Nature as such is lawful. Unless this were so, science would be impossible.

All Insight as Projective

The second basic weakness is an error of omission. This is the failure of the existentialists, except for Sartre, to give any analysis of knowing as a distinct mode of being, and their common tendency to identify it with an active tendency or project. Thus Heidegger, as we have noted, merely refers to knowing as a revealing mode of *Dasein* without attempting any exact analysis of what this mode of being is. This again is an over-reaction to idealism, which reduced being to cognitive being. The existentialists, on the other hand, seem to reduce cognition to active or projective being. This leads Heidegger to an apparent rejection of the notion of truth as a relation of union or identity, and to a view of his own that is by no means clear, though it seems to conceive of truth in terms of a "light" diffused by *Dasein*, and thus passes over its evident relational structure.

These mistakes must be corrected by the new philosophy. To pursue an active project is not the same as to reveal something. Being manifested to the agent is, of course, an essential part of the human project. This is what causes the confusion. But though intimately united, the revealing is distinct from the acting. Hence this kind of self-awareness, which the existentialists greatly emphasize, is still objective or intentional in character. I am conscious of my action as it proceeds towards its goal. Obliquely and at the same time, I am conscious of my awareness, for in knowing the object, this knowing is itself revealed. The end is intentionally present before the mind. This awareness directs the project. The action sustains and realizes it. So intimate is this union of two sustaining phases, each of which exists only by reason of the other, that it is easy for us to slur over the difference, and to suppose that the two are one, the action being the knowing and the knowing being the project. The philosophy of the future will avoid this confusion.

In carefully examining the many problems involved in this intimate fusion of practical reason, it will be guided by the truth, already established, that noetic revealing is intentional in structure. Knowing cannot reveal without revealing something distinct from, and yet intentionally united with, itself. Knowledge is not a thing that gains a relation to another thing. Its whole being is rather a being-to. When actualized, it achieves nothing but a relational union with existence as it is. This relational being belongs to man. To gain the truth makes a difference to him. In this sense, the existentialists are right in holding that the entitative being of truth is human. As Heidegger says—*without Dasein no truth*. But something else also needs to be said.

This revealing being is relational. It has a term. The terminus of truth is always being as it is. This terminal or intentional being of truth does not belong to the knowing act, and is not relative to man. Whether it is known or not, it remains exactly as it is. Truth in this terminal sense is altogether independent of *Dasein*. Our knowing of the truth is a human act which depends upon us, and contributes to our being. But the truth that we know is entirely independent.

The Rejection of Reason and Explanation

The third basic ontological weakness of existentialism is its tendency to ground the principle of sufficient reason in a groundless human freedom, which leads to a disparagement of explanation as against description, and to a view of the universe as a surd chaos of brute fact. This is part of the pragmatic urge to reduce pure theory to practice. But because of the many facts to which it is opposed, it must be rejected by the new philosophy. This does not mean, however, that it will be able to accept any classical theory of sufficient reason without radical revision. The notion of ground or reason will almost certainly have to be widened.

Any factor which can be grasped by reason and clearly distinguished from other factors is a reason, even though it be a factor of indeterminacy or an existential factor of active tendency. This is all that is required for the intelligibility of the universe. We need not deny indeterminacy or creative advance in nature, as classical theories have sometimes tended to do. Most certainly we do not need to analyze the universe into a set of static essences. If the universe is intelligible, we must be able to analyze rationally any concrete occurrence into internal and intrusive factors that are intelligible. Nothing is said concerning what these factors must be. They may be determinate or indeterminate, static or creative. Active tendencies are certainly at work in the world of nature. Novelties do arise. Finite existence is a principle of dynamism.[8]

This does not mean, however, that it is self-explanatory. For something to come out of nothing with no ground is a contradiction—a supposed passage over the unbridgeable gulf that separates being from nothing. The principle of sufficient reason, which asserts the intelligibility of the universe, not its exhaustive intelligibility to man, will be defended by the new philosophy. But many problems will need to be solved. Almost all attempts which have so far been formulated to demonstrate the principle of sufficient reason on the basis of the law of contradiction have really begged the question. New attempts must be made. New light must be shed.

There is an objective factor of potency or indeterminacy in nature which can be clearly grasped. But there is also a factor of cognitive vagueness and confusion which may pervade the whole of human experience in all its phases. Its failure to focus the intentionality of all awareness has prevented modern empiricism from recognizing this. But the act of being aware is distinct from its object. Hence the very same object may be apprehended with various degrees of clarity and confusion. Without rational analysis and judgment, our sensory apprehension is always confused. This can be brought into clarity only by the exercise first of rational discrimination and analysis, which breaks down the composite object into its various phases or reasons. Then these must be reintegrated by definition and judgment. The idea that sense presents us with clear and distinct atomic impressions is an *a priori* prejudice fraught with the most serious consequences. The elimination of this rationalistic, and anti-empirical conception, together with its many consequences, is a first duty of the new philosophy. It should lead to a new approach to the principle of sufficient reason.

BEING-IN-THE-WORLD

The human person is not an isolated mind-thing whose being is atomic and self-enclosed. Wherever man is found, there is also a human world in which he struggles and cares. This worldliness is not an accident that merely happens to man. Being-in-the-world is an essential relational aspect of his being. Here the existentialists are certainly correct, and Heidegger's disciplined descriptions have clarified certain phases of this structure. He is certainly right in pointing out that it is integral, and in some sense prior to any entity or set of entities that is in-the-world. Hence to explain the world as the grand collection of all those entities which are already in the world is no explanation at all, but only a barren tautology. He is also right in calling our attention to the temporal aspect of world structure. The world is more than a spatial container. Events and processes are in this world. It is in some sense also a time container. How, then, can time be contained?

Theoretical Clarification of Projective World Horizons

The existentialists refer us to the purposive structure of human care that runs ahead of itself, and thus places time within the limits of its chosen project. Primordial perception always takes place within such a practical horizon. What we perceive lies within a field. This field structure has been carefully studied by Merleau-Ponty.[9] But things and events are not only spatially but also temporally placed within an ultimate world horizon. Heidegger and Sartre have gathered evidence of great weight to support this view. There can be no question that what we may call the ordinary world of everyday has this practical structure. We speak in this way of the financial world, the international world, the world of the engineer, and that of the farmer, referring in an eminently inclusive sense to all those objects which may have any favorable or unfavorable connection with a long-range project of some kind. What, then, is *the* world?

Following the indications provided by common usage, the existentialists tell us that it must be all things whatsoever, seen in their relation to an ultimate or final project of man. Such projects

are open to free and creative choice. Hence the world of one culture differs from that of another, and even the worlds of persons
so far as they realize their freedom. Your world is the way you
order things and processes in relation to your final purpose. This
view is certainly suggested by Heidegger, and stated with unmistakable clarity by Sartre. It leads us to conclude not only that
without a world there would be no humanity, but also that without humanity there would be no world—nothing more than a
meaningless chaos of brute factuality. This practical subjectivism
is open to serious question. There are certain facts that it simply
does not explain. These facts will not be ignored by the new
philosophy.

The practical worlds of free persons and cultures *ex hypothesi*
differ from each other. We all at least dimly realize, however, that
the cosmic world, in which our entitative acts of thinking and of
striving take place, is one. This ultimate world-unity is not
coherently explained by the theory.

Since cosmic events are unfinished and indeterminate, they may
be fitted in different ways into divergent human projects. This
is certainly true. But these events also have a hard and stubborn
structure not subject to human choice and control. Every human
project must be fitted to this structure, if sheer fantasy and catastrophe are to be avoided. Our only access to it is through pure
theory. Cosmic facts must simply be grasped as they are. There
is, therefore, a theoretical component in every sound project that
is not grounded on fantasy. Engineering is based on theoretical
physics, medicine on physiology. Sound human projects must also
be based on just such a purely theoretical anthropology as the
existentialists themselves have been developing with considerable
insight, merged, unfortunately, with certain grave mistakes. One
of these is their failure to recognize the theoretical component
that enters into every project of whatever kind.

It is with respect to this theoretical component that world
structures overlap, and that communication between those committed to different world projects is possible. Thus men try to
defend and to justify their projects by reference to theoretical
evidence accessible to all. On the existentialist view, there is no
such evidence. Hence the justification of one world view as against

another. Even any intelligible communication between the two is quite impossible. But this runs counter to well-known facts. Philosophic communication does occur. Certain projects are recognized everywhere as being less unjustifiable than others.

Our first vivid sense of an independent existence that weighs upon us and stubbornly resists us, that frustrates us and finally shatters us, is first gained from the practical awareness that is fused with our activities. But as soon as we reflect on this, and recognize that it is so, pure theory is at work. Only in this way do we gain a clear insight into the global structure of being that both infuses us and surrounds us. This concept underlies all the rest, including those by which we apprehend our projects. It is only by focusing it to some degree of clarity that we can distinguish its various levels and kinds. In order to be *at hand,* in Heidegger's sense, the artifact must *be.* We can do nothing about this all-enveloping being. We can only gaze upon it and wonder, which is a theoretical experience. It requires leisure and detachment from practical preoccupations. Hence in individual and cultural life it comes late. We know the being-for of things before we know their being. But being-for is only a certain mode of being, which it presupposes. Being-in-the-world is not being as such. In the cosmic order, being is prior. This evident priority of being is not explained by the Sartrian theory, or by any other form of practical subjectivism.

The Human vs. the Cosmic World

In trying to gain some understanding of the cosmic world, we are confronted with many problems and mysteries. How these problems may be answered and these mysteries understood by the philosophy of the future, we can only dimly anticipate. The existentialist suggestion that the cosmic world is chosen by man will certainly be rejected. Even these thinkers are forced to recognize that human existence-in-the-world as such is not a human construction. The projective structure of our being is not a human project. We find that we, ourselves, and the world-views that go with us, are encompassed by a cosmic world that overarches all of them, and deeply transcends those which have no place for the hidden depths of mystery.

The first reaction of a sanguine mind, when it discovers this fact of transcendence, is to interpret it as pure chaos and disorder. If the human order is not all-encompassing, as idealistic philosophy falsely supposed, if it is only a tiny island in a vast surrounding ocean of being, we will first be inclined to say that this is no order at all. The spirit of man creates its own order. This premise of idealism is still accepted. But the world itself is foreign and strange. It is no order at all, but a wilderness of brute absurdity. This is the existentialist reaction. Man has been thrown by senseless forces into a being devoid of sense. If there is to be any meaning, this meaning must be created by man out of the meaningless. Human existence, indeed, must be devoted to this hopeless task. What is man against the universe?

The philosophy of the future will certainly call attention to the dubious subjectivist premise of current existentialism. Is ontological order a human creation? Does the law of contradiction fail to hold? Are the laws of nature a human construction, or are they grounded in actual tendencies that are determinate and repetitive? Are moral laws made up by man? Or are they grounded in fixed tendencies of human nature, and enforced by natural sanctions? In the light of these questions and the answers they suggest, the philosophy of the future will probably decide that while there is a creative aspect in the early stages of any noetic enterprise and in the first formulation of true principles, this is subordinate to a deeper aspect of revelation and discovery. What we wish to know ultimately is not an order that we have invented, but the order that is really there. Here and there we have already caught glimpses of such an order.

If this were not so, our reliance on disciplined science would be a bald delusion. This order is full of obscurity and mystery. Our knowledge of it is extremely partial and very weak. From the little we know, it seems remote from the forms of practical order that are subject to human choice and imposed by man on himself—much more remote from some of these than from others. But to say that it is no order at all is not only to go beyond the evidence but to contradict such evidence as we possess. It is not surprising that subjectivism, after the agelong grip it has gained on the modern mind, should take some time to die.

We have now discovered with gruesome clarity that the ideal-istic conception of the oneness of man with the universe, the friendly spirit behind phenomena, is an error. Whatever else it may be, the world is not like a human project. But the only al-ternative to human order is not absolute disorder. To think in this way is to betray an underlying subjectivism. It is an attempt to impose arbitrary limits on the range of our intelligence. These presuppositions are necessary. We cannot look at things in any other way. Only such and such a limited perspective is possible for us. Human order alone is possible. Such dogmatism is an invitation to closer examination of the evidence. Time after time it has been shown that the evidence does not support such arbi-trary restrictions. It is not likely, therefore, that Heidegger's idea of the circular nature of the phenomenological method will be supported. True empiricism is rather the constant escape from such circles of *a priorism*.

But the recognition that we are in such a circle is the first step in transcending it. The existential rebellion will, therefore, be understood as a last stage in the collapse of idealistic humanism. The world orders of materialism, idealism, and other *isms* are only human constructions. No longer can we confuse any of these with the order of the world as such. The next step is to take them less seriously, to open our minds to being. Instead of trying to fit the evidence into these narrow frames, or bewailing the absurdity of the world when it stubbornly refuses, a harder attitude will be adopted. Instead of fitting the world to our frames, let us rather fit our frames to the transcendent order of being, as it may be glimpsed here and there by contemplation. Instead of arbitrarily limiting our theory by the subjective demands of practice, we may eventually see the need of grounding our practice on the wider and firmer grounds of that real structure which can be revealed only by pure theory.

In its interpretation of world structure, the philosophy of the future will pay close attention to the intentionality of human thought. The entitative act of revealing, by which being is con-ceived, is a dated operation, relative to man. This act of revealing is brought forth by man. In this sense, man exudes his truth as a bulb radiates its light. Without man, or something analogous, there would be no such revelation. But these acts are relational in structure. They terminate in an object that is distinct. Hence no act can directly intend itself. I cannot now think *of* the individual act that I am thinking here and now. Such being follows the theory of types. It can include something only by making it a part of itself. But thought can unite with an object of *universal* scope. I may think not of this individual act but of cognitive act in general. In this way, via the universal object, I may think of the very thought that I am now thinking, for this is an instance of thought in general.

In the same way, all metaphysical reflection violates the theory of types, for it strives after all-pervasive generalizations which apply not only to everything else but also to itself. The cosmic world is such an all-inclusive, intentional object. It applies to all things, including the entitative act by which it is conceived. I myself and my acts of conceiving are really in the world that is the intentional object of certain conceptions. But unless the object is sharply distinguished from the revealing act, I must confuse the two, and my being-in-the-world will be interpreted as the being of the world in me. Every form of subjectivism can be traced to a similar neglect of intentionality.

BEING WITH

The existentialists are keen observers of human action in the concrete. Hence they have unanimously recognized that being-with-others is an essential relational aspect of human being as such. But they have given us no exact analysis of this being-with, and no coherent explanation of how it is possible. Both Kierkegaard and Jaspers have seen that this involves what we call *communication,* and they have struggled with some of the simpler problems which first arise in connection with any attempt to describe this complex and mysterious phenomenon. Even Merleau-Ponty considers only the rudimentary levels of material communication through which I may be sure of the other *with whom* I exist. He refers only casually to conceptual discourse, and within the limits of this perspective rightly holds that there is a lived solipsism which is insuperable.[10]

The Failure to Account for Communication

Modern epistemology has reduced cognition to the presence of a datum or quale within a subjective container. Modern logic has fallen into the hands of technicians who have been interested exclusively in the manipulation of symbol-things, and who have paid no attention to the signifying functions of concepts and judgments, which are the proper object of a humane logic. This neglect of intentional structure has made it impossible, not only for Kierkegaard and Jaspers but for anyone, to arrive at descriptive formulae which will do justice to the higher levels of rational communication. The mind is a thing imprisoned within an impenetrable containing surface. In terms of these metaphysical assumptions, the so-called problem of how I can know the content of another mind becomes at once insoluble.

Kierkegaard's accounts of what he called indirect communication may describe the sort of thing that happens when we try to interpret the behavior of a stubborn and recalcitrant child. It certainly does not do justice to rational discourse. Jaspers' account of existential communication may apply to the diplomatic war in words in which those of opposed interests are often engaged. It certainly does not apply to theoretical argument. The existentialists have given us only the bare beginnings of a phenomenology of human communication. To develop this into a responsible discipline is a desperate need of our time.

This is a fertile field for philosophical description and analysis which will probably be subjected to disciplined investigation in the near future. It would be rash indeed to predict any detailed results, but we may hazard a few guesses concerning more basic matters.

Towards a Realistic Theory of Communication

Disciplined study, I think, will show that there are different levels of communication, which differ in the kind of sign that is used, the mode of meaning and interpretation, the way in which the parts of the discourse are connected together, and finally in the mode of communion that is achieved. Three of these levels are especially important. For the sake of convenience, we shall name them the material, the formal, and the philosophical. In brief, they may be described as follows.

MATERIAL COMMUNICATION. Material communication is more accessible to the quantitative methods of "science," and has been subjected to some careful study and analysis by social psychology. It plays a certain role in all communication, though its importance diminishes at the higher levels. We are all vaguely familiar with it, and refer to it in common speech as eloquence, rhetoric, and persuasive style. Such knowledge as we have of it has been exploited, sometimes with a rather weird success, in what we call the techniques of mass propaganda and advertising. In terms of producing mass responses of an active character, it can be very effective. But in terms of transmitting the awareness of one person to another, it is crude, insensitive, unreliable, and generally inadequate.

Such communication operates by natural signs, such as gesturing, tone of voice, and facial expression, which do not call forth conceptual meanings, but active modes of response like interest, hatred, and fear. Those who try to communicate in this way must focus their attention on material signs. Those who are proficient in presenting such signs are said to be gifted with rhetoric. Those who respond are called sensitive. The meaning to be conveyed is a subjective image and the practical attitude associated with such an image. All definitions are ostensive. Nothing is ever defined in conceptual terms. The discourse takes the form of a story or tale in which discrete incidents are loosely strung together by relations of time and place. Psychological association takes the place of ontological structure. Instead of argument, there is suggestion. Phases and aspects are not distinguished. There are few subordinate clauses, and qualification is lacking.

The listener to such a discourse may grasp the same brute object that is being talked about. But beyond this point, agreement is uncertain. He never knows exactly what is being said, because the whatness is never focused. The best he can do is to respond with a roughly similar image, and a similar mode of response. The result is an empathy between the speaker and the listener

—either sympathy or antipathy. But since the object is indeterminate, this relation is always unstable. We never know how the other is really responding. We have to guess at this from his overt modes of reaction. When the situation becomes more clear, we are apt to find that sympathy has turned into antipathy, and antipathy into sympathy. If this were the only way in which we could communicate, the subjectivists would be correct. We could have no direct access to other minds. But amongst adults, this level never occurs alone. It is always fused with some elements of formal communication, which has a very different structure.

FORMAL COMMUNICATION. This is the level of intelligible, abstract discourse. Because of its detachment from practical interest, and its partiality, the existentialists scorn it as impersonal and unauthentic. But it is at this level primarily that the human individual is able to escape from his subjective loneliness, and to gain a direct access to the content of an alien mind. Instead of natural signs with active or "emotive" meanings, this formal discourse uses arbitrary symbols with abstract conceptual meanings. Little attention is paid to the material signs. Instead of this, the speaker may be asked to define his terms. If he merely points and gapes at a concrete blur, this is not deemed satisfactory. He must analyze it into its distinct aspects, and show how they are related.

Ontological necessity takes the place of psychic association. Evidence is not merely mentioned; it is carefully analyzed, and then asserted in a universal form. Once basic assertions have been made and accepted, we try to find reasons for further statements. Such discourse is full of qualifications and subordinate clauses. Persuasion takes the place of innuendo and suggestion. We cannot understand it by images and attitudes alone. We must not only recognize the same concrete blur, we must follow the analysis into abstract phases and relations, and understand the universal whatness that is being said.

The result is no mere empathy but agreement or disagreement concerning the same. It is important to realize that unless we mean the very same, disagreement is impossible. Those who always mean something different merely pass each other by. To achieve disagreement is a crucially important step out of the confused obscurity of unconscious conflict. We cannot disagree with someone without having gained a direct access to what is in his mind. We know *what* he thinks, and sometimes *why* (objectively) he thinks it. The whole issue is lifted into a luminous area pervaded by the light of reason. We no longer have to guess or infer. We have gained a direct access to what is in his mind.

The agreement which is achieved at this level is far more stable than any sort of sympathy: hence the relative stability and unanimity of science, which always uses the abstract concepts and impersonal methods of formal communication. Disagreements at this level are also more stubborn than emotional antipathy. The most stubborn ones are rooted in philosophical issues. Are these insuperable, as is often supposed? The answer will depend on how we interpret the third level of discourse. But before we consider this, we must consider two possible objections to the preceding analysis.

CAN I HAVE DIRECT ACCESS TO ANOTHER MIND? The first objection will be raised by the subjectivist. He will point out to us that we are first presented with a physical sign, either spoken or written. This sign, when it reaches us, is no longer in the speaker. How then can it give us any direct access, apart from inference, to the inner consciousness?

A careful consideration of this question will lead us to the distinction between a natural sign and an artificial symbol.[11] A natural sign, for example a cloud, is a concrete event in nature, connected by accident with its *signatum*. Thus it is possible for a physical cloud to exist without actual rain. The *signatum* is another concrete event, subject to wide variation, which may or may not occur. Hence inference is always involved in the interpretation of natural signs, like moans and grunts and growls.

A verbal symbol is also a concrete event in nature. But the word has been singled out by arbitrary, conscious stipulation to signify its meaning. Once it is recognized as a symbol, therefore, this connection is not accidental. As soon as we are presented with the symbols of a foreign language, we know that they must have a meaning. Furthermore, this meaning is not another concrete event, subject to indefinite variation, but an abstract concept that is always one and the same wherever it occurs. Hence when we know that a speaker is using linguistic symbols and knows the language, inference is not required in passing to the *signatum*. The symbol is a relation to its universal meaning. Either we understand this relation all at once, or we do not understand it at all. If we come across the relation father-of, we do not have to infer that there is a son. The meaning of a word may be grasped with varying degrees of clarity. It does not have to be inferred.

So far as we can conceptualize the contents of our experience and connect them with the arbitrary symbols of a language, we can transmit them without any loss or alteration to another mind. So far as this mind can express a conceptual and judgmental awareness, we have *direct* access to it, and may learn to think not something similar but the very same. It is in this way that we achieve disagreement and agreement, and may escape from that subjective loneliness which belongs to us as material organisms locked up within our spatial dimensions. But now we must consider another and more formidable objection that is raised by the existentialists.

IS EXISTENTIALIST ARGUMENT POSSIBLE? Universal concepts are always abstract and partial. They unite us only with aspects of the concrete, never with the concrete itself. This is ultimately responsible for the partiality of the perspectives of "science," which rest on the use of concepts that are abstract and univocal. Such concepts may enable me to share certain limited phases of my experience with other minds. But how about my concrete world as a whole? How about myself as a person in my concrete acts of existing, which are peculiar and private to me? These are too rich to be covered by any univocal concepts or judgments.

These are the things that matter most. They cannot be communicated by means of mere abstractions. I cannot actually *be* the existence of another, and neither he nor I can know this by concepts which are one and the same for all. The attempt to communicate the whole of my awareness, therefore, is bound to shatter. It must be vague and indirect. By the use of imagination and empathy, I may infer what the other person is really like. But such guesses are always hazardous. At best they may lead me to something roughly similar, not to the man himself as he really is. I must live my concrete existence alone by myself, and he must live his. Our attempt to achieve existential communication can be nothing more than a vague and friendly conflict between views that never really meet. Such is the existentialist position.

In their disciplined reflections, these thinkers have not taken us any farther. But in their actual procedure, they have given us certain fruitful suggestions as to how this impasse may be overcome. And surely it must be, for it stands squarely opposed to certain facts which are accessible to all. The concrete structure of an existential world can be intelligibly formulated. Such a formulation is precisely what we call a philosophy, and philosophical disagreement and agreement does occur. How is this philosophical mode of communication possible?

PHILOSOPHICAL COMMUNICATION. Qualities may coincide in the same region of space. They do not pervade each other. Hence when the experience is conceived as a set of properties or qualia, it becomes impossible to focus those philosophic structures which pervade concrete experience and hold its manifold aspects together. These are all relational in character. Many phases and aspects that may be *logically* isolated are *really* integrated together in such relational unities. Relation is not a being-in-itself but a being-to which may pervade the whole of a complex manifold, from its foundational sources to its termini. Thus all the necessary characteristics of an entity may be united together in an essential unity. They are all either constitutive of or dependent upon a complex essence. The nature of man pervades every human trait, so that human sickness, for example, has to be distinguished from the sickness of a brute animal. The understanding of such pervasive relations brings us close to the concrete.

We have had occasion to notice the atomism of modern thought, and its tendency to think of relation, not as pervading its terms, but rather as a bond, or a rod, lying in *between* the terms from which it is quite distinct. This mode of thought blinds us to the philosophic protocols, and keeps us far from the concrete as it is really given. The existentialists have broken radically with this philosophic atomism.

As we have noted, all the basic concepts of Heidegger's existential anthropology are relational complexes which have to be expressed in such hyphenated phrases as being-in-the-world, with-others, ahead-of-myself, as-already-in, the revealing-of-an-object, etc. The insight into such structures as these enables us to grasp the whole of our being without the partiality that attaches to all univocal abstraction. Thus every phase of my being is in-the-world with nothing of myself omitted, and everything of which I am aware is fitted into the world order. This structure pervades the whole of my experience.

But, we may say, another person has his own being. His experiences may be different from mine, and he may fit them together in a different order. Hence Heidegger's being-in-the-world is a mere equivocation.

This conclusion, however, does not necessarily follow, once we see the relational nature of this existential structure. Even though each distinguishable phase of a relational complex may be diverse from the corresponding phase of another such complex, there may still be a proportional similarity between the whole of one and the whole of the other. Thus the phrase, being-in-the-world, may refer without equivocation to an indefinite number of such relational instances. In spite of their diversities, each one may be proportionately similar to the rest. It is, in fact, only in this way that Heidegger's existentials may be vindicated against the charge of equivocation which has been urged against them.

As a matter of fact, the same charge may be urged against every genuine philosophic concept which applies necessarily to such a vast range of diverse instances that they cannot all be covered by a single univocal concept. Nevertheless, it does not follow, as the modern logician is apt to suppose, that such concepts are equivocal. These concepts are rather analogous. Between their different instances there is a relational similarity.

Thus the existentialist literature gives us many cogent examples of the way in which concrete existence may be understood by pervasive relational concepts based on proportional similarity. It is by the forging of such far-reaching concepts that philosophi-

cal discourse becomes possible. Once I have clarified my understanding of what world structure really is, I may compare
different types of this structure, and may argue with one whose
world structure is entirely alien from my own. The agreements
which may result from such modes of philosophic communication
are more basic and far-reaching than all others. Similarly, the
disagreements which may result are the most radical that can be
subjected to an empirical test and made intelligible. In such
philosophical argument, it is not divergent scientific theories
concerning something in the world which are at stake. It is
rather two alien worlds which are clashing. The issue is being
itself.

Since the attainment of authentic cultural unity depends on
the realization of such deep-level unity between free persons, it
is a matter of the utmost importance that this mode of existential communication should be more clearly understood, and that
adequate tools for maintaining it and checking it be further
refined and perfected.

The existentialist thinkers have laid the first foundations for a
sound phenomenology of human communication. But the back-
ward state of contemporary logic has greatly hampered them in
carrying on this task. The disciplined study of this obscure and
complex process, which underlies the whole social life of man,
and which has been completely neglected by modern logic, will
be a primary concern of the philosophy of the future.

BOUNDARY SITUATIONS

Jaspers' conception of the boundary situations will probably
be accepted by the new philosophy with certain important re-
visions and qualifications. These limiting situations are the most
concrete and unmistakable manifestations of human finitude.
Idealistic philosophy, especially in the pantheism of Hegel,
tended to slur over this radical human finitude, and to merge it
with the infinity of the absolute spirit. Such delusions have been
removed from the popular mind by the scientific barbarism of
the twentieth century, whose methods of mass propaganda, as
well as physical and mental torture, have revealed with luminous
clarity the fragility and dependence of the individual mind and

personality. These existential limits are pervasive philosophic facts on which the limited techniques of science are quite incapable of shedding light. They are open only to philosophic investigation and analysis. Hence the existentialist emphasis upon them is altogether justified. Three mistakes, however, call for correction.

Three Mistakes Requiring Correction

It is true that nothing can be done practically about the genuine limits of our nature. To dream of removing them is absurd. In the end we must simply face them, and meet them as best we can. But some light can be shed on them by pure theoretical description and analysis. The important existentialist thinkers have given us welcome light of this kind. What is Heidegger's well-known discussion of death but a disciplined description of the existential phenomenon? [12] Explanatory theories may be devised, though they take us so far beyond the range of available data, and must involve such a large element of inference, that decisive verification is most difficult to obtain. Nevertheless, these inescapable limits are open to theoretical investigation, and while we may never hope to eliminate them entirely, we may hope, in the light of such knowledge, to reduce their negating effect and, so to speak, push them back. In any case, the idea that they are wholly opaque to rational analysis must be categorically rejected. As Hegel rightly pointed out, to set up a limit is already to transcend it theoretically.

In the existentialist literature, these boundary situations are sometimes, not always, confused with avoidable evils, as is most evident in the case of guilt. This mistake must be corrected, for finitude, though a heavy weight to be borne, must be sharply distinguished from those avoidable privations which are rightly referred to as *evils*. It does not follow, of course, that these limits are good. Negations are never good, and while they are not privations, these limits are negative. The authentic ones are barriers beyond which our activity cannot go. They are not subject to human control, and certainly are not self-imposed. They point unmistakably to a transcendent reality which gave us a finite nature, not in any sense devised by us, and surrounded us with alien existences. As such, they should neither be welcomed nor evaded. They must simply be understood as accurately as possible in the light of pure theory, accepted as necessary, and then thrust back, so far as this is possible, by practical endeavor.

These limits certainly imply a fixed and determinate human essence, or nature, which is held in common by every member of the human species. The recognition of these boundary situations is, therefore, quite inconsistent with the tendency found among many existentialists to reject the notion of a stable human nature. As a matter of fact, each one of the boundary situations considered by them is traceable to a determinate aspect of this complex nature. We may illustrate this by considering them briefly one by one.

Situationality

The human person is always in a situation, striving to fulfill his tendencies amidst a nexus of surrounding persons and forces, which is at least confusedly revealed to him by mood and feeling. He may devise clever schemes for meeting a given situation, but no sooner is he out of one than he finds himself in another. Like all other ultimate limits, this situationality of human existence reveals the finiteness and fragility of human nature, surrounded as it is by alien and disruptive forces. In addition to this, however, it shows that the individual exists in an imperfect and tendential way, always seeking to fulfill a need or lack in the same stream of temporal succession which sweeps along all other entities of nature. It also shows that he naturally possesses cognitive powers of feeling and practical reason which can manifest his own existence, and that of other agencies around him. What is chiefly omitted from the existentialist accounts is any explicit reference to that power of theoretical insight, which they themselves exemplify, by which we may describe, classify, and illumine these situations as they come, and by which, if we take them seriously, we may guide ourselves towards authentic action.

Chance

The deterministic denial of chance is an attempt to explain away a disconcerting limiting factor by *a priori* speculation.

Experience shows clearly that men are subject to unpredictable coincidences at all times. To re-emphasize this fact is sound empiricism. It shows that human nature includes a factor of indeterminacy that is open to an indefinite range of diverse influences, and is largely opaque to human intelligence. It is certainly possible, however, to distinguish the most harmful kinds of accident to which we are subject, and to take precautions against them in a general way. By this theoretical means, the impact of such accidents may be reduced, but never entirely eliminated.

Struggle

The assertion that struggle and conflict is a necessary limiting condition of all human life is more questionable. It may be true that this has always happened in the past. But such universality is not the same as necessity, and it is hard to see anything in human nature as we now know it to justify the thesis. It has been defended by certain existentialists, including Jaspers and Sartre, because of their failure to recognize the facts of direct, conceptual communication, and their exaggerated emphasis on the material isolation of the lonely individual.

Suffering

Suffering is certainly an inescapable boundary situation of man. The more authentic the man, the more he is bound to suffer intellectually, morally, and even physically. This reveals the weakness and dependence of all aspects of our nature on passing and unstable external forces. The most harmful modes of suffering may be classified and anticipated in a general way. Under the guidance of sound theory, their effects may be reduced to some degree, but never eradicated. Every man is bound to suffer. Even the process of intellectual and moral growth is arduous, painful, and isolating. This is why those who are more developed suffer more deeply. The existentialist discussions of this subject are morally sound and full of insight.

Guilt

The same cannot be said of the existentialists' treatment of guilt, which certainly implies avoidability. Hence guilt cannot be an inescapable boundary situation. No man can be blamed for that which is inevitable. The theory of Jaspers and Heidegger that in taking over the defective being into which I have been thrown without my choice, I am necessarily tainted with guilt, rests upon a confusion of this moral quality with finitude. This finitude is a sad and weary burden. It is not the same as guilt. There is no doubt a collective guilt which affects the whole world into which the child is born. This is shared by all, and should be voluntarily recognized and taken over by each individual. Once having occurred, it may be inescapable, and in this respect like a boundary situation which follows with strict necessity from the nature of man. But collective guilt is not strictly but only *hypothetically* necessary, on the condition that it has once occurred. There was a time when it might have been avoided.

Death

The existentialist thinkers have performed an important serv- ice in recalling our attention to the actual phenomenon of per- sonal death. They have shown with great cogency and clarity that this is something more than the objective biological stop- page which can be observed from the outside. The limited methods of science can shed no light on this inner, existential phenomenon, which is open only to philosophical description and analysis. This is a way of existing endfully which happens, if it happens authentically, within the moment, here and now. It is only within this perspective that human existence in the world can be grasped in its wholeness. These insights have been taken over from the Christian tradition, but they have been developed in penetrating ways, and related to modern knowledge by Heidegger especially.

But in spite of their cogent criticism of many naturalistic dogmas, the existentialists have taken over some of these without sufficient examination. Thus Heidegger seems to assume that death is to be accepted phenomenologically as a passage into nothingness. But as Plato first pointed out, this is to go beyond the actual phenomena. All we really observe is a separation of the body from that which animates it. Whether this last factor persists or vanishes into nothingness is not observed. How we decide this issue must depend upon inference and theory, which the existentialists have so far neglected. This neglect will certainly be corrected by the philosophy of the future.

We have now completed our critical examination of the existentialist phenomenology and metaphysics. These philosophers have actually used a radically empirical method which has had the effect, as it always must, of reviving metaphysics as a responsible empirical discipline. We have seen, however, that certain mistakes still need to be corrected. Interpretation must be more sharply distinguished from description than it is by Heidegger, and the former more clearly subordinated to the latter, if genuine and strict phenomenology is to be achieved. Pervasive relational protocols are the peculiar object of philosophical concern. The existentialists have shed much light on certain of these which are bound up with human existence. But other beings than man need to be approached from the same point of view through a purely theoretical ontology.

– 8 –

Philosophical Anthropology

THE APPLICATION of genuinely empirical methods to the pervasive data of experience has once more made it possible to raise the question about being, and to pursue general ontology in a careful and responsible manner. As we have seen, however, the existential phenomenologists have so far not concentrated their efforts on this basic task which still lies open before us. Their major attention has been focused on the peculiar existence of man to which our inner experience gives us special access. In this field, their investigations have already led to results of really startling significance.

They have shown that the structure of experience is intentional, and have given us what is, in the setting of modern epistemology, an essentially new view of the nature of human awareness. They have also shown that human projects are intentional. This has enabled them to shed further light on the practical life of man. These researches have finally revealed the unique mode of temporality which distinguishes this being. It is now clear that the gulf between man and sub-human beings is much wider than is usually supposed, and that the ontological categories tacitly presupposed by prevalent modes of psychological and anthropological research are inadequate even to describe the actual facts, to say nothing of explaining them. Man simply does not exist as a thing, an organism, or an artifact.

These results are as yet almost wholly unknown to philosophers and social scientists in the English-speaking countries. They run counter to firmly-ingrained prejudices. Hence it will take some time to accomplish a critical assimilation. But in their major outline it is now clear that these results will be accepted by the empirical philosophy of the future. It is already apparent, however, that certain gaps will have to be filled, and certain errors corrected. It is dangerous to predict what is going to happen in a field that is now in such rapid movement, but it may be interesting to hazard a few guesses concerning the future development of the existentialist theories of awareness, care, and human temporality.

HUMAN AWARENESS, A REALISTIC VIEW

Epistemologists in the near future will no longer be able to evade the question, What is awareness? It is now not only clear that some kind of answer to this ontological question is presupposed by everything that is said in this field, but also that commonly-accepted physicalist assumptions are not in agreement with evident facts. As over against this traditional subjectivism, the new phenomenology is moving in a realistic direction. More accurate descriptions of certain phenomena have been achieved, but explanation has not yet been attempted. Practical awareness has been sharply focused, but theoretical cognition has been neglected. The philosophy of the future will certainly attempt to fill these gaps. In doing so, it will probably be led to make certain corrections which we shall now try briefly to indicate.

COGNITIVE BEING

First of all, it will be clearly recognized that cognition does not consist in the bringing forth of some new entity within a "container" of some kind. Such ontologically primitive conceptions have now had their day. They have been closely examined, and have been found to be thoroughly inadequate to the facts. Awareness is not a different kind of *thing*, but a distinct mode of being, manifesting itself in many levels or modes, several of which are found together in man. This cognitive mode of being is characterized by several traits which, in their entirety, mark it off from the thing-being which is most familiar to us.

First, it is relational rather than substantial. It is an outward reaching being-to rather than a subjectively centered being-in. Unlike many relations with which we are familiar, it does not originate in a determinate foundation which restricts the range of its possible terms, as my capacity to eat limits the kinds of food that will nourish me. The knowing power arises from a completely indeterminate foundation that does not restrict its terms in any way. In itself, this potency is an utter emptiness without internal structure of any kind. Any determination which is received must come from the outside, not from within; from the term alone, not from the foundation.

Thus it may exist as an outstretched emptiness ready to be filled with any structure, but in itself not determined at all. This emptiness, of course, is not sheer nothingness. It is an intensive mode of existing and acting, which underlies all actual cognition. This relational activity is what we mean by revealing and manifesting. Even when entirely lacking determination, the act reveals itself. Thus with my eyes open, groping in the dark, I am aware that I do not see. When in doubt concerning a rational problem, my mind is aware that it does not know.

When the power achieves determination, it is filled from foundation to term. In theoretical cognition, the relational structure is clearly divided into a subjective and an objective pole. The object always predominates, and is more clearly revealed. But the subjective pole is also manifested, less distinctly. All awareness is self-revealing. In practical cognition, the object is more complex, and there is a more intimate fusing of the awareness with certain of these objective phases. Thus in the experience of pleasure or satisfaction, it is much harder to distinguish the awareness from the object with which it is so closely united. We refer to them both by the single word pleasure, but an exact analysis can distinguish the two.

Human awareness is a union of the noetic power with subjective being, and the major problem of the theory of knowledge is first of all to describe, and then to explain this union and its different types. Genuine progress will be conditioned by an accurate knowledge of the ontological structure of the entities surrounding us, which are the primary objects of awareness. The failure of many epistemological theories to engage in such meta-physical "speculation" has led them into avoidable oversimplifica-tions and inconsistencies. Each entity around us, including our-selves, is made up of two distinct but united principles, the essence which marks it off from others, and the act of existing which brings it out of nothing. If we were not able to gain an awareness of both these phases, we should never know anything as it is. But the ways in which we cognize them are quite distinct.

A determinate whatness can be abstractly focused and absorbed into the knowing power without the matter and the other traits that individuate it. In this state of solitude, it may then be identified with an indefinite number of instances. The green color of the leaf is materially conveyed to my eye by the physical light. The seeing power of my eye is able to assimilate the sensi-ble green as such, without the matter. In this state, it will be identified with the reflected light, as long as it continues to affect the eye, and distinguished from other colors. This theory of the *species impressa* is still in a crude and undeveloped form, but in its major outlines it was clearly thought through in classical times. It is in some such manner as this that the determinate characteristics of things are known; first of all in a very blurred way by sense, and then more exactly and abstractly by what we call rational concepts. But how do we know the act of existing? Classical thought never formulated a clear and complete answer to this question. It cannot be evaded by the philosophy of the future. The solution will probably be worked out along lines already suggested in the recent phenomenological investigations of Nicolai Hartmann.[1]

HOW DO WE KNOW EXISTENCE?

I am my own act of existing. There is no way in which I can actually be an alien existence. It is this evident fact, together with a general disparagement of structure, that has called forth the radical existentialist critique of objective knowledge. To know something is to be it, as the idealists maintained. But to bring another person before me as an object of sense and reason is certainly not to be that person. His act of existing is non-transferable, and remains inviolate. No objective knowledge of

existence is possible. Hence to understand anything as a mere
object is to squeeze the existence out of it, to degrade it and
misunderstand it. My own existence I can know, for I am this
existence. But alien existence is beyond my reach. It is in itself,
and opaque to all objective intelligence. This is the gist of an
existentialist critique of theoretical knowledge which, as we
have seen,[2] has been urged with great cogency and has become
widely influential. It will not be accepted by the coming philosophy for the following two reasons.

The first reason is the hidden idealistic premise on which the
argument rests. It is not true that to know a thing I must be it
with no qualification at all. It is enough if I become the thing
in a certain sense,[3] if I can unite with its formal structure, and
can discriminate between its existing and non-existing. Such
discrimination does not demand complete coincidence. The second reason is that this criticism, if consistently developed, will
finally jeopardize all knowledge, including that of my own existence. To know is a certain mode of being which cannot be
identified with being as such. This, indeed, is presupposed by
the argument. Hence from the fact that I exist, which may be
granted, it does not follow that I know.

It is true that in revealing various objects, my acts of knowing
are also revealed. But it is always the object that is most clearly
manifested. Hence if this manifestation is open to question, the
other is even more dubious. The most accurate awareness that I
have of myself is certainly possessed in an objective form. If all
objective knowledge is a distortion, then I have no accurate
existential knowledge of myself. These consequences are against
the facts. Hence the existentialist critique must be rejected. But
this means that we must be able to give a coherent account of
how existence, as against essence, can be known. Can such an
account be given? I believe that it can be given along the following lines.

It is through the practical feeling and reflection closely united
to my active tendencies that I first become aware of existence.
These modes of awareness are organically related to active urges,
and work in unison with them. They are not self-energizing, but
are brought into act only by existential action to which they are

objectively sensitive. They vaguely feel and abstractly grasp my
activities as they proceed. Like all cognitive powers, they are
self-revealing and sensitive to the privative state of inactivity.
Hence, though they are not existentially one with these acts, they
can discriminate between their being and non-being.

Thus I know the difference between digging and resting, swim-
ming and floating. This practical awareness also cognizes alien
forces that break in on my acts to frustrate or to help them. I
feel the resistance of the rock that strikes my shovel, and the lift
of the waves that rock me as I float upon the surface of the sea.
This does not mean, of course, that I become petrified or lique-
fied. But my awareness becomes vaguely identified with what
they are, and sharply discriminates between the presence or
absence of their existential powers. It is thus through practice
that I first come to know existence. But later, pure theory also
gains access to such knowledge, with the aid of feeling and sense.

It cannot gain such knowledge by itself alone, for after the
first abstractive acts have been performed, theoretical reason is a
self-activating power which can construct new concepts and judgments by itself. Without reference to the senses, it would never
be able to discriminate accurately between those which refer to
mere possibilities and those which are concretely exemplified.
How does sense do this?

My sense of touch assimilates the sharp corner of my table top
as I feel it pressing my fingers. But my fingers are not turned
into wood. They, and the power of feeling they contain, preserve
their own mode of existing. This mode, however, is self-revealing.
It sharply discriminates between the empty state of feeling nothing, and that of fulfilment, when the outside pressure brings it
into act. It distinguishes something really pressing from the
absence of this state. Reason, paying attention to such an experience, and far more accurately abstracting the formal properties
involved, may then learn that they are not possibilities, but
actualized here and now in the pressure I am feeling. This truth
may then be expressed in the judgment: this (confused and concrete object of sense) corner of the table top (conceptual analysis)
is (judgment of existence).

All such judgments of existence must contain concrete nouns, proper names, or demonstratives which refer, via reason, to the objects of sense. A formal identification is achieved with the corner of the table top. But there is no existential identification. Reason does not entitatively turn into a corner. With the aid of sense, however, it discriminates the existence of this form in actual act, and asserts that it is so. The noetic relation terminates in a distinct existence with which formal identity is achieved. We may call this terminal union a noetic identity, which must be sharply distinguished both from the mere reception of a causal impulse, and from complete existential identity.

The reception of a physical influence is a necessary but not a sufficient condition for sensory awareness. The effect is distinct from its cause. Hence there is no identity at all. No knowledge is involved. In the case of perfect self-union, there is no existential difference. So human knowledge is certainly not involved. Such awareness always includes an aspect of formal identity, and an aspect of existential difference which is responsible for the objective nature of knowledge. This object is known. Formal identity is involved. But it is always known as something other that retains its existential diversity. This fusion of sameness with difference is properly referred to as noetic union or identity.*

This analysis, I believe, is intelligible to anyone whose ontological horizons have been expanded by some phenomenological study, and is generally in accordance with the facts. It needs to be clarified and expanded at many points by further investigations of the facts. Such clarification, refinement, and expansion can be expected of the new philosophy.

---

* Identity as a relation always involves an aspect of duality, which is nevertheless transcended in some way. Thus the duality of S and P in a meaningful proposition is transcended by the oneness of S and P in the intentional object (Veatch, *Intentional Logic,* pp. 156-169). In the same way, the successive incidental differences of a continuous process are transcended by its essential unity. Hence we refer to its identity from beginning to end.

The noetic act exists as an indeterminate relational form, grounded in the knowing agent. The object is determinate and has its own ground. This duality is overcome when the empty relational form is terminated by the object. We find here a peculiar type of relational union, but also that combination of existential diversity together with formal unity which is characteristic of every kind of identity.

PRACTICAL AWARENESS

Heidegger's theory of an original mode of awareness that is neither theoretical nor practical has resulted in an account of the latter. This will have to be abandoned. All knowledge is either one or the other. The distinction is basic, and cannot be overcome without violence to the facts. Practical insight is the more primordial, and comes first in human experience. It has the intentional structure which is essential to all awareness. But the subjective pole of this structure is fused with active tendency, which is always revealed with a peculiar subjective poignancy at the center of the practical horizon.

Thus my feeling of effort is the effort, and my feeling of satisfaction is the satisfaction. But while the experience is dominated by this subjective pole, there is always an objective horizon of existential forces that is also dimly manifested. I am struggling with something opposing me. I am pleased with something I have accomplished. Since these urges belong to my being and are always active as long as I live, my moods and feelings are not subject to the same control as my theoretical reflection, which may be started or stopped more or less at will. I cannot turn my moods on and off in this way. They are always present, revealing existential powers of my world as they really are in relation to my moving appetites and tendencies. This practical awareness never dissociates itself from these subjective urges to attain the absolute emptiness of radical doubt and wonder. The quietistic desire to escape from all action is itself an urge with its own moods and feelings.

All our so-called sensations and feelings are originally fused in this way with appetition. It is only by long training and discipline that some of them may be freed from this bondage, and brought into the service of theoretical reflection. In their original condition, which can never be totally abandoned, they reveal my subjective temporal being, the future which I project ahead of myself, the past I still have and have been, and the present which either separates the two by self-indifference or joins them by authentic choice. They also hazily reveal my situation in the world of active forces that support, weigh down, or frustrate me.

This awareness is fused with tendencies which are unfinished, and shares this indeterminacy with them.

It is concerned not merely with the anticipation of a future, but with its active projection. Unlike theory, it never arrives at a state where alternatives are impossible. As over against theory, its horizons are restricted and its point of view biased. But while it is vague in its apprehension of essence, it gives us a hazy but indubitable insight into the active existence of ourselves and the entities around us. The existential phenomenologists have given us many illuminating insights into this projective awareness, and the primordial world of practice which it reveals. These studies will certainly be continued in the future. But the disparagement and neglect of theoretical awareness must be corrected.

THEORY

Theoretical awareness always comes later in time, and is achieved only with effort and arduous practice. It attempts to gain a detachment from practical concern and situation. This is attained to some degree in what we call a *point of view*. Here the observer tries to free himself from all practical bias, and to remove himself from his limited situation to an external position from which he can apprehend things as they really are. Usually, however, practical presuppositions still remain, and the new position, while less subjective and restricted, is still a human situation. As these perspectives become broader, however, as in disciplined philosophical enquiry, they approach the pure nothingness of radical wonder into which reality can be assimilated as it is without internal warping. As the subjective pole approaches this nothingness of pure indeterminacy, it can give itself more completely to the "object," and can achieve a more accurate union with it.

This union is not existential. The knowing remains relational and detached. It does not as a whole become the object. But it is terminally identified with it,[4] assimilating every essential structural phase with clarity, recognizing its existence, and sharply discriminating its existential mode from others. I cannot be the inner existence of this object. But I can know that it is there. I can grasp whatever structure it may have, and even its active energy from my practical awareness of struggling with it or with similar things. This cognitive union enables me not to become the thing entirely without qualification, but to become the thing in a certain way by terminal identification.

The cognitive indeterminacy from which I start, and which underlies the whole noetic enterprise, is constantly revealed, and enables me to distinguish being as such from nothing. Hence it is most important to recognize that this mode of cognition has no limits. Any being of any sort may become such a "terminal object," including the most intimate phases of subjective existence and practical action. As we have often had occasion to point out, the existentialists have themselves been applying this detached attitude of pure phenomenology to the lived existence of the human subject, with singular success. Heidegger's book is not subjective existence as lived. It is detached theoretical cognition in objective terminal union with the human subject. We cannot find out what practical awareness is by struggling to realize it and use it in striving for a goal of endeavor. Its self-revelation is very vague and confused with alien factors. To find out what it really is, we must gain objective detachment, and examine it with the abstract methods of pure theory.

Unlike practical awareness, such theory is always divided into a subjective and an objective pole. I can distinguish my acts of conceiving and judging from the intentional objects in which they terminate. These intentions (the objects of logic) are dimly revealed in the operations of theoretical insight which focus on the object. But they may be sharply and clearly manifested by further acts of second intention. No range of being is closed to such apprehension. Hence its content is much richer and its horizons broader than those of practical awareness. This occurs automatically, at least at the level of mood and feeling. But theory requires discipline, and is subject to rational control. No "sensations" are originally theoretical. They must be specially trained and adapted before they can function in this seemingly "artificial" context.

Pure theory is not concerned with the active projection of a future ahead of itself, and the fitting of all things into this projective point of view. It tries rather to detach itself from all such frameworks, and to attain an unrestricted perspective from which being can be grasped as it is. Starting in a condition of complete indeterminacy which is open to all alternatives, it seeks for fulfilment in such complete union with its object that other alternatives are excluded. It seeks not to determine its object, but to be determined by it; not to create, but to assimilate. The objects of theory may be stretched out into the future, past, and present, but though its operations are dated, they seek to attain a dateless detachment from which time itself and its many modes may be clearly distinguished and seen as they are. It is for this reason that the great insights of philosophy are indifferent to time, and repeatable in diverse situations.

The phenomenology of theoretical awareness has been neglected. We may anticipate a sustained development of it in the future. In the history of human culture and in the life of the individual person, it comes as a late and fragile growth, requiring leisure from pragmatic tasks and intensive inner discipline. It never occurs in the concrete without practical consciousness, which usually subordinates it to its needs. Although this supremacy of the practical over the theoretical has been defended by Kant and many of the existentialist thinkers, it is almost certainly incorrect.

When judged in terms of pure cognition, the insights of pure theory are more accurate and more adequate than those of practice, which give us only a relative knowledge of the thing in relation to our projects. If we wish to know what the thing is in itself, for example practice, we must turn to theory. In addition to this, the horizons of pure theory are broader and its structural knowledge much clearer. For these reasons, it is evident that practice itself requires theory, if it is to be developed to the most intensive degree. Theory alone can distinguish between ends that are really grounded on nature, and those that are arbitrary projections. It can extend the limits of our practical world by inference and by the observation and study of many objects having no direct connection with practice.

It is from practical awareness that we gain our first, most direct and poignant knowledge of existence. But it never sharply focuses pure structure. Hence without the clarifying influence of theory, it falls into vagueness and confusion. In subordinate modes of technological endeavor, like engineering and animal husbandry, it is theory that guides practice. This is clearly the natural order of subordination. In the direction of individual life as a whole, it is very rare, and those who sometimes approximate to it are regarded as fanatics. In the direction of cultural life, it has never even been approximated. Here practical considerations have always reigned supreme. Probably they always will. We may perhaps hope, however, for an intensive development of pure theoretical anthropology, and those normative sciences that must be based upon it. When this occurs, the sound direction of human action will at least be possible.

A HUMANE AND REALISTIC LOGIC

These theoretical advances will be greatly aided by the development of a genuinely humane logic which will be in close touch with the intelligible reflections of men about the world in which they exist. This new discipline will recognize the intentional structure of those logical tools, such as concepts, propositions, and arguments, by which we understand reality. It will make a sharp distinction between instrumental signs which have an existence and a physical structure of their own, apart from what they signify, and formal signs whose whole being is exhausted in the exercise of their signifying function. These formal signs are the peculiar object of logical study.

It is the function of this discipline, in close cooperation with epistemology and ontology, to study the nature of these intentional tools and the ways in which they must be ordered, if the truth about existence is to be attained. As soon as the existence of formal signs is recognized, instrumental symbols will cease to be the exclusive object of attention. Symbolism and nominalism arise from a failure to recognize the existence of intentional structure in intelligible discourse. It cannot be corrected by *a priori* argument, but only by closer phenomenological attention to the facts. As soon as these facts become evident, certain errors may be corrected, and logic may once again be brought into vital contact with the real reflections of men about reality.

Real definition will be understood as a crucially important

step in the elimination of that vagueness which permeates all the immediate data of experience as they are first given. Both *definiendum* and *definiens* refer to the same structure, and through this to the same class of individuals. But this does not mean that all definition is purely nominal, reducing to a mere equivalence of instrumental signs. There is an important difference between the *definiendum* and the *definiens,* which can be understood only in terms of the distinction between intentional reference and its object. Both sides of the equation signify the same object. But they signify it in very different ways. The *definiendum* refers to it in a way that is vague, unanalyzed, and implicit; the *definiens* in a way that is clear, exact, and explicit. Thus a sound definition is neither a barren tautology nor a contradiction. It is a vital step in the process of gaining insight, a clarification of the intentional mode of apprehension.

When the nature of general concepts, especially the analogous concepts of ontology, has been more exactly analyzed, the so-called paradoxes of logic will be solved without reference to a dubious theory of types which stands in the way of any careful study of the pervasive data of experience. It will be recognized that such intentions are founded on proportional similarities of relational structure, and that they may be self-referential without directly intending themselves. Through its reference to intentional structure in general, there is no reason why "concept" should not refer to itself.[5] With this impediment removed, we may anticipate an intense revival of interest in those relational structures which pervade the immediate data of experience, and which have been so long neglected by the atomistic and nominalistic prejudices of modern "empiricism."

The disciplined investigation of intentional structure which we may expect from the new logic will enable it to distinguish between purely intentional relations like that of subject to predicate, which are the proper object of logical study, and real relations like that of tendency, father-of, and greater-than, which are the concern of different scientific disciplines. The subjectivistic notion that the former must in some mysterious way be isomorphic with the latter will certainly be abandoned. In order to understand reality as it is, we must first separate its distinct phases and then reunite them. To do this, we must carry out certain mental operations, and set up certain intentional relations which have no counterpart in the object, though they may result in the establishment of an intentional identity with this object.

It will be seen that complex relational structure, if it is to be grasped at all, must be grasped by a single complex concept all at once. But the sharp distinction between such a concept and the judgment of existence will also be clearly seen. This is because the act of existing *in rerum natura* never occurs without such structure, but belongs to a different order of being. The mind achieves terminal union with this act only in the proposition that is true or false. The notion that the meaning of a concept is changed in any way by the existence or non-existence of objects in its extension will have to be abandoned. It is only in the proposition that a concept gains such a reference. Existence, of course, has many modes. But every proposition refers to existence in some one mode. When these principles are clearly seen, logic will no longer be plagued by the attempt to reduce categorical propositions to hypothetical enthymemes, which are not propositions at all.

When these confusions are resolved, the new logic may turn its attention to basic questions which call for disciplined consideration. How more precisely is the act of existence apprehended? Is it by a judgment? If so, what is the predicate of such a judgment? Can we formulate such a judgment without making use of the concept, being? What is the status of this concept, and how is it derived? What precisely are the different modes of existing, and how are they expressed by different propositional forms? How, and in what different ways, does a proposition enable its terms to designate real existence? These questions cry out for definite and detailed answers. More light needs to be shed.

The new logic will have to devote intensive effort to the study of those intentional forms by which we apprehend relational structure. It will have to recognize that while categorical assertions can never be reduced to arguments, hypothetical forms are often employed to express relational properties. Many new types of such structure have now been brought into the light. To understand them clearly is of the most extreme importance, not only in the restricted sciences but in ontology as well. The new logic will never confuse these real relations with the logical relations by which they are intentionally known. Hence it will resist the temptation to suppose that the discovery of new types of relational complex must involve new types of inference. Such new types of inference have not yet been shown.

We may also anticipate that the long-neglected intentional distinction between immediate and mediate inference will be revived, refined, and further developed.[6] In immediate inference, we pass to a new symbolic formulation which refers to the same existent fact, whereas in mediate or genuine inference we pass to a new fact not already known, but potentially involved in the premises. Such inference must involve at least two premises and a middle term. One premise must refer intentionally to a causal or tendential relation in reality. The clarification of these facts will certainly require that we abandon the peculiar notion of implication as a mysterious relation holding between two propositions, the real ground of which is vague and indeterminate. The ground of all genuine inference is a causal connection *in rerum natura*. Without this, no inference is possible. Three propositions are required to express such an inference, not two. This much is already clear. But ontology needs to shed more light on these existential connections and the peculiar inductive and hypothetical processes by which they become known.[7]

This must serve as a brief indication of the new developments which may be expected of the intentional logic of the future. This logic will no longer restrict itself to the study of those mechanical procedures which may be found in calculating machines, and which play a subordinate but not a determining role in the referential acts of human awareness. The calculating machine may be marvelously complex and efficient in performing repetitive functions. But in its intricate machinery we find no concepts, no propositions, and no arguments. It knows nothing about the whatness of things, whether they exist, and why. In short, it lacks intentionality.

This extraordinary referential factor pervades all the logical operations of men. These operations may sometimes involve the mechanical manipulation of instrumental symbols. But something more than this is always involved—the attempt to gain an intentional union with reality. Our logic is a vital part of the noetic enterprise of man, and cannot be properly understood in isolation from it. Hence the logic of the future will be a humane logic concerned with the nature of those formal signs and those ways of ordering them which are required for noetic truth about existence.

Since our insight is practical as well as theoretical, the new logic will devote itself to both fields, and will be divided into a logic of practice and a logic of theory. The former will study the signs and signals that are used to express our urges and acts in projecting, desiring, and commanding, and the intentional order of our scheming, planning, and deliberating. This science will have to maintain a close rapport with ethics and philosophical anthropology, a field that has long been neglected. The existentialist phenomenologists have done some spade work here, but for the most part it is unexplored. In the future, it will receive the attention that it deserves.

But practical reasoning cannot be sound unless it is governed by theoretical insight. Hence theoretical logic, which is governed by the norms of truth, will retain its position as the prior discipline. In the future, it will be more clearly understood than ever before that the intentional objects of this discipline cannot be adequately described and analyzed without the aid of ontological insight into the real structures to which they refer, and epistemological insight into those cognitive acts of which they are an essential part.

Even now, we are beginning to grasp the crucial importance of conceptual communication as the necessary foundation for all genuine human communion. We may expect, therefore, that the logic of the future will break with the indifference of the past, and turn its attention to this dark and problematic field. Beginning with the task of concrete phenomenological description, which the existentialists have often met so adequately in other realms, this logic of humane discourse will then attempt to explain the general nature of this mysterious phenomenon, and to describe and analyze its various levels.

CARE

The existentialists have not added much to our knowledge of logic and theoretical awareness. But with respect to practical awareness and the structure of human action, their discoveries have been epoch-making. We have already noted the essentialist drift of modern thought, and its tendency to ignore active tendency and its different modes. So far as action has been recognized, its manifold manifestations have been reduced to that sort of drift or drive from a finished past into a non-existent future that is found in non-human artifacts and things. This over-simplified ontological prejudice has resulted in the fantastic attempt to understand human action without reference to that factor of purpose which everywhere pervades it. This reductive behaviorism is now a marked feature of Anglo-American "psychology." [8]

The phenomenologists of contemporary Europe have not only shown the empirical inadequacy of such conceptions, but have clearly revealed their ground in that traditional neglect of ontological data which goes back to the beginnings of modern philosophy. It is not simply that certain properties of man have been ignored. This would be serious enough. The error is more basic. The very way in which man exists had been misconceived. This distorts and vitiates everything else that we know, which is misfitted into a mistaken framework. The major outlines of this existentialist phenomenology of human action were presented in Chapter IV. We shall now refer only briefly to the salient features of this revolutionary analysis, with a few comments on certain corrections that need to be made.

NEW LIGHT ON HUMAN ACTION

The new phenomenology has shown conclusively that what we call "sensation," "emotion," "mood," and "feeling" originally occur in an active context, and have an intentional structure. To think of them merely as physiological disturbances within the organism is to misconceive and even to decapitate them. Physiological disturbances are doubtless involved, but these are only a partial phase of a complex referential structure that includes

PHILOSOPHICAL ANTHROPOLOGY

much more besides. The intentional object of which I am afraid cannot be examined in a laboratory by quantitative methods. It may not physically exist at all. Such methods are, therefore, wholly inadequate. It exists only as an intentional object of mental anticipation with some ground, fanciful or real, in observable fact. It can be understood only in the light of the future that I have projected ahead of myself.

This projective being, and the moods and feelings attending it, are not open to the quantitative methods of "science," though they may be phenomenologically described and analyzed. On some of these, such as fear, hope, and fidelity, the existentialist analyses have already thrown a much needed light. These methods will certainly be further developed and applied in the anthropology of the future. In the light of such investigations, the so-called results of behavioristic psychology will have to be completely reformulated, and fitted into a radically different framework which can do justice to the known facts.

It is their sensitiveness to pervasive world structure that has enabled the existentialists to focus for the first time the strange and significant feeling of dread. The intentional object of this emotion is no specific thing or event, but my whole lost and distracted being-in-the-world. Because of those last real possibilities which loom before me, I dread this integral existence. The existentialists have given us many diverse versions of this theme. But there can be little question that this strange feeling plays a vital role in human existence, and that it will continue to attract the attention of future anthropologists as the most original and basic form of fear. Heidegger's interpretation of it in terms of authentic future existence, combined with Kierkegaard's brilliant analysis of the allied feelings of melancholy and despair, will probably withstand criticism. The focusing of this philosophic emotion, and the recognition of its moral significance has been a triumph of phenomenological description and analysis.

As we have suggested, Heidegger's attempt to subsume theoretical apprehension under the rubric of care is subject to serious question. But his analysis of self-projection into the future and the threefold structure of care is sound. We must think of this as a brilliant phenomenological contribution to the study of final causation begun in ancient times. It has discovered new ranges of evidence to confirm the theory. If this evidence had been better known in the past, we might have been spared the recent fantastic attempts to interpret human conduct as a complex of purposeless drives and urges. In addition to this, the European phenomenologists have shown that final causation is not something accidental, but is basically ingrained in our being.

Sub-cognitive tendencies are formally determined from behind to move towards a goal that is non-present and non-existent. Human tendencies, on the other hand, move towards a goal that is intentionally present as a phase of our being. Our practical awareness is not confined to a passing present. It can move ahead of us into this projected future, where it may stand firm and guide our present action. The existentialists are certainly right in thinking of this as a primary guiding phase of our existence. We certainly cannot understand a person, or adequately judge him, without gaining some insight into his unfinished projects. Personal existence is something more than a mere succession of passing instants.

The image of the stream of consciousness is wholly inadequate to express it. Every part of the stream is now present. The past and the future are non-existent. But I am not merely my present now. I am also the past that I have been, and the future projected ahead of me. The flow of a stream is formally determined by gravity and its bed. But the flow of my life, so far as it is really human, is guided from the future that I have projected ahead of myself. It is in the light of this future, thus projected and revealed to me, that I choose in the present moment to take over my past in finally decisive action. Heidegger's threefold analysis of care as ahead of itself, as already in the world, as being with, will probably be accepted. I am not a being who may have or dispense with purposes. I am a purposive being.

The existentialist contributions to the phenomenology of death are also of major importance. They have certainly shown the incapacity of naturalistic and pan-objectivistic interpretations to account for the more important existential phases of this mysterious and long-neglected phenomenon. In this sense, death is not something universal. It concerns me as an individual. It is not a replaceable, interchangeable function, but something I must face by myself alone. It is not an event that I will observe in the future, but something that I must either evade or face authentically here and now.

Nothing more clearly indicates the need for expanding our over-simplified and overly-restricted conception of empirical fact. Here is an empirical fact of which I am quite certain, but which I shall never observe. Books on ethics slur over this fact, but the existentialists have cogently demonstrated its profound moral significance, and no conscientious moralist can now afford to overlook their descriptions and interpretations. It is in the light of death that my real existence is most clearly disclosed. In this perspective, I can discern my last unsurpassable possibilities. It is only from this final position that I can see my life as a whole. In so far as it is ever clearly understood, moral integrity will be found to be closely connected with the thought of death. These important insights will certainly be assimilated, clarified, and elaborated in the philosophy of the future.

More question can be raised concerning Heidegger's view of conscience. His rejection of the courtroom theory will almost certainly be accepted. Conscience is not merely a criticism of specific acts after they have once been performed. It is rather a voice that comes from a distance, and calls me to authentic action. It does not talk or argue about this or that, but appeals to my whole being. The sense of distance conveyed by the call easily suggests supernatural interpretations, which Heidegger is probably right in rejecting. It is better to interpret this as coming from my own last possibilities, summoning me to final and decisive effort. The voice of conscience comes out of me from beyond. All this is probably sound.

But the notion of inevitable guilt is far more dubious. This is a reversion to the Puritan ethos and the courtroom scene. But guilt does apply to a specific act and only when it is finished. Then the judgment of guilt is final. Conscience no doubt makes such judgments. But when it calls to me from my projected future, I am not yet finished, and therefore neither guilty nor non-guilty. Certain final possibilities lie ahead of me, though I may die the next minute. Conscience summons me to take over a past that is finite, weak, and already laden with specific guilt. But if I were finally and inevitably guilty, if nothing more could be done, this would not be a call but a voice of judgment. As long as conscience calls, there is still hope. It summons me to final decision that I will abide by unto death. It calls me to authentic action. Here again Heidegger is right.

But this is hard to reconcile with his rejection of any stable principles or norms. The authentic is open to wide ranges of flexibility, but it is certainly not entirely indeterminate. If this were so, it would lose all meaning. Authentic action is not a chaos, but an ordered pattern based upon the structure of human nature. When this order is violated, I am guilty. But until this irrevocably penetrates through the whole of my being, conscience calls me to final action within the limits of natural law, and in accordance with the spirit of man. It is views of this sort that will be thoroughly reviewed, criticized, and refined in the philosophy of the future.

THE SELF AS SUBJECT AND OBJECT

The Sartrian view that choice is the same as awareness cannot be sustained. When the active factor in deliberation is discounted, this leads to a one-sided rationalism in which desire is reduced to a condition of passive servility. When theoretical awareness is disparaged, on the other hand, this must lead to a voluntarism in which reason becomes the servant of projective desire, as in Heidegger and Sartre. Neither of these extreme views is borne out by the facts, which point rather to a complex process of give-and-take to which pure theory, practical reason, and appetite all make important contributions. This intricate process of choice begins with the call of conscience. It can be maintained in a sound condition only by arduous discipline which prevents any one factor from tyrannizing over the rest, and holds all three together in a cooperative "political" union. The important phenomenological studies of Paul Ricoeur [9] have now revealed this process of practical deliberation as the source of that knowledge of myself as both subject and object, united in an existential unity, which is presupposed by all later action and theoretical reflection.

In planning and deliberating, I become aware not of objects

but projects, of myself as I am going to be. This awareness is intentional. I am aware of my project and objectify myself in it. But in this awareness, I am also aware of myself—not from a detached point of view, but now as a practical awareness joined with active striving and seeking, the self that I am. Such an awareness is not completed and clarified by falling into any sort of detached observation. This will rather interrupt or destroy the voluntary act. It can be completed and clarified only by an act of conscious decision which bridges the gulf between a possible project and the self that I am. It is by this pre-reflexive awareness that I know myself as a living existential unity which, because of three defects, I cannot achieve by theoretical reflection alone. Theory apprehends the self (1) only as an object, (2) from which it is permanently detached, and (3) from which it is separated by a time gap. Practical awareness overcomes these defects.

In the first place, it grasps the self not in relation to an alien object, but in relation to a proper project of its own: it knows the self in relation to the self.

In the second place, the conscious act of choice, which decides to enact the project, is not divorced from the project, but by this very act unites with it and accepts it as its own. The self that actively knows *in this way* becomes the self that is objectively known. From this moment on, I recognize the act as my own, both while it is being enacted and after its enactment. Unless I deny myself, I know the act as mine, and am ready to acknowledge it. This is that sense of responsibility, that readiness to answer for my acts, which expresses the basic awareness of myself as a conscious and unified existence.

In the third place, there is no temporal gap between the self that apprehends and that which is apprehended. During the very same interval that I am grasping the project and its enactment, it is being grasped and enacted by me. In this peculiar process, the self that knows and the self that is known are not alien, but united by a firm contemporaneous bond embracing strands of action as well as awareness. It is in this way, not by theoretical reflection, that we become aware of ourselves as unified, active, and conscious beings.

By theory we can know the universal norms of human action

which cannot be violated without the imposition of inexorable natural sanctions, and the spirit of humanity that must guide and pervade authentic life. This pattern, however, is universal and abstract, and leaves vast areas open for creative freedom of choice, not only with respect to means but with respect to intermediate ends as well. In projecting *the* detailed course of action, sound practical judgment, in union with tendency, will follow the general guidance of theory in a complex process of interfusion.

When functioning properly, reason does not issue commands to an obedient slave, nor does appetition make blind leaps into a dark obscurity. It is a process of creative interaction to which each factor makes a contribution that is conditioned by the other. It ends with a final choice in which I take over myself as objectified in the future and the past. Even though overt action may be held in abeyance, it originates at the moment of choice.[10] From this moment on, the person is fully prepared like a lighted fuse, and ready to act decisively at a given signal. More light will be thrown on this process of creative self-projection by the moral phenomenology of the future.

TIME AND HISTORY

Essences are fixed and timeless. The act of existing is dynamic and temporal; hence in our language we express it by verbs which are tensed. The neglect of this ontological factor, and the attempt to reduce it to, or contain it within, a tenseless structure is characteristic of essentialist thought, as we have noted. The existentialists, in rebelling against this abstract intellectualism, have once again raised the fundamental problem of time, which is always the center of active attention when metaphysics is really alive. Different modes of being are characterized by different modes of time. We cannot deal with the one in a disciplined way without also dealing with the other. The existentialist thinkers have not only raised the problem of time; as we have seen, they have developed views of striking interest and originality. Will these views be sustained by a disciplined study of the evidence? Here we must give a divided answer.

HUMAN TIME AND WORLD TIME

Heidegger has certainly shown, in the light of a cogent mustering of evidence, that human existence temporalizes itself in a unique manner. In their authentic modes at least, the three ecstasies of time are not separated from each other in an advancing succession out of the past, through the present, and into the future. They are rather held together in an integral order where each finds a distinctive place. In this order, it is not the past but the future which has priority. It is not the past which precedes the future, but the projected future which precedes the past. Authentic existence comes out of this future to take over the past in the moment of decision.

It is clearly wrong to describe this existence as a succession of discrete nows, in each of which the past and the future are completely non-existent. The past weighs me down and limits me. If I am to act, I must objectify it, hold it, and take it over. It is not a now no longer existent, but something with a peculiar existence of its own which I have been. The future also is not properly understood as a now that is not yet there. Much of what is intentionally stretched before me may never become a now at all. But it is now an essential phase of my being that stretches ahead of me. I can place myself "there," and from this vantage point determine and direct my action. This existential time does not constantly advance with an even flow. Sometimes it is quicker and sometimes slower. Furthermore, it is not going to proceed on and on indefinitely. It is most certainly limited by my death. These facts are indubitable, and they are accessible to all with sufficient patience to investigate them. In a general way, they must be accepted.*

This human temporality, which belongs to our existence, offers a sharp contrast to what we have called world-time. Everything that we know, including ourselves, seems to be involved "in" this universal time. We can visualize it only as a streamlike flow from the past (which is first), through the present, and into

* For an illuminating study and revision of Heidegger's views of time, cf. Maurice Merleau-Ponty, "La Temporalité," *La Phénoménologie de la Perception*, pp. 469-495; and de Waelhens, *Philosophie de l'Ambiguité*, pp. 292-308.

the future. We can describe it only as a succession of nows. A given now may be the fulfilment of a past potentiality, and may be potentially ripe for the future. But the now alone is fully actual. The past which once existed is no longer actual, and the future which may be is not yet. The flow of this world-time is everywhere even and regular. Otherwise our measurement of the different velocities of moving stars and galaxies would be meaningless. Nowhere does this time ever move more quickly or slowly.

Even though it may be impossible for physicists to locate themselves on different moving bodies and measure exactly this regular flux, it must exist. Otherwise their motions would have no beginning, no end, no duration, and would lapse into a blur of indeterminacy. At this moment, all things in the physical universe, however they are moving, are actually contemporaneous, whether or not we can determine this by physical instruments. Furthermore, this world-time is not necessarily finite. So long as anything exists, it will include origin, duration, and destruction, and may flow on indefinitely. This time sweeps everything along in its even passage, including our physical motions, our desires, and our acts of thought.

This world-time is so evident that Heidegger has to grant it some status. As we have seen, he tries to interpret it as an unauthentic debasement of human time, resulting from indecisiveness and laxity. In any case, it is a derivative phenomenon dependent on the more basic mode of human temporality. This subjectivistic contention results from the almost exclusive concern of the existentialists for human reality, and from their general neglect of other modes of being. It may contain some elements of truth. But as it stands, it must be rejected for many reasons.

The main reason is that Heidegger's own exposition of human temporality presupposes the existence of world-time. The future is said to be ahead of me. But without world-time, no sense can be given to this assertion. The future now belongs to my being, and is intentionally present before me. It is ahead of me only as measured by the all-inclusive flow of world-time. It may be present to me in a peculiar intentional sense of presence. But as measured by world-time, it is not yet fully actual, and therefore lies ahead of me. According to Heidegger, I am certain that I shall die. When will this happen? I am now uncertain about this *when*. But sometime it will actually occur at a definite *when* in world-time. I can also anticipate what will happen in this time after my human temporality is finished.

Heidegger, of course, admits that things will still go on after the death of an individual, and even after the death of the race.[11] But this certainly implies that human temporality, peculiar as it may be, is nevertheless included entitatively within the all-encompassing flux of world-time. My acts of projecting the future, remembering the past, and choosing in the present, must unroll in world-time. Thus they can be dated. For all these reasons, the notion that this universal flux can be dismissed as an aberrant mode of human time cannot be accepted. This subjectivistic view will not survive in the future. Non-cognitive being temporalizes itself in the mode of world-time. We ourselves share in this mode of being. Hence our existence also is measured by this time.

THE INTENTIONALITY OF HUMAN TIME

The fact that our existence is measured by world-time does not mean, however, that human existence, in virtue of the intentional powers that belong to it, does not also temporalize itself in another quite distinctive manner of its own. Our theoretical awareness can grasp the tendential structure of things, and, on the basis of such insight, can bring the future before itself in the intentional act of prediction. Such an object becomes present to us in a peculiar relational mode of being to which our nature gives us access. Our practical awareness, working together with desire, can project a personal future ahead of us, and can make it intentionally present in the same way. This projected (not predicted) future is an even more intimate phase of our concrete existence. The entitative act of projecting it occurs in world-time. But the intentional future itself is not yet actual. Of course it is not nothing. But it possesses only that relational mode of being which belongs to the terminal object of an intentional act. Without this act, it would be nothing. But as the objects of such acts, the past and the future do become real for us.

It is through our possession of this cognitive power that we are freed from the chains that bind things and artifacts to a fleeting present moment, and become mobile in time, projecting an objective future ahead of ourselves, and holding on to the past we know we have been. *Entitatively* we are embedded in the steady flux of universal time. But *intentionally* we can wander as we will, and gain access to the past and future which entitatively are not. This temporal mobility is a distinctive phase of our existence, which enters into everything that we do and are. Unless this intentional being is sharply focused, as the new phenomenology has focused it at last, any attempt to understand human action must end in fantastic distortion, reduction, and delusion. The existentialists have shown this by a cogent presentation of concrete evidence.

Human existence is entitatively measured by world-time. But as an intentional being, man possesses a peculiar temporality of his own. This part of the existentialist doctrine is certainly true. It is also true that man possesses a strong tendency to slur over this unique intentional phase of his being, and to misunderstand himself as a complex thing-object wholly immersed in the flux of world-time, like stars and planets, chemical compounds and artifacts. This way of misunderstanding himself, which is as widespread as man, usually has its roots in moral laxity and indecisiveness, and is bound to express itself in ways of existing that are unauthentic and inhuman. This part of the existentialist doctrine is also true.

To think of ourselves as objects wholly immersed in the ceaseless flux of time is certainly a degrading mistake. But we need not pass to the other extreme and deny the existence of world-time. This is also a serious mistake, which will be avoided by the philosophy of the future. Its radical empiricism will force it to serious grapplings with the problems of time and existence. The insights of the new phenomenology will be carefully criticized and refined. When freed from error, they will lead at once to further problems requiring serious and disciplined attention. How are world-time and intentional time related in the being of man? How does he participate in both? There is a sense in which human temporality is entitatively included in the flux of world-time.

But there is also a sense in which world-time, as the object of an intention, is included within intentional time.

Can human temporality transcend world-time? If so, what is the precise nature of this transcendence, and what are its concrete manifestations? How are the parts of world-time linked together? Are these parts punctual nows? If so, what lies between? Does the continuity of world-time imply the notion of a specious present? If so, how are the notorious difficulties of this conception to be overcome? Is there any difference between our conception of world-time as a universal measure, and the actual events of the world process? How is it that these manifold motions and events are subject to a common measure? These basic questions will not be evaded in the future. We may expect that they will elicit ontological doctrines of far-reaching scope. Without the formulation of such metaphysical doctrines, the study of human action must remain a mere stumbling in the dark.

THE HISTORICITY OF MAN

The existentialists have also given us many discerning thoughts on the meaning of history. They are doubtless right in attacking the prevalent view that history is only a special current in the stream of world-time, steadily advancing out of the past into a future of prolific and fascinating novelty. This theory thinks of the past as a stable basis for further development into those novel forms which always attend the motions of life. It even identifies freedom itself with this chance or novelty.[12]

The new phenomenology has called our attention to the fact that this ignores the peculiar intentional being of man which enables him to project his future ahead of himself, and to hold to the past that he knows he has been. From this point of view, human history is this projective future taking over the past, and man himself is not properly viewed as an object immersed in a flux of events. Human being intentionally *is* the future and the past. Hence it is true to say that man's very existence is historical.

The past is not merely a basis for further advance, but an objective burden that our conscious action must take over. Hence it weighs on us and limits us. The future is dark, uncertain, and filled with opposed alternatives between which we must decide.

The present is a terrifying responsibility which we try to evade by running away to an imaginary past or a Utopian future. Automatic progress with respect to such basic existentials as love, hope, and fidelity is certainly a delusion. Hence freedom is not the same as novelty. The most desperate acts of freedom are performed in trying to achieve continuity and repetition, which will at least here and there dam up the all-consuming streams of novelty. These criticisms are certainly justified.

As the existentialist sees it, the historian himself is a part of history, and cannot become detached from his own historicity. His function is not merely to understand a past event as something there that once happened in a moment long since vanished, but rather to understand this event historically as an act with its own futurity, taking over its past in decisive action filled with risk and uncertainty. The so-called "events" of history are not all there, over and gone. They never were all there. They are tinged with the same futurity that still lies before us. It is the duty of the historian to single out those futurities which are genuine, to study their failures and frustrations in the world of the past, to interpret them, and finally to repeat them before his contemporaries in his own thought and action.

This view is sound in many ways, but it suffers from over-simplification. The entitative acts of history are dated in world-time. It is part of the function of the historian to sift the available evidence, and to describe the most important of these acts as accurately as is possible. But the beings who performed them are stretched out into their own past and future. It is an even more essential duty of the historian to interpret this peculiarly human historicity, which was never completed, and is still unfinished. In order to do this, he must be able to distinguish "real" possibilities from those that are unauthentic, to interpret the shattered fragments of those that are still accessible in the past and present of world-time, and finally to show us that these possibilities are relevant to us, and how they may still be repeated.

The critical phase of this process is the distinction between "real" and spurious possibilities. Heidegger makes use of this distinction in his discussion of history,[13] but does not explain it. Such a distinction necessarily implies the capacity of theoretical reason to discover stable norms for human conduct, both individual and social, which are grounded on human nature, and accessible to disciplined investigation. The intelligible judgment and interpretation of history requires the application of such norms. How may we discover them? Many men have thought that they knew. But many were deluded. Do such natural norms really exist? Is our theoretical reason equal to the task of disclosing them? This brings us to the field of ethics where, as we have seen, existentialist thought has been very active.

What are we to think of the moral philosophy of existentialism? Can it be defended? Will it be sustained by the critical empiricism of the future? It is to these questions that we shall now turn.

– 9 –

Realistic Ethics

WE HAVE already called attention to the sharp separation of norms from facts which has marked the course of Western philosophy since the time of Kant. At the present time, this isolationist position is most cogently and persuasively presented to us by the ethical intuitionists. When we examine this position, we note its incapacity to account for the moral phenomena of obligation and justification, which seem to bridge the supposed gulf between fact and norm. In the experience of obligation, I recognize a value. But this is not all. The value is relevant to my concrete existence as I am here and now, and binds me to act. If norms are divorced from fact in an isolated realm of their own, how is this binding power to be explained? The theory does not answer. Furthermore, men seek to justify themselves as they are, and the acts that they have actually performed.

This is a search for values relevant to their existence. Men turn to moral philosophy for disciplined help in carrying on this perennial search. To offer them normative objects to be gazed at—objects having no ground in the facts of life—is not really to help them. It is rather an intellectualistic irrelevance, an academic missing of the point.

This difficulty has led other schools of thought, like utilitarianism and emotivism, to turn to the factual sciences of psychology and sociology. Here, perhaps, we may gain some light on the actual norms that govern men. So the naturalist turns to the diverse patterns of pleasure and interest which may be found among different peoples and tribes. Here are particular objects that men do actually prize, and the task of ethics is simply to describe and to analyze these interests with the help of psychology and anthropology. This view leads to a sterile and confusing relativism. Furthermore, it does not account for obligation, a fact which needs to be explained. Because men happen to desire something, it does not follow that they ought to desire it. To observe an interest theoretically from a detached point of view, either in myself or in another, is not to feel the peculiar subjective urgency that belongs to an obligation.

This difficulty has led others to the theory of emotivism, which identifies obligation with the immediate feeling of urgent appetition which may be proclaimed by the use of expressive language. But this is of little help in accounting for justification. Certainly I cannot justify a desire by merely proclaiming its urgency. Justification is universal and intelligible to all men. It involves the cognitive use of reason, and the assertion of propositions that may be true or false. Furthermore, the difficulties of a subjectivistic relativism are not diminished by making it even more extremely irrational than it already is. Where are we to find norms that can hold all men under real obligation, and which are grounded on observable facts?

The realistic tradition of natural law was submerged by idealism during the last century, but now once again it is being revived. This is a unique type of moral theory, sharply distinct from intuitionism, Kantianism, naturalism, and emotivism.[1] It is the only realistic moral theory that has been persistently cultivated in our Western tradition from classical times to the present day. In the current confusion of ethical thought, it can give us genuine help and guidance, largely because of the sound ontology which underlies it.

According to this theory, good and evil are not fixed properties or qualities, but modes of existing. The fulfilment of essential needs and tendencies is good. That of incidental desires and interests is also good, provided they do not obstruct the former. The warping and obstruction of essential needs and coordinate interests is evil. To exist in a condition of ordered activity is good; to exist in one of disordered frustration is bad. This theory bridges the supposed gulf between fact and value. It discloses norms that are grounded on those incomplete tendencies which constitute the active existence of man.[2] Hence it is not subject to the difficulties which arise from the intuitionist separation of fact from value.

It recognizes an active subjective urgency that belongs to the tendency working within us and propelling us to action. Hence, unlike naturalism, it can give an intelligible account of obligation. But it shows us that the direction of these tendencies is determined by a formal structure of human nature that is shared in common by all men. This structure is open to observation. That general pattern of human action which is always required for the active realization of this nature, the natural law, is subject to rational investigation and analysis. Such analysis, in fact, is required for the sound guidance of individual and social action. Hence this theory is not subject to the objections which have been urged against relativism and the extreme irrationalism of emotive ethics.

In the context of modern thought, it is a radically novel point of view which can shed much needed light on the burning problems of the contemporary world. It is no wonder that it is now receiving world-wide attention, and that the classic texts in which it has been most carefully formulated and expressed are once again being studied with care.

This realistic ethics will admit of no synthesis with views (like utilitarianism and emotivism) which find no stable ground for norms beyond variable pleasures and propensities, nor with those (like intuitionism) which assert a radical separation of goodness from existence. What is its relation to existentialism? The classical and Christian origins of Kierkegaard's thought would seem to make an affirmative answer at least possible.[3]

EXISTENTIALIST ETHICS AND NATURAL LAW

Is there a sense in which the seemingly opposed positions of existentialist ethics and natural law supplement each other? Is a genuine synthesis possible? We shall divide our discussion of these questions into the following sections: essentialism and existentialism in ethics; classical ethics; existential norms; the possibility of a realistic synthesis; and the ethics of the future.

ESSENTIALISM AND EXISTENTIALISM IN ETHICS

Recent study of the classics has revealed a marked essentialist trend in these works which was not clearly noticed before. This trend is incidental and not required by the ontological structure revealed by realistic analysis. According to this view, every finite being is constituted by two vectorial principles: essence, which determines it and marks it off from other entities, and the act of existing, which expresses itself in active tendencies. Man is no exception. He also possesses a specific human nature that determines the direction of his existence. Authentic human action, therefore, will be subject to two sorts of limiting conditions or norms.

In the first place, man is under an obligation to perform those acts which are required to realize the physical, intellectual, and social needs that belong to him by nature. He may, of course, fail to perform such acts. But since these needs are inescapable, he is then subject to natural sanctions. If health is neglected, he will suffer from disease. If education is neglected, he will suffer from confusion and ignorance.

But in the second place, he is also under an obligation to perform these acts in a free and spontaneous manner which agrees with the mode of existing open to him, and with its external limiting conditions. Since these conditions also are inescapable, any failure to act in this way will be followed by inexorable sanctions. Thus if voluntary freedom is neglected, he will be subject to the sanctions of servility or rebellion. Each human individual is constituted not only by a limited essence, but also by a limited mode of existing. Each of these imposes upon him certain norms and sanctions which he ignores at his peril.

In any real entity, essence and existence, of course, are intimately fused. Each has being only by virtue of the other. Authentic human existence involves not only a determinate pattern of action, but its concrete realization in the world. In actual life, it is impossible to separate the actualization from what is being actualized. These two phases of concrete existence, however, are

really distinct (though inseparable), and can be isolated by rational analysis. Furthermore, as we have pointed out, it is the
essential structure that is more intelligible and more readily focused by the human intellect. It is not surprising, therefore, that
in the early history of classical ethics it was this phase of determinate structure that was first clearly grasped.

This earlier ethics gave us a disciplined analysis of human
nature, distinguished its major capacities, and clarified the hierarchical order of subordination required for normal functioning.
It formulated a clear conception of the ideal human life which
was of lasting significance. But it paid less attention to those
fragile existential processes and acts of choice, by which alone this
structure can be realized in concrete history, and the inescapable
barriers which limit them. Classical ethics laid such an emphasis
upon the hierarchical order of functions and duties that it neglected the free mode of existence, which is required if these are
to be performed with existential authenticity. It was too oblivious to autocracy and benevolent forms of tyranny that left the
natural order intact.

Since the time of the late Middle Ages, this failure has been
recognized, and has brought forth various movements for the
elimination of restraints on personal liberty. This existential
freedom, however, was never coherently analyzed and integrated
with the genuine insights of classical thought. It was conceived as
an anarchic antinomian force, rejecting all fixed limits, and entirely opposed to the ordered conceptions of ancient thought.
The essence of man was thus set at odds with that free existence
which alone can actualize it. This suicidal conflict has had a
tragic history in post-Renaissance life and thought. Modern man
has been presented with a fatal dilemma. He may choose either a
natural law and rational order, which crushes out all human
freedom, or a lawless liberty that knows no rational bounds. Each
of these extremes has been closely approximated many times over
in the course of modern life.

Philosophers, watching this suicidal struggle, have been led to
conclude that there are no genuine norms with a basis in nature.
Existence as such is blind, chaotic, and indifferent to value, which
is an arbitrary creation of man. Ontology has been abandoned as

an outmoded relic of antiquity, and any conception of a universal ethics has been discarded as a naive delusion of fanatics. No disciplined effort to describe existence and its varying modes was undertaken. The assumption underlying all these views is that existence is a surd and unintelligible factor, entirely opaque to rational description and analysis.

This modern dogma is also shared by many of the existentialist thinkers. They maintain that subjective existence, and, in particular, the free act of existing, is ineffable, surd, and even absurd. But in spite of these repeated declarations, they have managed to give us intelligible descriptions of its manifold manifestations, and of its inexorable limits. They have at last shed rays of light into this abyss of obscurity, and have begun to undermine a traditional dogma so long encrusted in modern thought that it is hard for them to grasp the real significance of what they are doing.

To those, however, who can view their work with some detachment, it is clear that they have shed some light on the acts and modes of human existing. We cannot shed light on anything without coming to understand something of the norms which govern its authentic being. The classical analysis of human nature revealed certain natural laws and norms founded on this determinate nature. The new existential ontology has now begun to reveal certain norms of another kind—norms based on the limited modes of human existing. These relational existential norms are the inner core of the existentialist ethics. They are all embodied in the concept of authentic existence which has now emerged, and which we have already studied.

What is the precise moral significance of this concept? Can it withstand careful criticism? Is it complete and self-sufficient? Let us now attempt to deal briefly with these important questions.

CLASSICAL ETHICS

We have already pointed out that it is impossible to attain a complete separation of essence from existence, even in thought. Nevertheless, we are able to focus the one as over against the other, and thus to achieve, on the one hand, an essential perspective on some being; or, on the other hand, an existential perspective which reveals significant differences. We may reduce these differences to three.

In the first place, essence is determinate. It marks a thing off, and separates it from other entities of a different kind. Existence, on the other hand, is indeterminate and diffusive. It binds one entity to others by action and passion. When we regard man from an essentialist point of view, therefore, we see all his acts and relations as springing from his intrinsic nature, and tend to ignore those external beings to which he is existentially bound, and which implacably limit his action. To focus these extrinsic bonds and limits, we need to grasp his existence.

In the second place, we must note that the most intelligible phase of the human essence is not singular but universal. From this point of view, we think of man in general, not of the weak and fragile individual who exists. This universal essence is also necessary, in the sense that it must be possessed by any individual man. In such a perspective, the dependence and contingency of the human person is masked.

Finally, existence is active and tendential; whereas essence is quiet and inactive. Essential categories are fixed traits and structural properties. Existentials, on the other hand, are modes of acting. When we look at man in this way, we focus not so much *what he is* as *how he acts*.

Classical ethics was based on an essentialist view of human nature. Existentialist ethics is based on an existentialist view. As a result of this, it has revealed new existential norms never clearly focused before.

Classical philosophy knew of practical reason,[4] and gave us a disciplined analysis of it as a cognitive faculty rooted in the nature of man. But it did not study the active modes by which this power realizes itself in ordering a *world* of things and artifacts. As a distinct faculty, it may belong exclusively to us. But its active realization puts us in relation to a vast field of surrounding entities, ordered together within a world structure that is an unavoidable phase of our existence. This being-in-the-world was ignored by classical thought which, on the whole, regarded external things from a theoretical point of view, and made no sharp distinction between the thing as it simply is, and the thing as it is for practice. It distinguished between true art and false art, moral virtue and depravity, as these affect the human agent. But it never focused the way in which these so-called virtues and vices are intentionally involved in all the objects of our concern, and how they are reflected in an unauthentic and an authentic being-in-the-world.

In this respect, the existentialists are more rationalistic than their realistic ancestors. We cannot live well without a decisive insight into the order of the world in which we exist, an awareness of our own role in establishing this order, and a sharp sense of the radical difference between persons who possess this cognitive power, and things which have no world of their own, but inertly exist without thought or self-direction.

The ancients knew of the social needs of man. They recognized him in general as a political animal. Their intentional logic enabled them to give a coherent account of theoretical communication which is basically sound. We still have much to learn from their illuminating descriptions of justice and friendship in general. But personality is an existential category, not a set of properties and traits. It is a way of existing in freedom and love, rather than a kind of function to be performed. No matter what I am doing, I may do it in personal freedom or in an impersonal routine. The essentialist perspective of the ancients, which led them to concentrate on the analysis of human nature in general, prevented them from sharply grasping this distinction. It is implicit in many of their discussions, but they never revealed it with unmistakable clarity and distinctness.

No matter how necessary a function that an individual is performing may be, if he does not do it spontaneously from free choice, something is lacking. Classical philosophy saw many specific traits and faculties that mark us off from the brute animals. But to achieve authentic human existence in the concrete, these abstract faculties must be realized in an authentic personal mode. The ancients recognized this only implicitly. Hence they never clearly focused the danger of that collapse into impersonal anonymity, which is the major problem of our time, and which the existentialists have analyzed with such penetrating clarity. In spite of our rational nature, we may live and exist like machines.

The ancients knew that our human faculties and our human nature in general were strictly finite. But they paid less careful attention to the inexorable barriers which threaten and limit our fragile existence. No sharp distinction was made between situation and point of view, problem and mystery. We find a most penetrating analysis of chance and fortune in Aristotle's *Physics,* but later on it was diluted and qualified by theories of providential determinism. Suffering, conflict, and guilt were not clearly focused as barriers which the individual must face as a result of his own decisions. With the coming of Christianity, they were regarded as religious problems, and were removed from the field of philosophical ethics. In the *Phaedo,* Plato has given us a poignant and revealing study of personal death which suggests many of the existentialist themes. These themes were also developed and refined in the Christian tradition, but they were not sustained in secular moral thought. The authentic facing of these existential limits, as over against impersonal evasion, was not clearly focused and dealt with in a disciplined way among the classical moral virtues and vices.

EXISTENTIAL NORMS

The existentialist analysis of awareness is basically realistic, as we have already noted. Phenomenological procedures presuppose a capacity to understand human existence as it actually is. Furthermore, the references to awareness as a process of revealing and disclosure make little sense without the tacit assumption that we exist with others in a world many facets of which we may know as they really are. Sartre is most explicit in clearly stating this underlying realistic doctrine, and in attempting to justify it. This attempt, as we have seen, is neither altogether clear nor coherent. It is especially weak on theoretical awareness. Traditional realistic theory is far more intelligible, and is more firmly grounded in a disciplined analysis of accessible facts. But in spite of these weaknesses, the existentialists have called our attention to certain aspects of practical awareness which have never been clearly noticed before. For example, their accurate descriptions have unmistakably revealed the intentionality of its operations.

Our decisions and projects are not isolated events locked up inside of a subjective agent. They refer to a world of objects that is always revealed, either unauthentically or authentically. The plans and projects of individual persons and cultures do not merely differ as internal acts. They involve different ways of ordering the world. In the practical issues of human life, it is not merely forces but opposite worlds that are clashing. The human individual is not a self-enclosed substance with certain relations incidentally attached to it. His very being is intentional in structure. His existence in the world is determined by his projects. This has never been so clearly seen before. Moods and feelings have been regarded as inner passions or disturbances due to the working of physical causes. The new phenomenology has shown the inadequacy of this widely-accepted point of view. These moods and feelings are intimately connected with our projects, and like them possess an intentional structure of their own, which may be described and analyzed in a disciplined way that has never been attempted before.

Certain norms involved in these newly-revealed structures have now become quite clear. If we are prepared to listen to it, true theory may be of great assistance to us in authentically organizing our practical world. But whether or not we receive its aid, we are responsible for this world order; and it is a responsibility very hard to bear. Phenomenological analysis has now shown many ways in which this responsibility is commonly avoided. One of these is a rigid determinism, emanating from theoretical misconceptions, but strongly supported by existential weakness and lethargy. Thus men run away from their freedom by thinking of themselves as things externally moved by a reign of universal cosmic law. They constantly seek to justify outworn schemes of value by assuming that they are supported by divine sanction or an imagined natural order. These evasions have now been carefully observed and described. Natural law would have been defended far more effectively in the past if these phenomena had been better known.

Freedom first manifests itself to us in the peculiar feeling of dread, whose object is not some innerworldly threat, but the whole unauthentic structure of our everyday being-in-the-world. As I catch a glimpse of the real possibilities open to me, all this becomes suddenly cloudy and meaningless. We tend to reject this first indication of freedom as something neurotic and morbid. But the new phenomenology has presented us with cogent evidence to show that this also is an attempt to escape from freedom. Dread is the most original and authentic form of fear—the fear for our genuine existence. Here is a well-founded existential norm, not clearly noticed or described before the time of Kierkegaard.

The new analysis of human care as involving the three ecstasies of time—future, past, and present—is a discerning contribution to the ontology of man—a contribution which has also suggested important existential norms not hitherto clearly focused. There is an authentic as well as an unauthentic mode of caring, which are sharply opposed. Authentic existence recognizes its own finitude, and projects itself to the final end. This future takes over the past in a moment of decision which holds the ecstasies together with wholeness and integrity.

Unauthentic existence temporalizes itself in a very different way. The ecstasies disintegrate into a succession of discrete nows. As time goes by, we may lose ourselves in imagining a Utopian future or an idyllic past, but in either case the real moment escapes us, and our action wobbles and vacillates, or else sinks into an inflexible routine.

It is by decision alone that we cut ourselves off from this endless postponement. Such existence holds itself to a final future with fixed integrity, and is free and flexible in the given situation. Ethics is here concerned with the radical being of man. Moral character is expressed in the mode of temporalization. It is also expressed in the way we understand and live our history.

Human history is not to be accurately understood as a mere succession of nows proceeding from the past into the future. This rests on a debased view of man, which in turn leads to further unauthenticity. Even when we forget them, the three modes of time are integrally fused, and cannot be separated without doing violence to being. The past is still unfinished, and we cannot understand it properly without grasping the real possibilities that were and still are fused within it. To grasp these possibilities is to make up our own minds, and to take a stand. History is a discipline of freedom which elicits choice. Novelty inevitably emerges from the great time stream, which finally devours both ourselves and all our works. Freedom does not lie in abandoning ourselves to its ceaseless flux of the ever new. It lies rather in standing firm, not clinging stubbornly to past events now over and out of place, but in holding tightly to the real future that has been transmitted to us by living traditions, and realizing them, so far as we are able, in the new situations facing us. Here also is an existential norm.

In their analyses of conscience, the new phenomenologists are not interested in what conscience says. They are interested in it rather as a dynamic mode that lasts throughout life, and which may be maintained in authentic and unauthentic ways. The original phenomena, when closely studied, indicate that it is the call of our distant care, ahead of ourselves, from which we have become lost and alienated. It summons us to arouse ourselves, and to grapple with time before it flows past. To think of it as an *ex post facto* judgment on isolated acts and omissions is a serious restriction of its full, positive significance. This existentialist suggestion takes us beyond the interpretation of Socrates, who thought of conscience as a negative warning voice. It will be seriously criticized and examined by the philosophy of the future.

It is from their painstaking analysis of the phenomena of choice that the existentialists have derived what they consider to be the most basic norms of ethics. Here also they are not concerned with the actual content of what is chosen. They are interested rather in the ways we choose, and in the existential norm that emerges from this distinction. Authentic choice is mine. I must know that I am choosing, and bear the responsibility for it. In so far as external factors have influenced me, its significance is diminished. Furthermore, this mode of choice must concern possibilities that are thought through to the very end. If I choose only within certain limits for this time or that, I am letting something else make the last determination for me, and am not pressing myself to the final limit. It is only by projecting myself to this final future, and choosing it to take over the objective past I have been, that I can achieve any real integrity. These ways of holding myself in being through time are independent of all specific content.

This is true of all the norms we have just considered. They are not determinate traits or properties. They are existential norms, ways of being that are active and dynamic, and must be maintained through the whole of life. Furthermore, these norms are not invented or constructed by man. They are grounded on human existence itself, its necessary modes and limits. This existence is authentic when it really is itself. It is unauthentic when warped or deprived. This is certainly a realistic conception. Imaginary, constructed values are no good at all. Real goodness lies in achieving, acting, and existing.

Finally, it is noteworthy that each of these norms includes a theoretical as well as a practical component, a way of understanding as well as a way of acting. Thus I cannot authentically be with others unless I understand them as persons, and sharply distinguish between persons and things. I cannot authentically temporalize myself without having some true feeling for the integral structure of human time, though this feeling may never become conceptualized. Thus sound insight and action reinforce each other. The same is true of their opposites. The more I misunderstand myself as a mere thing in time, the more degraded my action becomes, and vice versa. In theory, we may separate awareness from action. But as phases of our being, they are closely fused and interdependent.

This general conception of the existential norm will almost certainly be accepted by the philosophy of the future. Many of those we have considered will also be accepted after disciplined criticism. But are these norms self-sufficient? Can they really stand alone?

THE POSSIBILITY OF A REALISTIC SYNTHESIS

Freedom is not a natural but an existential norm. It is not an ordered set of determinate tendencies, but a way of realizing them in the concrete that is peculiar to man. It is grounded in the human act of existing, and its limits have now been described with great accuracy and penetration. As a result, we have been presented with the most lucid and profound analysis of the norm of freedom that has been developed in modern times. Because of essentialist trends of thought, this norm was not clearly focused in ancient times, and remained only implicit in classical thought. This neglect was reflected in the philosophical acceptance of the institution of slavery, with certain qualifications, and in the failure to see the danger of feudal autocracy and oppression.

When the modern rebellion came, it was supported by an antinomian conception of freedom that was often formulated in conscious opposition to classical rationalism and natural law. This abstract ideal of an unrestricted freedom has ignored certain rights and duties founded on human nature. This has called forth the vigorous reaction of Marxism, which has gone to the opposite extreme of giving such an exclusive weight to material rights that freedom is almost completely submerged. But its criticism of the abstract liberal ideal has been urged with deadly effect. As the ancients well knew, freedom cannot be achieved without regard for the essential needs of human nature. As the Marxists point out, the starving and the uneducated cannot be free.

Existentialism is a profound and searching statement of this liberal ideal. Like other modern statements, it is marked by a strong antipathy to theoretical reason and the stable norms of natural law. The setting up of such principles is interpreted as an attempt to evade responsibility, and their enforcement (in agreement with Hobbes and Locke) as an undue restriction of freedom. But in spite of this professed anti-rationalism, the phenomenological procedure is clearly theoretical. This has led to a more accurate description of the fragile, contingent existence of man, and to a clearer analysis of freedom and its natural limits. On the basis of this existential analysis, perhaps the most accurate that has yet been given, we are able to see with striking clarity not only the strength but the weaknesses of the liberal ideal, and the supplementary insights it requires to become self-sufficient and defensible.

We may grant that the world of practice is ordered with reference to our chosen projects. But we do not need to grant that this choice is necessarily ungrounded and arbitrary. This human world really exists in relation to us, but it is included within the all-encompassing reality of the world itself, which is accessible only to the methods of detached observation and theory. Such insight is required for the sound direction of our free choices. The existentialists themselves have demonstrated this by their penetrating descriptions of human existence and the normative inferences they have drawn, which are clearly grounded on these. Practical reason without theory cannot clearly understand itself, and becomes confused and capricious.

Certain structural differences between persons and things have been analyzed before. But the new phenomenology has focused other profound differences in the modes of temporalization, and has shed further light on the whole distinction. It must not be forgotten, however, that this has been done by a descriptive procedure which makes use of universal concepts and judgments. The theory of practice is theory, not practice. By their persistent attack on theory, the existentialists are undermining the ground on which they themselves stand. This attack is an unfortunate confusion which certainly requires correction. Their illuminating studies of practical reflection and projection need to be supplemented by similar studies of theoretical reflection and its complex relations with practice. Such studies are needed to shed even a minimum light on the neglected topic of communication, and on that human mode of being-with which the existentialists have rightly accepted as a brute datum, but as yet have signally failed to clarify.

They have cogently described certain barriers which inescapably limit our existence. We have pointed out that some of these, like necessary guilt, are open to question. But on the whole, these descriptions are accurate. Why is existence thus limited? As such, it is not restricted to any specific determinations. Otherwise, it could not be shared by entities of radically different kinds. The ultimate source of these limits must, therefore, lie in the determinate nature of man. It is this nature which pins our existence down, and subjects it to inexorable conditions. It is not existence as such that condemns us to human freedom and to death. It is rather the human nature we bear that determines the mode of our being, and sets the ultimate boundaries. The existentialist study of these boundaries needs to be connected with an exact analysis of this common nature, which has not yet been realized.

Human existence temporalizes itself in a most distinctive manner. Much new light has been shed on the way in which the three ecstasies of time are held together, and on the peculiar priority of the future. These are welcome additions to the classical theory of final causation. It is true that our very existence is historically and temporarily "stretched." But the intentional nature of this "stretching" has not been sufficiently clarified. Here the classical view has something to contribute. Furthermore, it is important to understand that while we have our own mode of human temporality, we also participate in a universal world-time. It is "in" this time that we hold the past and project the future. It is in this time that the present moment is really passing. The existentialists have ignored world-time and its relations with human temporality. As we have seen,[5] many problems cry out for solution. A close study of the intentional structure of human memory and projection is a prerequisite for any basic clarification.

New light has also been shed on the way in which conscience calls from the future to the existing individual person. We have been told that it is more than a critical judge; that it summons us to authentic action. There is no doubt some truth in these suggestions, but they are incomplete as they stand. They tell us nothing of *what* conscience says. This is an indeterminate ethics with no specific content. Surely my conscience tells me something. It does not call me merely to action, but to action of a certain kind. The existentialists give us no help here. No doubt they will say that the content must differ from culture to culture and from individual to individual, depending on their historic situations and circumstances. But this is merely to relapse into a chaos of relativism, which is incompatible with the existence of ethics as in any sense a rational discipline. The existentialists have described certain modes of action that are everywhere and for everyone authentic. Can we believe that these existential norms are lacking in all structure—that they have no connection with the formal traits that make us human? This is hard to believe.

The ethics of the future will struggle to fill this gap, and will almost certainly look for aid and guidance in fulfiling this essential task to the great realistic tradition of natural law. The goal set before us is not merely to exist, but to exist in the most intensive way as human beings. Existential norms are not fixed properties. That is true. But neither are they blind acts. They are ways of existing whose structure is rooted in our nature. Why is it that authentic existence is stretched into the future and the past? Because of the intentional cognitive power that we possess by nature.

The existentialists have certainly deepened our understanding of the crucially important phenomenon of choice; but in this field also their theories are marred by a certain weakness. Heidegger tells us that we should be guided by our real possibilities, and should choose them rather than spurious counterparts. But he never explains this important difference. How are we to distinguish the one from the other? We are to make a final choice involving the whole of our being. But when we ask what kind of life, then, is worthy of such devotion, we are left with a shrug of the shoulders. What we choose apparently does not matter.

This assertion is extremely dubious. The kind of act we choose does matter. It is easy to find muddled fanatics who have embarked with whole-souled commitment upon hairbrained schemes which they find in the end to have brought untold misery, not only upon themselves but upon their fellow men as well. This lack of specific principle gives to the whole existentialist ethics a strange quixotic tinge that has often been noted.[6] Like certain versions of Kantian ethics, it is wholly formal in structure, and lacks material content. This content could be supplied by the classical ethics of natural law, to whose realistic structure existentialism is closely allied. Such a synthesis of existential and natural norms will doubtless be attempted in the future.

THE ETHICS OF THE FUTURE

If civilization survives the crises of our troubled time, we may expect the discipline of ethics to be intensively developed and cultivated in a manner that is without precedent. Without rational guidance, freedom withers away. Hence we may expect it to be expressed in many literary forms, and taught in both high school and university at different levels of complexity. This is not the place, of course, to attempt any detailed exposition. But we may hazard a few guesses concerning the structure of the new ethics, based on the living trends of thought we have been studying.

Men are no longer interested in norms that are invented by themselves, or in norms that are supposed to inhabit a special realm of their own, divorced from the facts of nature. We can anticipate with some confidence that the new ethics will be concerned with norms that are grounded on observable facts. The physicalist view of human nature may survive for some time in areas where science continues to be confused with philosophy, and uncritically worshipped as the only path to knowledge. But for all those who are capable of an unbiased study of the empirical data as they are given, and their number must increase if free culture is to survive, this age of quantitative idolatry is past.

There is, of course, a physical phase of human nature. Men are bodily beings. This will be clearly recognized. But there is a cognitive factor which is not open to quantitative methods of investigation and which is equally important. This will also be clearly recognized and studied by those methods of phenomenological description and analysis to which it is open. Men possess a common nature which determines the general direction of essential tendencies. But the realization of these tendencies, which is the object of ethical concern, has conditions of its own. The ethics of the future will, therefore, direct its attention to existential as well as to natural norms.

It will aim at discovering not only what natural need must be satisfied, but how it can be satisfied in a free and authentic manner as well. Natural law must be reconciled with existential freedom. A mere addition of the two will be insufficient. The two traditions must be united. Only such an integral synthesis of what is really best in our Western tradition will provide us with a sound and disciplined answer to Marxism. Many insights of the new phenomenology will be refined and developed in this realistic philosophy of freedom.

But the classical analysis of man will certainly be retained, at least in its major divisions. We cannot escape from the fact that our nature is originally endowed with powers of theoretical apprehension, self-projection and choice, and capacities for sensory desire of many different kinds. A careful examination of these powers clearly indicates that natural order of subordination which is expressed in the conception of the cardinal virtues. Reason is clearly the most far-reaching and penetrating of our cognitive faculties. Hence wisdom has the first place amongst the virtues. Under its guidance, the choice-making power should render to each being its due with justice, and persist in its rationally charted course through every danger and obstacle with courage. The many drives and interests to which our nature is susceptible must be allowed their proper place, but under the deliberate control of temperance, which fits them into our rationally chosen projects.

The traditional classification of the appetites will no doubt have to be changed in certain respects, but the Aristotelian description and analysis of certain passional virtues will be retained intact. As long as men exist on the earth, they will be concerned with money and material things, with honor and self-respect, and finally with their fellows. Unless these tendencies are brought under rational control, they will lead us to obsession and disaster. Hence the classical virtues of generosity, greatness of soul, and friendliness will never be out of date. This general pattern of action is grounded on human nature, and will certainly be allotted a central position in the new ethics, together with a considerable amount of the descriptive material and interpretation which has been developed in the past. But the moral necessity of realizing this pattern as a free projection, under the limited conditions of human existence, will also be more clearly recognized than ever before. Here the new ethics will draw on the factual insights of modern phenomenology.

More emphasis will be placed on the active factor in moral deliberation, and on the need for creative originality in the ordering of rational projects. These projects will not be viewed as incidental additions to a substantial being already there, but rather as an essential phase of an unfinished personal existence. Their intentional structure will also be more clearly envisaged with their objective correlate in the structure of the personal world of action.[7] As the free person orders his projects, so is the order of the world in which he exists. Different types of world structure, both authentic and debased, will be studied and analyzed. But the need for the guiding light of theoretical reflection will also be sharply stressed.

Real possibilities will be clearly distinguished from those that are spurious, on the basis of natural law. A real possibility is one which agrees with the essential structure of our nature, and the pattern of action required to fulfill it. A spurious or unauthentic act is one which conflicts with what is essentially human and unworthy of the spirit of man. No claim will be made for moral omniscience or a casuistic omnicompetence. But the capacity of disciplined moral reflection to offer sound and relevant guidance to all individuals, whatever their circumstances, will be cogently defended.

The suggestions of recent research concerning the positive role of conscience in calling the person to decisive choice of his real possibilities will probably withstand criticism, as will also the close relation between moral integrity and the thought of death. No study of ethics will be complete without a careful consideration of human mood and feeling, and especially of the peculiar emotion of dread, which is so rich in moral significance. In this field, the preliminary work of the existentialists will certainly be most carefully sifted, developed, and refined.

Of all the cardinal virtues, it is courage that stands most in need of reinterpretation and revision. The classical accounts of this virtue are dominated by political and militaristic conceptions which are now dated and irrelevant to contemporary life. We have reached the point where either war or civilization itself must vanish. So if there is to be any ethics in the future, it will have to purge courage of those belligerent and provincial elements with which the classical accounts are unfortunately loaded. But this, of course, does not mean that courage itself is passé. An even higher place will certainly be allotted to personal courage in the scale of natural values. Its essential role in firmly facing death and the other boundary situations will need to be strongly emphasized.

But the desperate need for maintaining personal choice and autonomy in a world increasingly threatened by the standardized thoughts and responses brought forth by the webs of technology will constantly be brought to the attention of students, young and old. Without sacrificial zeal and devotion in meeting this threat, authentic existence will wither away. In this area, the existentialist literature is filled with precious insight.

This new ethics will attempt to combine in an integral synthesis the solid structure and rich content of the classics with the spirit of freedom which dominates the best moral thought of modern times. The penetrating insights of the new phenomenology—being-in-the-world, boundary situations, the priority of the future, conscience as a call, human integrity in the light of death, and final choice—will all be taken up into this synthesis. But they will be given a firm and solid structure grounded on the nature of man. Mere commitment is not sufficient. It makes a great difference what it is to which I am committed. Some light on my responsibilities as a human person can be shed by the disciplined study of human ontology. It is to these that my conscience calls me; for these that I feel dread.

When these facts are clearly recognized, the aura of ultimate relativism, fanaticism, and absurdity which has so far weakened and confused the existentialist literature will finally be removed. This will be an ethics of human freedom, authentic existence in the pursuit of grounded choice. It will not be the ethics of an unlimited and inhuman liberty, of supposed integrity in the pursuit of a quixotic whim. Such an ethics cannot be precisely developed and cogently defended without the close cooperation of such allied disciplines as ontology, epistemology, and a genuinely humane and realistic logic.

In social ethics, we may hope for a parallel development; though in this field, as we have noted, existentialist thought has so far been quite sterile because of its lack of a humane logic, and a resulting incapacity to deal with the processes of communication which underlie the social existence of men. The realistic tradition has much more to offer in these fields, and we may expect a profound re-examination and development of these suggestions in the near future. But the essentialist trend that has so far marked the history of this tradition has prevented it from doing justice to the claims of personal freedom.

The social philosophy of the future will certainly make a serious and persistent attempt to correct this fault. In order to do this, the basic insights of natural law must be united with those of our liberal social philosophy. The possibility of such social philosophy, in which the best thought of the West may be soundly and clearly integrated, is indicated by the recent United Nations Declaration of Human Rights. This Declaration includes the material rights emphasized by Marxists, the rational rights to information and education found in classical thought, as well as the rights of personal liberty, participation in the formulation of public policy, protection from violence, fair trial, etc., which have dominated modern political thought.

Material rights and duties are founded on the human body and its needs, rational rights on the intellect, political rights on the human capacity for choice, and the right to work and social status on the social nature which each person shares in common with his fellows: hence the document's fourfold division. The social philosophy of the future will seek to clarify these basic rights and duties in a body of coherent doctrine, and to show more precisely how they are grounded in the structure of human nature and the limiting conditions of its existential realization.

This social philosophy will sharply distinguish the human group from any form of animal swarm, or hive, or herd that is based on automatic drive or instinct. No such automatic drive to social cooperation is found in human nature. Instead of this, we find intellect and the capacity for rationally guided action. The new philosophy will, therefore, see in human communication the very life blood of the human group. In cooperation with a humane and genuinely empirical logic, which does not yet exist, it will study this obscure and long-neglected phenomenon in its material, formal, and especially its existential manifestations—attempting to clarify the role which they severally play in the maintenance of sound social life, as well as in its breakdown and disintegration.

More clearly than ever before, this new philosophy will recognize that free persons cannot be led to voluntary cooperation without a sound and coherent understanding of what they are doing. It will, therefore, see that the unity of a soundly-ordered human culture rests not primarily on blood, or soil, or autocratic conditioning, but rather on a shared world view that can be coherently explained in the light of evident fact, and that can call forth willing devotion. This group ideology must be sound as well as appealing. Nothing more terrible can happen to a human culture than the breakdown of its ideology. No human group can long remain in a healthy state unless its primary energies are constantly poured into the critical and communicative functions of rational education.

Future social thought, with the aid of philosophy, will be basically concerned with formulating such an ideology. It will concern itself with the comparative study of group ideologies, and with a disciplined analysis of that vast array of historic evidence, already starting to be revealed, which can shed further light on the close relation between the structure of such ideologies and the rise and fall of civilization.

Notes

CHAPTER 1. THE BREAKDOWN OF MODERN PHILOSOPHY

1. Feigl and Sellars, eds., *Readings in Philosophical Analysis*, p. 14.
2. *Ibid.*, p. 399.
3. *Ibid.*, p. 47.
4. *Ibid.*, p. 12.
5. *Ibid.*, p. 22.
6. *The Concept of Mind*, pp. 214-215.
7. Feigl and Sellars, *op. cit.*, p. 391.
8. Sellars and Hospers, eds., *Readings in Ethical Theory*, p. 398.
9. Feigl and Sellars, *op. cit.*, p. 21 note.
10. *Ibid.*, p. 400.
11. Sellars and Hospers, *op. cit.*, p. 397.
12. Feigl and Sellars, *op. cit.*, p. 25.

CHAPTER 2. SÖREN KIERKEGAARD

1. *The Journals of Sören Kierkegaard*, p. 147.
2. *Ibid.*, pp. 357-358.
3. *Critique of Pure Reason*, A599-600, B627-628; cf. Müller ed., pp. 515-516.
4. *The Journals of Sören Kierkegaard*, no. 1042, p. 366.
5. *Ibid.*, nos. 582-583, p. 156.
6. *The Concept of Dread*, p. 38.
7. Cf. *The Journals of Sören Kierkegaard*, p. 332 (note 967); cf. *The Concept of Dread*, pp. 38-39.
8. *The Concept of Dread*, p. 139; cf. p. 55.
9. *Ibid.*, p. 142.
10. Cf. especially *Either/Or*, vol. 1, pp. 29, 234-239.
11. *Ibid.*, p. 234.
12. Cf. *Either/Or*, vol. 2, pp. 172-181; *The Sickness Unto Death*, pp. 32-123; and *Concluding Unscientific Postscript*, pp. 230-231.

13. Cf. *Concluding Unscientific Postscript,* part 2, ch. 1-3. This is the clearest statement of those existential principles which play a basic role in Kierkegaard's thought.

14. These diverse ways of existing are described in *Either/Or* and *Stages on Life's Way.*

15. Cf. *Either/Or,* vol. 1.

16. Cf. *Ibid.,* vol. 2.

17. Cf. *Works of Love,* especially pp. 15-37 and 110-125.

18. *Ibid.,* pp. 75-110.

19. *Ibid.,* pp. 32-33.

20. *Loc. cit.*

21. Cf. *Concluding Unscientific Postscript,* pp. 383n, 389, 463; *Works of Love,* pp. 85-87; *Journals,* nos. 617, 662, 962, 1134.

22. *Concluding Unscientific Postscript,* pp. 109-110; 121, 206, 274-281, 352-353 *Either/Or,* pp. 210-211.

23. *Concluding Unscientific Postscript,* p. 280; *Either/Or,* pp. 141, 149, 210.

24. *Concluding Unscientific Postscript,* pp. 129-134.

25. Cf. *ibid.,* pp. 147-152.

26. Cf. *ibid.,* pp. 376-385.

27. Cf. *Either/Or,* p. 141.

28. Cf. Hegel, *System der Philosophie,* vol. 10, pp. 382 ff., especially pp. 409-446 *(Der Staat)*

29. *The Decline of the West,* p. 106; cf. *Untergang des Abendlandes,* vol. 1, 11-14 ed., p. 153.

30. For a penetrating and poignant analysis of these tendencies, cf. *The Present Age.*

31. *Journals,* no. 614, p. 179.

32. *Ibid.,* no. 1293, p. 489.

33. *Ibid.,* p. 490.

34. *Der Begriff der Ironie.*

35. *Journals,* nos. 578, 1000, 1232.

36. *Ibid.,* nos. 638, 1224, 1291.

37. *Ibid.,* no. 414.

38. Plato, *Euthydemus* 290C1.

39. Cf. Plato, *Sophist* 263; Aristotle, *Metaphysics* 1051B31-1052A5.

40. *Statesman* 258E.

41. *Ibid.,* 260A-B.

42. *Nicomachean Ethics,* Book VI, especially ch. 2 and 9.

43. Cf. Plato, *Republic* 429C-E and Aristotle, *Nicomachean Ethics* 1140B25-30.

44. *Nicomachean Ethics,* Book VII, ch. 10.

45. *Laches* 188C; cf. *Republic* 395C-397.

46. Cf. Plato, *Republic* 352E ff.

47. *Nicomachean Ethics* 1097B25-29.

48. *Training in Christianity,* pp. 240-246.

49. *Journals*, no. 1226; *Works of Love*, pp. 12-13.
50. Cf. pp. 76-78.
51. *Concluding Unscientific Postscript*, pp. 312-322.
52. *Confessions*, Book I, ch. 1.
53. Cf. *Concluding Unscientific Postscript*, pp. 68-74.
54. *Journals*, nos. 32, 356, 582, 1067; *Concluding Unscientific Postscript*, pp. 267-270, 273-280.

CHAPTER 3. THE NEW EMPIRICISM AND ONTOLOGY

1. *The Philosophy of Existence*, p. 87.
2. *Loc. cit.*
3. *Ibid.*, p. 78.
4. *Ibid.*, p. 94.
5. Cf. *ibid.*, ch. 4.
6. Heidegger, *Sein und Zeit*, pp. 52-89.
7. *Ibid.*, pp. 27-39.
8. Jaspers, *Philosophie*, vol. 1, pp. 213-214.
9. *Ibid.*, pp. 222-223.
10. Marcel, *Metaphysical Journal*, pp. 9-12.
11. Jaspers, *op. cit.*, pp. 229-230.
12. Heidegger, *op. cit.*, p. 88; Sartre, *L'Être et le Néant*, p. 149; Jaspers, *op. cit.*, p. 62.
13. Marcel, *The Mystery of Being*, vol. 1, pp. 92 ff.
14. *Philosophie*, vol. 2, ch. 10.
15. *Ibid.*, pp. 336 ff.
16. *Sein und Zeit*, p. 159.
17. *L'Être et le Néant*, p. 429.
18. Cf. *ibid.*, pp. 12-13.
19. Cf. *ibid.*, p. 12.
20. *Metaphysical Journal*, p. 322.
21. *Man Against Mass Society*, p. 119.
22. *Loc. cit.*
23. *Sein und Zeit*, p. 38. (Tr. Wild)
24. *Loc. cit.*
25. *Ibid.*, sec. 6, p. 21 *et passim*.
26. *Ibid.*, p. 43.
27. *Existentialism*, p. 18.
28. *Ibid.*, pp. 15-20.
29. *Ibid.*, pp. 45-46; cf. p. 87.
30. *Man Against Mass Society*, p. 85.
31. Cf. Heidegger, *Sein und Zeit*, secs. 15-16, 25-26, 51-53.
32. *Ibid.*, p. 120.
33. *L'Être et le Néant*, pp. 308-310.
34. Cf. *ibid.*, pp. 268-269; Marcel, *Metaphysical Journal*, p. 161.

35. *Sein und Zeit*, p. 154.
36. *Über den Humanismus*, p. 7; cf. p. 19.
37. *L'Être et le Néant*, p. 429.
38. *Sein und Zeit*, p. 42. (Tr. Wild)
39. *Ibid.*, pp. 42-43.
40. *Ibid.*, p. 43.
41. *L'Être et le Néant*, pp. 639-642.
42. *Ibid.*, pp. 701-702.
43. *Man Against Mass Society*, pp. 94-95.
44. *Sein und Zeit*, pp. 134-135.
45. *La Nausée; roman*, p. 167. (Tr. Wild)
46. Cf. *L'Être et le Néant*, pp. 121-127.
47. *Was ist Metaphysik?* pp. 42-44.
48. *L'Être et le Néant*, p. 142.
49. Bollnow, *Existenzphilosophie*, pp. 17-27.
50. *Later Poems*, pp. 109-110.
51. Cf. Jaspers, *Man in the Modern Age*, pp. 134-135; Heidegger, *Sein und Zeit*, pp. 168-169.
52. *Philosophie*, vol. 2, ch. 3, especially pp. 53 ff.
53. Cf. *ibid.*, ch. 7.
54. *Loc. cit.*
55. *Ibid.*, p. 204.
56. *Ibid.*, pp. 216 ff.
57. *Ibid.*, pp. 230-231.
58. *Ibid.*, pp. 233 ff.
59. *Ibid.*, pp. 246 ff.
60. *Ibid.*, pp. 220 ff. and Heidegger, *Sein und Zeit*, pp. 237-260.
61. Cf. *Sein und Zeit*, secs. 46-51 for a careful study of the phenomenology of death.

CHAPTER 4.   HUMAN AWARENESS AND ACTION

1. *L'Être et le Néant*, p. 539.
2. Cf. Collins, *The Existentialists*, pp. 128 ff.
3. *Sein und Zeit*, secs. 29-44 and 67-82.
4. *Ibid.*, pp. 134 ff.
5. *Ibid.*, pp. 137 ff.
6. *Ibid.*, p. 139.
7. Cf. *Metaphysical Journal*, pp. 304-311.
8. *Mystery of Being*, vol. 1, pp. 49-50.
9. For fidelity, see *Du Refus à l'Invocation*, pp. 192-225; for hope, *Mystery of Being*, vol. 2, ch. 9.
10. *Sein und Zeit*, pp. 191 ff.
11. *Ibid.*, p. 145.
12. *Ibid.*, pp. 222-225.

13. *Ibid.,* pp. 152-153.
14. *Ibid.,* pp. 157-158.
15. *Ibid.,* p. 145.
16. *Ibid.,* pp. 37-38.
17. *Ibid.,* p. 37.
18. *Ibid.,* pp. 226-227.
19. *Ibid.,* p. 227.
20. *L'Être et le Néant,* p. 12.
21. *Ibid.,* pp. 25-26.
22. *Ibid.,* p. 26.
23. *Ibid.,* pp. 19-20.
24. Sartre, *L'Être et le Néant,* pp. 18-21.
25. Cf. "Les Temps Modernes," *Revue Mensuelle,* 9 and 10.
26. *L'Être et le Néant,* p. 142.
27. *Ibid.,* pp. 32-33.
28. *Ibid.,* pp. 139-145.
29. *Ibid.,* pp. 40-47.
30. *Ibid.,* pp. 128-139.
31. *Ibid.,* p. 57.
32. *Loc. cit.*
33. *Ibid.,* pp. 115-131.
34. *Ibid.,* pp. 40-47.
35. *Ibid.,* p. 60.
36. *Ibid.,* p. 57.
37. *Ibid.,* pp. 126-127.
38. *Ibid.,* pp. 144-147.
39. *Ibid.,* p. 144.
40. *Ibid.,* pp. 141-144.
41. *Ibid.,* pp. 549-561.
42. *Ibid.,* pp. 148-149.
43. *Ibid.,* pp. 521-541.
44. *Sein und Zeit,* p. 159.
45. *Ibid.,* pp. 54-55.
46. *Ibid.,* p. 160; cf. pp. 224-225.
47. *Ibid.,* p. 159.
48. *Ibid.,* secs. 31-33.
49. Cf. *ibid.,* pp. 71, 98-99, 114-115 *et passim.*
50. *Über den Humanismus,* pp. 33-34. (Tr. Wild)
51. *Loc. cit.*
52. *Sein und Zeit,* sec. 40.
53. *Ibid.,* p. 185.
54. *Ibid.,* p. 186.
55. *Ibid.,* pp. 187-188.
56. *Ibid.,* pp. 189-190.
57. *Ibid.,* pp. 190-191.

58. *Ibid.*, sec. 41; especially pp. 194-195.
59. *Ibid.*, pp. 191-192.
60. *Ibid.*, p. 192.
61. *Loc. cit.*
62. *Ibid.*, pp. 194-196.
63. *Ibid.*, p. 193.
64. *Ibid.*, p. 195.
65. *Loc. cit.*
66. *Ibid.*, p. 197.
67. *Ibid.*, pp. 198-199.
68. Cf. *ibid.*, sec. 65.
69. Cf. *ibid.*, sec. 81.
70. *Ibid.*, p. 422.
71. *Ibid.*, p. 423.
72. *Ibid.*, p. 426.
73. *Ibid.*, pp. 421-422, 424.
74. *Loc. cit.*
75. *Ibid.*, p. 404.
76. *Ibid.*, p. 426.
77. *Ibid.*, p. 405.
78. *Ibid.*, p. 424.
79. *Ibid.*, pp. 404-405.
80. *Ibid.*, p. 426.
81. *Ibid.*, p. 365.
82. *Ibid.*, pp. 422-423.
83. *Ibid.*, pp. 406 ff.
84. *Ibid.*, p. 425.
85. *Ibid.*, sec. 65.
86. *Ibid.*, pp. 328-331.
87. *Ibid.*, pp. 330-331.
88. *Ibid.*, p. 410; cf. p. 333.
89. *Ibid.*, p. 329.
90. *Ibid.*, p. 426.
91. *Ibid.*, p. 329.
92. *Ibid.*, pp. 326-331.
93. *Ibid.*, pp. 325-326.
94. *Ibid.*, p. 326.
95. *Ibid.*, pp. 332, 410.
96. *Ibid.*, p. 425.
97. *Ibid.*, p. 338.
98. *Ibid.*, pp. 408-411.
99. *Ibid.*, pp. 422-423.
100. *Ibid.*, p. 424.
101. *Ibid.*, secs. 72-77.
102. *Ibid.*, pp. 378-379.

103. *Ibid.*, p. 378.
104. *Loc. cit.*
105. *Ibid.*, p. 388.
106. *Ibid.*, p. 380.
107. *Ibid.*, p. 381.
108. *Ibid.*, pp. 384-385.
109. *Ibid.*, pp. 380-381.
110. *Ibid.*, pp. 385-386.
111. *Ibid.*, p. 391.
112. *Ibid.*, p. 392.
113. *Ibid.*, pp. 388-389.
114. *Ibid.*, pp. 395-397.

CHAPTER 5. EXISTENTIALIST ETHICS. INTEGRITY AND DECISION

1. *Philosophie*, vol. 2, p. 182.
2. *L'Être et le Néant*, pp. 127-130, 508-516, 639-642.
3. *Sein und Zeit*, pp. 245 ff.
4. Cf. *ibid.*, sec. 50.
5. *Ibid.*, p. 250.
6. *Ibid.*, pp. 250-255; cf. p. 262.
7. *Ibid.*, pp. 263-264.
8. *Ibid.*, p. 264.
9. *Ibid.*, pp. 264-265.
10. *Ibid.*, pp. 265-266.
11. *Ibid.*, secs. 46-53.
12. Cf. *ibid.*, secs. 54-60.
13. *Ibid.*, p. 271.
14. *Ibid.*, pp. 271-272.
15. *Ibid.*, sec. 56.
16. *Ibid.*, pp. 277-278.
17. *Loc. cit.*
18. *Ibid.*, secs. 35-37.
19. *Ibid.*, p. 273.
20. *Ibid.*, pp. 280 ff.
21. *Ibid.*, p. 277.
22. *Ibid.*, pp. 283-286.
23. *Ibid.*, p. 291.
24. *Ibid.*, pp. 285-287.
25. *Ibid.*, p. 294.
26. *Ibid.*, sec. 62.
27. *Ibid.*, pp. 305-306.
28. *Ibid.*, pp. 307-308.
29. *Ibid.*, p. 300.
30. *Ibid.*, p. 306.

31. *Ibid.*, p. 307.
32. *Ibid.*, p. 308.
33. *Loc. cit.*
34. *Metaphysical Journal*, p. 213.
35. *Ibid.*, p. 186.
36. *Ibid.*, p. 216.
37. *Loc. cit.*
38. *Ibid.*, p. 220.
39. *Man in the Modern Age*, pp. 40-41.
40. *L'Être et le Néant*, p. 122.
41. Cf. *ibid.*, p. 669, and his discussion of the viscous, pp. 701-702.
42. *Ibid.*, pp. 137-138; cf. *Existentialism*, pp. 30-33.
43. *L'Être et le Néant*, p. 134; cf. pp. 652-654.
44. *Ibid.*, pp. 508-516.
45. *Existentialism*, pp. 20-25.
46. *Sein und Zeit*, pp. 114-130.
47. *Ibid.*, pp. 121 ff.
48. *Ibid.*, p. 119.
49. *Ibid.*, pp. 126 ff.
50. *Journals*, no. 1293.
51. Heidegger, *Sein und Zeit*, p. 127.
52. *Loc. cit.*
53. *Ibid.*, pp. 167 ff.
54. *Ibid.*, p. 168.
55. *Ibid.*, pp. 171-172.
56. Cf. *ibid.*, secs. 54-57.
57. *Ibid.*, pp. 173-174.
58. *The Philosophy of Existence*, pp. 2-3.
59. *Man in the Modern Age*, pp. 34 ff.
60. *Ibid.*, pp. 40-41.
61. *Ibid.*, p. 49.
62. *Ibid.*, pp. 134-135.
63. *Ibid.*, pp. 64-65.
64. *Ibid.*, p. 65.
65. *Loc. cit.*
66. *Ibid.*, p. 165.
67. *Ibid.*, p. 241.
68. Heidegger, *Sein und Zeit*, p. 264.
69. Cf. *Philosophie*, vol. 2, ch. 3.
70. *Ibid.*, pp. 60-73.
71. Cf. pp. 183-184 and 206-214.
72. Jaspers, *Philosophie*, vol. 2, pp. 208-216.
73. Heidegger, *op. cit.*, p. 300.
74. Cf. *ibid.*, pp. 299-300 and 307-308.

75. *Philosophie,* vol. 2, pp. 216-219 (chance); pp. 230-233 (suffering); pp. 233-246 (conflict).
76. *Ibid.,* p. 230.
77. *Ibid.,* p. 247.
78. *Ibid.,* p. 248.
79. Cf. especially Heidegger, *Sein und Zeit,* pp. 235-267.
80. *Ibid.,* pp. 253-254.
81. Cf. pp. 81-84.
82. Heidegger, *op. cit.,* pp. 258-259.
83. *Ibid.,* pp. 260-267.
84. Cf. *ibid.,* pp. 309-310.
85. *Ibid.,* pp. 170-173.
86. Cf. *ibid.,* pp. 49-50.
87. *Ibid.,* pp. 188-189.
88. *Ibid.,* pp. 175 ff.
89. *Ibid.,* p. 122.
90. *Loc. cit.*
91. *Ibid.,* pp. 420 ff.
92. Williams, "The Myth of Passage."
93. Heidegger, *op. cit.,* p. 424.
94. *Ibid.,* pp. 323 ff.
95. *Ibid.,* pp. 378 ff.

CHAPTER 6. EXISTENTIALISM AS A PHILOSOPHY

1. *Philosophie,* vol. 2, p. 340.
2. *Ibid.,* ch. 1.
3. Cf. for example, *ibid.,* pp. 150-163 entitled "The Phenomenology of Will."
4. *Ibid.,* vol. 1, ch. 4; *The Perennial Scope of Philosophy,* pp. 148-149.
5. *Philosophie,* vol. 2, ch. 1.
6. *Existenzphilosophie,* pp. 62-63.
7. *Philosophie,* vol. 3, ch. 4.
8. *Ibid.,* vol. 1, pp. 13-19; vol. 2, ch. 1.
9. *Ibid.,* vol. 2, ch. 3.
10. Cf. Jaspers, *Vernunft und Existenz; 5 Vorlesungen,* pp. 34-57.
11. *Perennial Scope of Philosophy,* pp. 31-33; cf. *Philosophie,* vol. 3, p. 39.
12. *Philosophie,* vol. 3, pp. 160-164.
13. *Ibid.,* ch. 4.
14. Cf. *Perennial Scope of Philosophy,* ch. 2, especially pp. 25-30 and 34-37.
15. Jaspers, *Vernunft und Existenz,* p. 60.
16. *Ibid.,* p. 69.
17. *Philosophie,* vol. 2, pp. 182 ff.
18. Jaspers, *Vernunft und Existenz, 3 Vorlesungen,* pp. 57-82.

19. *Way to Wisdom,* pp. 96 ff.
20. Cf. Jaspers, *Perennial Scope of Philosophy,* pp. 158 ff.
21. Cf. *ibid.,* pp. 170 ff.
22. Cf. Jaspers, *Philosophie,* vol. 2, pp. 180-181.
23. *Ibid.,* p. 185.
24. Cf. *Way to Wisdom,* pp. 85-87, 93-99; cf. *Perennial Scope of Philosophy,* ch. 2.
25. Cf. *Way to Wisdom,* pp. 86 ff; *Perennial Scope of Philosophy,* pp. 138 ff.
26. *Philosophie,* vol. 3, pp. 219 ff.
27. *L'Être et le Néant,* pp. 34, 124.
28. *Ibid.,* pp. 53 ff.
29. *Ibid.,* p. 655; cf. *Existentialism,* p. 18.
30. *Existentialism,* pp. 45 ff.
31. Cf. pp. 90-95.
32. *L'Etre et le Néant,* pp. 150-218.
33. *Ibid.,* pp. 201-218.
34. *Ibid.,* pp. 185-196.
35. *Ibid.,* pp. 255-268.
36. Cf. *ibid.,* pp. 477 ff.
37. *Ibid.,* pp. 720-722.
38. *Ibid.,* p. 669.
39. *Existentialism,* p. 55.
40. Cf. *L'Être et le Néant,* pp. 701-702.
41. Cf. *Metaphysical Journal,* Preface, p. xiii.
42. *Ibid.,* p. 292; cf. *Man Against Mass Society,* p. 52.
43. Cf. *Man Against Mass Society,* p. 90; *Mystery of Being,* vol. 1, pp. 204-205.
44. Cf. *Metaphysical Journal,* Preface; and *Mystery of Being,* vol. 1, p. 94.
45. *Metaphysical Journal,* p. 331.
46. *Mystery of Being,* pp. 117-119.
47. *Ibid.,* p. 119.
48. Cf. *ibid.,* pp. 211 ff.
49. *Man Against Mass Society,* pp. 67-68.
50. *Mystery of Being,* vol. 1, pp. 204 ff.
51. Cf. *Man Against Mass Society,* p. 85.
52. *Mystery of Being,* vol. 2, p. 125.
53. Cf. *Metaphysical Journal,* p. 34.
54. *Man Against Mass Society,* p. 48.
55. *Mystery of Being,* vol 1, p. 181.
56. *Ibid.,* p. 87.
57. *Man Against Mass Society,* p. 100; cf. *Mystery of Being,* vol. 1, pp. 171-172.
58. *Mystery of Being,* vol. 1, p. 219.
59. *Ibid.,* pp. 181 ff.
60. *Ibid.,* pp. 125 ff., 134.

61. *Man Against Mass Society*, p. 86.
62. *Mystery of Being*, vol. 2, p. 5.
63. Cf. *ibid.*, vol. 1, pp. 91 ff.
64. *Ibid.*, pp. 100-101.
65. *Ibid.*, pp. 91 ff.
66. *Ibid.*, p. 123.
67. *Ibid.*, p. 126.
68. *Ibid.*, p. 122.
69. Cf. *Man Against Mass Society*, pp. 71-72.
70. *Sein und Zeit*, especially pp. 15-27.
71. *Ibid.*, pp. 95-101.
72. *Metaphysica* 998B22.
73. *Sein und Zeit*, pp. 11-19.
74. *Ibid.*, p. 145.
75. *Über den Humanismus*, especially pp. 5-9 and 42-45.
76. *Ibid.*, p. 19. (Tr. Wild)
77. Cf. *ibid.*, pp. 24 and 37.
78. *Sein und Zeit*, pp. 186-187.
79. Cf. Sartre, *L'Être et le Néant*, pp. 115-130 *et passim*.
80. *Über den Humanismus*, p. 22.
81. *Sein und Zeit*, p. 38.
82. *Über den Humanismus*, pp. 39-43.
83. *Ibid.*, p. 19.
84. *Ibid.*, pp. 36-37.
85. Cf. *Erläuterungen zu Hölderlin's Dichtung*.
86. *Über den Humanismus*, pp. 36-37.
87. *Ibid.*, p. 37.
88. *Vom Wesen des Grundes*, p. 28, n. 1, referred to in *Über den Humanismus*, p. 36. (Tr. Wild)
89. *L'Être et le Néant*, p. 708. (Tr. Wild)
90. *La Nausée*, p. 178. (Tr. Wild)
91. *Philosophie*, vol. 3, p. 227.
92. *Vernunft und Existenz*, p. 121, n. 2. (Tr. Wild)
93. *Existentialism*, pp. 37-38.
94. Berdiaev, *Slavery and Freedom*, p. 26.
95. *Ibid.*, p. 59.
96. *Le Sursis, Roman*, p. 285.
97. Dufrenne and Ricoeur, *Karl Jaspers*, p. 214, n. 14.
98. *L'Être et le Néant*, p. 502. (Tr. Wild)
99. *Journals*, p. 62.

CHAPTER 7. REALISTIC PHENOMENOLOGY AND METAPHYSICS

1. *Phénoménologie de la Perception*, pp. 10-40; cf. De Waelhens, *Une Philosophie de l'Ambiguité*, pp. 61-93.

2. Cf. De Waelhens, *op. cit.*, pp. 399 ff.
3. Cf. Ricoeur, *Philosophie de la Volonté*, pp. 41-52 and especially pp. 187-202.
4. *Sein und Zeit*, pp. 12-13 and 338, n. 1; cf. De Waelhens, *La Philosophie de Martin Heidegger*, pp. 295-316.
5. Cf. Wetter, *Der dialektische Materialismus*, pp. 520-524 and 557-562.
6. Cf. Aristotle, *Nicomachean Ethics*, Book VI.
7. *Works of Love*, pp. 32-33.
8. Cf. Wild, "Tendency: Ontological Ground of Ethics."
9. *Phénoménologie de la Perception*, especially pp. 10-12, 30, 250, 381-382, and De Waelhens, *Philosophie de l'Ambiguité*, pp. 98-104.
10. *Phénoménologie de la Perception*, p. 411; cf. pp. 406-416.
11. Cf. Wild, "An Introduction to the Phenomenology of Signs."
12. *Sein und Zeit*, secs. 46-53.

CHAPTER 8. PHILOSOPHICAL ANTHROPOLOGY

1. Cf. *Zur Grundlegung der Ontologie*, pp. 151-242.
2. Cf. pp. 94-95, 98, 152-153, and 180-183.
3. Aristotle, *De Anima III*, 429B31.
4. Cf. Parker, "Realistic Epistemology."
5. Cf. Veatch and Young, "Metaphysics and the Paradoxes."
6. Cf. Veatch, *Intentional Logic*, pp. 385-392.
7. Cf. *ibid.*, pp. 316-335.
8. Cf. Skinner, *Science and Human Behavior*.
9. *Philosophie de la Volonté*, pp. 37-57 and especially pp. 148-180.
10. *Ibid.*, p. 39.
11. *Sein und Zeit*, p. 330.
12. Cf. Hartshorne, *Beyond Humanism*, pp. 162-164.
13. *Sein und Zeit*, p. 394.

CHAPTER 9. REALISTIC ETHICS

1. Cf. Wild, *Plato's Modern Enemies and the Theory of Natural Law*, pp. 64-71 and 204-230.
2. Cf. *ibid.*, ch. 7.
3. Cf. pp. 45-53.
4. Cf. Plato, *Statesman* 258E-259D; Aristotle, *Nicomachean Ethics*, Book VI, 1149B9 ff.
5. Cf. pp. 243-247.
6. Cf. Bollnow, *Existenzphilosophie*, pp. 120-121.
7. Cf. Ricoeur, *Philosophie de la Volonté*, pp. 41-52.

Bibliography

A. BOOKS

Anderson, J. F., *The Bond of Being*, Herder, St. Louis, 1949.

Aristotle. *Works*, W. D. Ross, ed., Clarendon Press, Oxford, 1908-52.

Augustine. *Confessions*, E. B. Pusey, tr., Everyman ed., J. M. Dent, London, 1907.

Berdiaev, N., *Slavery and Freedom*, Charles Scribners & Sons, New York, 1944.

Bergson, Henry, *Creative Evolution*, Holt, New York, 1911.

Berkeley, George, *The Works of George Berkeley*, Fraser ed., Clarendon Press, Oxford, 1901.

Bollnow, Otto Friedrich, *Existenzphilosophie*, W. Kohlhammer, Stuttgart, 1949, 3rd ed.

Broad, C. D., *The Mind and Its Place in Nature*, Harcourt Brace, New York, 1925.

——, *Scientific Thought*, Kegan Paul, Trench, Trubner, London, 1923.

Brock, Werner, *Existence and Being*, Regnery, Chicago, 1949.

Cohen and Nagel, *An Introduction to Logic and Scientific Method*, Harcourt Brace, New York, 1934.

Collins, James, *The Existentialists*, Regnery, Chicago, 1952.

De Waelhens, A., *Une Philosophie de l'Ambiguité*, Publications Universitaires de Louvain, Louvain, 1951.

——, *La Philosophie de Martin Heidegger*, Éditions de l'Institut Supérieure de Philosophie, 1948, 3rd ed.

Dewey, John, *The Philosophy of John Dewey*, John Ratner, ed., Holt, New York, 1928.

——, *The Quest for Certainty*, Minton, Balch, New York, 1929.

——, *Reconstruction in Philosophy*, Beacon Press, Boston, 1948.

Dufrenne, M., and Ricoeur, P., *Karl Jaspers et la Philosophie de l'Existence*, Éditions du Seuil, Paris, 1947.

Eaton, R. M., *General Logic; An Introductory Survey*, Scribner's, New York, 1931.

——, *Essays in Critical Realism*, Macmillan, London, 1920.

Feigl, H., and Sellars, W., eds., *Readings in Philosophical Analysis*, Appleton-Century-Crofts, New York, 1949.

Hartmann, Nicolai, *Ethics* (Coit), Macmillan, New York, 1932.

——, *Philosophie der Natur*, Walter de Gruyter and Co., Berlin, 1950.

——, *Zur Grundlegung der Ontologie*, Walter de Gruyter, Berlin, 1935.

Hartshorne, Charles, *Beyond Humanism*, Willett, Clark and Co., Chicago, 1937.

Hegel, *Hegel's Science of Logic*, Macmillan, New York, 1929, vol. I.

——, *System der Philosophie*, Drittes Teil, *Sämtliche Werke* (Glockner), Frommans Verlag, Stuttgart, 1929, vol. 10.

Heidegger, Martin, *Erläuterungen zu Hölderlin's Dichtung*, Klostermann, Frankfurt-am-Main, 1944.

——, *Existence and Being*, Werner Brock, ed., Regnery, Chicago, 1949.

——, *Holzwege*, Klostermann, Frankfurt-am-Main, 1950.

——, *Sein und Zeit*, Max Niemeyer Verlag, Halle, 1931, 3rd ed.

——, *Über den Humanismus*, Klostermann, Frankfurt-am-Main, 1949.

——, *Was ist Metaphysik?* Klostermann, Frankfurt-am-Main, 1943.

Heinemann, *Existentialism and the Modern Predicament*, Oxford, New York, 1952.

Hicks, Dawes, *Critical Realism*, Macmillan, London, 1938.

Hume, *A Treatise of Human Nature*, Green and Grose, eds., Longmans, Green, London, 1874, vol. I.

Jaspers, Karl, *Existenzphilosophie*, W. de Gruyter, Berlin and Leipzig, 1938.

——, *Man in the Modern Age*, Eden and Cedar Paul, trs., Routledge, London, 1951.

——, *The Perennial Scope of Philosophy*, Ralph Manheim, tr., Philosophical Library, New York, 1949.

——, *Philosophie*, Verlag Julius Springer, Berlin, 1932.

——, *Vernunft und Existenz; 5 Vorlesungen*, J. Storm, Bremen, 1949.

——, *Way to Wisdom*, Ralph Manheim, tr., Yale University Press, New Haven, 1951.

John of St. Thomas, *Cursus Philosophicus Thomisticus*, Reiser, ed., Marietti, Turin, 1933, vol. I.

Jolivet, Régis, *Les Doctrines Existentialistes*, Éditions de Fontenelle, Paris, 1948.

Kant, *Critique of Pure Reason*, Müller ed., Macmillan, London, 1881.

Kierkegaard, Sören, *Der Begriff der Ironie*, Kaiser Verlag, München, 1929.

———, *The Concept of Dread*, Princeton University Press, Princeton, 1946.

———, *Concluding Unscientific Postscript* (Swenson), Princeton University Press, Princeton, 1944.

———, *Either/Or*, Princeton University Press, Princeton, 1944, 2 vols.

———, *Fear and Trembling*, Princeton University Press, Princeton, 1941.

———, *The Journals of Sören Kierkegaard* (Dru), Oxford University Press, New York, 1938.

———, *The Present Age*, Oxford University Press, London, 1940.

———, *The Sickness Unto Death*, Princeton University Press, Princeton, 1946.

———, *Stages on Life's Way*, Princeton University Press, Princeton, 1940.

———, *Training in Christianity*, Princeton University Press, Princeton, 1947.

———, *Works of Love* (Swenson), Princeton University Press, Princeton, 1946.

Krikorian, Y. H., ed., *Naturalism and the Human Spirit*, Columbia University Press, New York, 1944.

Lewis, C. I., *An Analysis of Knowledge and Valuation*, Open Court, Lasalle, Ill., 1946.

———, *Mind and the World Order*, Scribners, New York, 1929.

———, *Survey of Symbolic Logic*, University of California Press, Berkeley, 1918.

Marcel, Gabriel, *Man Against Mass Society*, Regnery, Chicago, 1952.

———, *Metaphysical Journal*, Regnery, Chicago, 1952.

———, *The Mystery of Being*, Regnery, Chicago, 1950, 2 vols.

———, *The Philosophy of Existence*, Philosophical Library, New York, 1949.

———, *Du Refus à l'Invocation*, Gallimard, Paris, 1940.

Maritain, Jacques, *Introduction to Logic*, Sheed and Ward, New York, 1937.

Merleau-Ponty, Maurice, *La Phénoménologie de la Perception*, Gallimard, Paris, 1945.

Mill, J. S., *Utilitarianism*, Dutton, New York, 1929.

Moody, E. A., *The Logic of William of Ockham*, Sheed and Ward, London, 1935.

Moore, G. E., *Ethics*, Home University Library, Holt, New York, 1916.

———, *The Philosophy of G. E. Moore* (Schlipp), Northwestern University Press, Evanston, 1942.

———, *Principia Ethica*, Cambridge University Press, Cambridge, 1922.

Perry, Ralph B., *General Theory of Value*, Longmans, Green, New York, 1926.

———, *The Moral Economy*, Scribner's, New York, 1909.

Plato, Loeb Classical Library, Heinemann, London, 1921-33.

Pritchard, H. A., *Moral Obligation*, Clarendon Press, Oxford, 1949.

Quine, W., *From a Logical Point of View*, Harvard University Press, Cambridge, 1953.

Reichenbach, Hans, *Elements of Symbolic Logic*, Macmillan, New York, 1947.

Ricoeur, Paul, *Philosophie de la Volonté*, Aubier, Éditions Montaigne, Paris, 1949.

———, *Gabriel Marcel et Karl Jaspers*, Éditions du temps Présent, Paris, 1947.

Rilke, Rainer Maria, *Later Poems*, Leishman, tr., Hogarth Press, London, 1938.

Ross, W. D., *The Right and the Good*, Clarendon Press, Oxford, 1930.

Russell, Bertrand, *Human Knowledge Its Scope and Limits*, Simon & Schuster, New York, 1948.

———, *Problems of Philosophy*, Holt, New York.

Ryle, Gilbert, *The Concept of Mind*, Barnes and Noble, New York, 1949.

Sartre, Jean-Paul, *L'Etre et le Néant*, Librairie Gallimard, Paris, 1949, 18th ed.

———, *Existentialism*, Philosophical Library, New York, 1947.

———, *La Nausée, Roman*, Gallimard, Paris, 1938.

———, *Le Sursis, Roman*, Gallimard, Paris, 1945.

Sellars and Hospers, eds., *Readings in Ethical Theory*, Appleton-Century-Crofts, New York, 1952.

Skinner, B. F., *Science and Human Behavior*, Macmillan, New York, 1953.

Spengler, O., *The Decline of the West*, Atkinson, tr., Knopf, New York, 1926.

———, *Untergang des Abendlandes*, Oskar Beck, München, 1920, vol. 1, 11-14 ed.

Tolstoi, Leo, *The Death of Ivan Ilyitch,* The Modern Library, New York.

Stevenson, C. L., *Ethics and Language,* Yale University Press, New Haven, 1944.

Toynbee, Arnold J., *A Study of History,* Oxford University Press, New York, 1947.

van Steenberghen, Fernand, *Epistemology,* Flynn, tr., Wagner, Inc., New York; B. Herder, London, 1949.

Veatch, Henry B., *Intentional Logic,* Yale University Press, New Haven, 1952.

Wetter, G. A., *Der dialektische Materialismus,* Verlag Herder, Freiburg, 1952.

Weyl, Hermann, *Philosophy of Mathematics and Natural Science,* Princeton University Press, Princeton, 1949.

Wild, John, *Plato's Modern Enemies and the Theory of Natural Law,* University of Chicago Press, Chicago, 1953.

———, Wild, ed., *The Return to Reason,* Regnery, Chicago, 1953.

B. ARTICLES AND ESSAYS

Ayer, A. J., "Critique of Ethics," in *Readings in Ethical Theory,* Sellars and Hospers, eds., Appleton-Century-Crofts, New York, 1952.

Dewey, John, "The Need for a Recovery of Philosophy," in *Creative Intelligence,* Holt, New York.

Frankena, W. K., "Moral Philosophy at Mid-Century," *Philosophical Review,* vol. 60, 1951.

Garnett, A. C., "Moore's Theory of Moral Freedom and Responsibility," in *The Philosophy of G. E. Moore* (Schlipp), Northwestern University Press, Evanston, 1942.

Parker, Francis, "Realistic Epistemology," in *The Return to Reason,* John Wild, ed., Regnery, Chicago, 1953.

Russell, Bertrand, "The Philosophy of Logical Atomism," *Monist,* vols. 28 and 29, 1918.

Santayana, G., "Three Proofs of Realism," in *Essays in Critical Realism,* Macmillan, London, 1920.

Sartre, Jean-Paul, "Les Temps Modernes," *Revue Mensuelle,* Paris, nos. 9 and 10.

Stevenson, C. L., "The Emotive Meaning of Ethical Terms," in *Readings in Ethical Theory,* Sellars and Hospers, eds., Appleton-Century-Crofts, New York, 1952.

Stevenson, C. L., "Ethical Judgments and Avoidability," *Mind*, vol. 47, no. 185, 1938.

Tarski, "The Semantic Conception of Truth," *Philosophy and Phenomenological Research*, no. 4, 1944.

Veatch, Henry, and Young, "Metaphysics and the Paradoxes," *Review of Metaphysics*, vol. 6, no. 2, Dec., 1952.

Weiss, Paul, "The Theory of Types," *Mind*, vol. 37, 1928.

Wild, John, "Analysis vs. Empiricism: Some Comments on Mr. Ryle's Concept of Mind," *The Philosophical Forum*, vol. 11, 1953.

——, "Berkeley's Theories of Perception: A Phenomenological Critique," *Revue Internationale de Philosophie*, nos. 23-24, 1953.

——, "An Introduction to the Phenomenology of Signs," *Philosophy and Phenomenological Research*, vol. 8, no. 2, Sept., 1940.

——, "A Realistic Defence of Causal Efficacy," *Review of Metaphysics*, vol. 2, no. 8, 1949.

——, "Tendency: Ontological Ground of Ethics," *Journal of Philosophy*, vol. 49, no. 14, July 3, 1952.

Williams, Donald, "The Myth of Passage," *Journal of Philosophy*, vol. 48, no. 15, July 19, 1951.

Index

Action
  authentic, 36-37, 158-59, 161-62, 216, 253
  and care, 100-3, 164- 236-41
  conscience and the appeal for, 121, 155, 265
  and the historic past, 113, 150
  and natural law, 252
  and notion of time, 103-9, 164, 243, 246
  role of feeling in, 98 f., 171
  and understanding, 76, 86, 94, 170, 182, 196, 198, 262
Analytic Philosophy
  emphasis on logical apparatus, 9 f., 131, 135, 145
  ethical theory, 21-4, 116, 251
  neglect of concrete experience, 11, 15, 18, 21, 57
  theory of knowledge, 16-63
Anthropology
  as aim of Heidegger and Sartre, 58, 72-84, 174
  and Heidegger's notion of time, 103, 106-9
Anxiety (see Dread)
ARISTOTLE, 16, 23, 31, 45 f., 175, 191, 258, 268
AUGUSTINE, 51 f.
Awareness
  authentic and unauthentic, 145-46
  causal theory of, 61, 94
  Jaspers' notion of, 151 f.
  as a mode of being, 221-23

  relation to practice, 86, 95, 98
  as relational, 60-61, 85, 90-91, 93-94, 189, 205-6, 222, 228
  Sartre's view of, 61, 90 f., 198-99, 229-30
Awareness: Practical
  aim of, 51
  classical notion, 46-47, 256 f.
  connection with action, 20, 37, 53 f., 155, 198
  as feeling a situation, 19, 216
  neglect of, by modern philosophy, 19-20, 28, 181
  as a source of knowledge, 33 f., 55, 86 f., 94 f., 163 f., 182-83, 203, 228 f., 240-41
  and time, 245-46
Awareness: Realistic Theory of, 221-36
  as act of discovery, 45, 191 f., 198-99, 229-30
  and notion of self, 241 f.
  its traits, 92, 205-6, 221-23
Awareness: Theoretical
  distinguished from practical, 46, 51, 53-54, 191 f., 229
  inadequacy of, 65 f., 88 f., 96-97, 139, 153, 162-63, 170 f., 182 f., 240, 263-64, 199-200
  and intentional activity, 19 f., 60-61, 86, 91, 145 f., 163, 170-71, 198-99, 205-6, 239-40
  neglect of, by existentialism, 197-98, 216, 221, 228-29, 258, 263-64

Awareness: Theoretical (*Cont'd*)
  and noetic acts, 19, 61, 68, 90, 145,
    191-92, 222
  opacity of, to boundary situations,
    81-84, 215
AYER, A., 21, 24

Being
  and appearance (Sartre), 160 f.
  and Aristotelian logic, 32, 70-71, 96,
    175, 195
  basis of classic texts, 11, 174
  and ethics, 47, 144
  Heidegger's problem, 174 f.
  and phenomenology, 58, 84, 90, 146,
    197
  priority of, 203, 213-14
  and relational structures, 68, 90 f.,
    169-70, 212 f., 232-33, 245
Being-in-the-world
  authentic and unauthentic, 126-29,
    256-57
  condition of human existence, 58 f.,
    67, 75-78, 201-3
  and death, 120
  decision as a way of, 117
  as disclosed by mood, 87
  as historical, 114
  as object of dread, 99, 237, 259-60
  realistic view of, 201-6
  and time, 106 f.
Being-unto-death
  and decision, 124
  Heidegger's analysis of, 119-21, 166,
    176
Being-with-others
  and anxiety, 136
  care as a way of, 101-2, 130, 138
  and communication, 206 f.
  condition of human existence, 59,
    67, 79, 100-1, 206
  "one" as unauthentic, 130 f.
BERDIAEV, N., 182-83
BERGSON, H., 27
BERKELEY, G., 20, 65
Boundary Situations
  and decision, 124
  errors in notion of, 215 f.
  as limiting (Jaspers'), 80 f., 139 f.,
    153, 214-15
  and "mystery" (Marcel), 168-69

and notion of history, 114-15, 150
  ways of facing, 139-43

Care
  as conative structure, 100-3, 237-38
  and conscience, 122 f., 261
  and death, 118-19
  theory as derivative from, 172, 237
  time at root of, 106-9, 148-50, 260-
    62
  unauthentic, 147
  world as field of, 75
Categories
  basic protocols, 64-72, 194 f.
  existential, 65, 69, 85, 117, 140, 257
Chance
  boundary situation, 70-71, 80-81,
    141, 217
  determinist notion of, 141, 216
  Sartre's notion of, 161 f.
Change
  and flux notion of Jaspers, 66, 71,
    152, 180-81
  and real possibilities, 195
  and structure, 161 f., 195
Choice
  as arbitrary, 162, 164, 180
  and classical ethics, 254
  and consciousness, 90 f., 182, 240 f.
  and dread, 35-37, 41, 71, 99, 108-9
  the "ethical way," 32, 29 f.
  and existence, 42, 58, 66, 124 f.
  necessity of, 70, 183
  and possibilities, 95, 102-3, 123, 240-
    242
  as unifying time, 107-10, 113-14,
    124, 155, 164, 227, 238
  as unifying world, 129
Christianity
  contrast between lived and
    preached, 28, 47-49, 50-51
Commitment
  and care, 102-3
  and the "ethical way," 39
  freedom from (Sartre), 166
  in hedonism, 38, 140-41
Communication
  and commitment, 50
  failure of existentialism to account
    for, 165, 184, 202, 207
  and freedom, 137-38, 270-272

and history (Heidegger), 112 f.
Kierkegaard's practical solipsism,
  52-53, 58, 79, 184
and logic, 235, 257, 271
and "other minds," 79, 206 f.
struggle and philosophical, 81, 138-
  39, 148, 153, 155, 165, 211-12,
  217
and unauthentic being, 131
Concrete Experience
  and accepted notion of time, 104-6
  danger of arbitrary selections from,
    11 f., 59, 62-63, 72, 167
  interest of existentialism in, 57-58,
    63, 160
  priority of, 11-15, 30, 194
  relational character of, 212-14
Conscience
  and choice, 240-270
  as *ex post facto* judgment, 121, 261
  "voice" of, 122 f., 131-32, 239, 261,
    265, 269

Dasein
  Heidegger's notion of, 65, 75-77, 94,
    120, 161, 171
  Jaspers' notion of, 152-53, 156
  in relation to understanding, 88 f.,
    175 f.
Death
  a boundary situation, 81-84, 118 f.,
    143, 218-19, 238-39, 258
  as disclosing my last possibilities,
    120, 124, 144, 147, 237 f.
  as a mode of existing, 119, 144, 218-
    19
  naturalist conception of, 82-84, 118,
    143-44, 218
  as revealing transcendence
    (Jaspers), 159
  and time, 109-10, 114, 149, 243 f.
Decision
  and authentic being, 129, 144, 243,
    260
  as core of freedom, 116-17, 124
  and guilt, 123 f.
  and possibilities, 120, 150, 175
  and situationality, 140-41
DESCARTES, 9, 14, 19, 21, 26 f., 91, 127
Dread
  and decisive choice, 108-9, 158

and hedonism, 38-39
Heidegger's notion of, 98-100
and impersonal "one," 132, 135-36
not identical with fear, 35, 98-99,
  145, 259-60
as revealing notion of ground, 71
significance of, 35, 120, 176, 237, 269

En soi
  Sartre's notion of, 61, 68, 71-72, 92-
    94, 161
Epistemology
  current subjectivism, 19 f., 59, 78-
    79, 145, 168
  Jaspers' skepticism, 152
  major problem of, 222
  phenomenalism's error, 61-62, 90,
    160
  weaknesses of existentialist, 181-83
Essence
  boundary situations and human,
    216 f.
  in classical philosophy, 31-65
  as coordinate with existence, 181,
    223, 253, 255-56
  distinguished from act of existing,
    17, 65, 169-70, 180-81, 194, 223 f.,
    242, 253 f.
  and existential characteristics, 66-
    67
  Husserl's error, 73, 190-91
  Jaspers' notion of, 66, 180-81
  Marcel's notion of, 66, 170
  Sartre's notion of, 66, 162-63
  and theoretical knowldge, 33, 37,
    189
Essentialism
  the "aesthetic way," 39
  in classical ethics, 256-58
  its difficulties, 31, 180, 242
  existentialism as rebellion against,
    28, 54
  major phases of, 28
  as scientific methodology, 17-18
  value as a property, 23
Ethics
  classical, 254, 256-58
  naturalistic, 250-51
  as a normative discipline, 22, 251 f.
  and practical cognition, 37
  a program for, 266-72

Ethics: Existentialist
  authentic and unauthentic exist-
    ence as core of, 125 f.
  and decision, 117 f., 183 f.
  and norms, 256 f.
  an ontological discipline, 47, 69, 84-
    85, 126, 148-50, 165
  weaknesses of, 183 f.
Ethics: Realistic (*see* Natural Law)
Existence
  active and passive modes of, 16, 233
  and care, 102-3
  and choice, 42, 47, 96
  in classical philosophy, 31, 256
  concept of, 31, 50-51, 73-75
  confusion of, with essence, 17, 169,
    174, 256
  human and non-human, 196
  judgments of, 225-26, 233 f.
  not a mere object of thought, 34,
    65, 74, 88, 223-24
  pervasive datum of experience,
    12 f., 30 f., 54 f., 168
  priority of, over essence, 32, 65
Existence: Authentic and Unau-
    thentic
  and care, 147-48, 260
  and choice, 44 f., 69, 99, 124-26,
    129
  existential norms, 255, 258-62
  good and evil as, 38, 41, 69
  Jaspers' principles of, 158
  notion of, 126-50
  and notion of time, 109-10, 148-50,
    246
  and paths open to *Dasein*, 155
  phases of, 252-53
  and possibilities, 88, 138, 146 f., 257,
    270
  and responsibility, 129-30, 142-43,
    147, 155, 164, 176, 183, 239, 261
Existence: Human
  awareness at core of, 94, 196
  and "being there," 118, 130-39
  and being-unto-death, 121 f., 176
  as communicable, 79
  its conditions, 58, 66, 99-100, 116,
    158, 163
  decision as determining, 117 f., 125
  error of "scientific" theories, 195-96,
    236

as full of tendencies, 67-68, 75, 85,
  170, 216, 252
Jaspers' normative principles of,
  158
normal, 35, 143
prior to essence, 66, 73
as "stretched" in time, 106-9, 122 f.,
  163, 243, 245 f., 265
and structure of care, 100-1
Existentialism
  its aim, 58, 74, 79
  its anti-intellectualism, 53-54, 73-74,
    181-82
  denial of sufficient reason, 71, 161-
    62, 179, 199-200
  and human communication, 79-80,
    139
  Kierkegaard: the seminal mind, 27-
    56
  notion of choice, 124, 183
  and notion of essence, 66, 180-81
  as rebellion against abstract objec-
    tivism, 9, 28 f., 167-68, 187
  subjectivist premise of, 59, 204
  theory of time, 103-15
  use of literary media, 30, 55
  weaknesses of, 164-65, 178 f., 197 f.
Existentials (*see* Categories)
Existenz (*see* Self)
External World
  an artificial question, 30, 57, 127
  and unauthentic being, 126-27

Fear (*see* Dread)
Feeling
  Kierkegaard's analysis of, 51, 55
  as mode of disclosure, 19-20, 35, 37,
    70-71, 87
  relation to cognition, 87 f., 145, 216,
    227, 259
  role in action, 98 f., 236 f.
FEIGL, H., 15, 18, 24
Freedom
  and choice, 42, 124 f., 158
  and classical ethics, 254
  confused with novelty, 115, 149-50,
    247-49
  as core of Sartre's ethics, 165-67,
    183 f.
  depersonalization as threat to, 133-
    39, 157-58, 172-73, 257-58

distinguishing persons and things, 42, 77-78, 161-62, 184, 257
and existential norms, 248-49, 259-63
Heidegger's analysis of, 118-26, 176
and law, 40-41, 197-98, 253, 263
to make oneself, 77, 136, 163
not a "thing," 38, 116-17, 125
as an ontological category, 117
possibility of, 35, 36, 137

Good and Evil
as ways of existing 41, 47, 69, 194, 251
Guilt
a boundary situation, 81, 142-43, 155, 218
and freedom, 158, 164
as message of conscience, 122 f., 147, 239-40
and moral law, 39
and norms, 122, 142, 183, 240

HARTMANN, N., 196-97, 223
HEGEL, 25, 28 f., 42, 54 f., 182, 185, 214 f.
HEIDEGGER, M., 58, 60 f., 79, 84-114, 117-151, 160 f., 173-78, 189 f., 213 f., 237-45, 248, 266
History
ambiguity of the term, 110-14
and Existenz, 156 f.
function of the science of, 111, 114, 149-50
men as, 112 f., 247-49
HUME, 11, 14, 17-20
HUSSERL, E., 73, 190

Idealism
confusion of being and mental being, 59, 64-65, 90, 91, 198
existentialism's break with, 28, 30, 57, 68, 82, 167
and Heidegger's concept of Lose, 69
a reductionist theory, 18, 77, 188
Sartre's reaction against, 160
Impersonal "One"
as dominating social life, 130 f.
Heidegger's view of, 130 f.
Jaspers' notion of, 133-39

Individual Person
as a center of care, 101 f., 190, 201 f.
distinguished by choice, 42
essence of, 74, 125, 152, 162-63, 197, 216 f., 253, 256
Jaspers and Marcel on, 58, 136, 157
and Kierkegaard, 29, 32, 43-44, 50, 52, 55, 184
Marcel on, 58, 171
and masses, 42-43, 52, 136 f.
not an object, 34, 41, 124, 128-29, 132, 138, 182-83
Integrity
and decision, 117 f., 123 f., 148, 260
and notion of death, 119 f., 150, 239, 269
Intentionality
of human experience, 188 f., 200, 205, 245-46, 259
and logic, 207, 229, 231 f.

JASPERS, K., 58 f., 80-82, 133-44, 151-60, 175, 206, 214 f.

KANT, 31 f., 61, 151 f., 230
KIERKEGAARD, S., 9, 26, 27-56, 57 f., 98, 114 f., 172 f., 206, 237
Knowledge
and boundary situations, 80-82
its focus on projects, 88, 90, 95, 130, 192 f.
Heidegger's two notions of, 89-90
as a mode of action, 86, 88, 94, 182-83, 198
as a mode of being, 198, 224
necessary condition of, 191-92
object of, 204, 225-26, 228
of transcendence, 154-55

LEWIS, C. I., 21, 62
Logic: Mathematical
and living discourse, 22, 97, 145
in relation to ontology, 95-96
Logic: Realistic
Greek logic as intentional, 96, 232 f., 257
as inquiry into human meaning, 97, 210 f., 231
of practice, 96-98, 235
Love
and real possibilities, 113-14

Love (*Cont'd*)
  and the "religious way," 40
  Sartre's exclusion of, 165
  and unauthentic care, 147

MARCEL, G., 57-66 *passim*, 86 f., 125 f.,
    151, 167-73
MARX, 25, 185
MERLEAU-PONTY, M., 188, 190 fn., 201,
    206, 243 fn.
Metaphysics
  in Anglo-Saxon universities: death
    of, 17
  as basic empirical discipline, 12, 16,
    64, 188, 219
  protocols of, 194 f., 219
  weaknesses in existentialist, 180-81
Mind
  as container of ideas, 19, 33, 59-60
  Heidegger's view of, 61
  Idealism and, 168
  Sartre's view of, 61, 163 f.
  as wholly private, 21, 207
Moods
  allied to dread, 36
  in relation to action, 98 f., 236 f.
  as revealing my being, 87, 227
  as revealing others, 79
  as revealing situations, 70-71, 87, 88,
    227
Moral Law
  and hedonism, 38-39
  Kierkegaard's skepticism regarding,
    183 f.

Natural Law
  and boundary situations, 264
  and existential norms, 258-62
  and freedom, 269-72
  and human action, 241-42, 259
  notion of good and evil, 251 f.
  and obligation, 252-53
  relation to existentialism, 252-72
NIETZSCHE, F., 27, 73
Nothingness
  as conditioning insight, 191 f.
  and death, 83-84, 218-19
  as guilt, 123
  the object of dread, 35, 71, 176, 181
  ontological concept, 70, 92-94, 176
  the *pour soi* as, 68, 92, 161, 166, 195

Ontology
  and existential norms, 255, 258-62
  Heidegger's, 33, 72-73, 174-76
  human, 72-84, 112 f., 130 f., 195-97
  Jaspers' rejection of a universal, 152
  Kierkegaard's lack of interest in, 32
  and natural law, 251 f.
  possibility of, 61-62
  in relation to logic, 231 f.
  Sartre's, 33, 160 f.
  weaknesses in existentialist, 197 f.

PASCAL, 27, 51
Phenomenology: Existentialist
  and cognition, 163 f., 190, 219, 258-
    59
  and communication, 52-53, 146
  a descriptive empirical method, 6-7,
    29-30, 54 f., 63, 91, 167-68, 188
  and "empiricism," 62-63, 188
  Jaspers' notion of, 72, 152
  weaknesses of, 179-80
Phenomenology: Realistic
  aim of, 190, 193, 200, 219
  role of pure theory in, 188 f., 193-
    94, 202 f., 215, 225, 229-31
Philosophy
  evidence for its modern breakdown,
    10-26
  first function of, 3-6, 10, 12, 22, 136-
    37, 138-39, 178
PLATO, 23, 28, 45 f., 66, 219, 258
Possibilities
  and anxiety, 71
  and authentic existence, 88 f., 94,
    119 f., 122 f., 141, 146, 148-50, 194,
    261-62
  as beyond dread, 99
  of *Dasein*, 66, 153, 156, 175
  and death, 119, 141
  as directing care, 100 f., 107-9, 147-
    48, 158
  of *Existenz*, 153
  as the heart of human history, 113-
    14, 248-49, 260-61
  of *pour soi*, 94-95
  in relation to understanding, 88 f.,
    96
  of things, 66, 195-96, 197-98, 200
Potency
  knowing as pure, 192 f., 222

as lacking in *en soi,* 161, 196
and nothingness, 93, 94, 191-92
Pour Soi
as non-being, 94-95, 161 f.
Sartre's notion of, 61, 68, 71, 125,
161-63
PROTAGORAS, 24

QUINE, W., 18

Reason
its abstractive capacity, 189, 225
indeterminacy of, 191 f., 222, 228-29
RICOEUR, P., 240
RILKE, R. M., 78
RUSSELL, B., 59, 60, 62
RYLE, G., 21

SARTRE, J. P., 33, 58-72 *passim,* 90-95,
125 f., 159-67, 179 f., 240
SCHLICK, M., 15
Self
as center of care, 101-3, 123 f.
consciousness of, 38, 53, 91 f., 100,
153, 241 f.
as contingent existence, 41, 124,
152, 195
and dread, 99
as dynamic, 53, 74, 166
Jaspers' notion of, 152-53, 156
as time, 107-9, 149, 247-49
Situation
and decision, 124, 140 f.
and human existence, 75, 140, 216
as revealed by mood, 80, 87
SOCRATES, 22, 30, 45, 47, 261
SPENGLER, O., 43
SPINOZA, 31
Structure
of being, 64, 67, 196
en soi as lacking, 94, 161, 180
as found in experience, 67, 169, 189,
197-98, 230, 253-54
of world, 75 f., 170, 201
Struggle
a boundary situation, 81, 190, 217
at social level, 113-14, 184
Suffering
a boundary situation, 81, 141, 217

Time
accepted view of, 103-6, 109-10, 148
futurity and human existence, 65-
66, 74, 100, 114-15, 119-20, 148-50,
243, 245, 247-49, 265
Heidegger's theory of, 106-9, 195,
243-45
history and the stream-theory of,
110-12, 114-15, 243-44, 247-49
Sartre's theory of, 163-64
its unity in care, 100-3, 148-50, 201,
260
and value (Jaspers), 159
world-time, 244-49, 265
Transcendence
being as, 175 f., 203 f.
and boundary situations, 215-16
Jaspers' view of, 153-54, 156, 158-59
Kierkegaard's concept of, 39-40
Marcel's view of, 173
Truth
accessible to individuals, 44
classical definition of, 45, 193
correspondence theory of, 68
as revealing being, 45, 68, 175-76,
199
stages in attaining, 193-94

Value
and duration, 159
not separate from existence, 69-70,
165, 250, 252
and obligation, 255
VEATCH, H., 226 fn.

"Ways of Life" (Kierkegaard)
the aesthetic way, 38-41
the ethical way, 39-41
and moral choice, 58, 183 f.
the religious way, 40-41
WILLIAMS, D., 148
World
as cosmos, 76-77, 127-28, 202
as limiting, 50, 204
as ordered by projects, 201-2 f., 268
pan-objectivist view of, 33, 38-39,
42, 108
as revealed by practical awareness,
53, 75, 95, 170, 201, 256 f.